D1165868

Harvard Historical Studies · *153*

Published under the auspices
of the Department of History
from the income of the
Paul Revere Frothingham Bequest
Robert Louis Stroock Fund
Henry Warren Torrey Fund

A Question of Balance

~ HOW FRANCE AND THE UNITED STATES
CREATED COLD WAR EUROPE

MICHAEL CRESWELL

HARVARD UNIVERSITY PRESS

Cambridge, Massachusetts, and London, England   2006

Copyright © 2006 by the President and Fellows of Harvard College
All rights reserved
Printed in the United States of America

Library of Congress Cataloging-in-Publication Data

Creswell, Michael, 1958–
   A question of balance : how France and the United States created Cold War Europe /
Michael Creswell.
      p. cm.
   Includes bibliographical references and index.
   ISBN-13: 978-0-674-02297-3
   ISBN-10: 0-674-02297-1
   1. United States—Foreign relations—France.   2. France—Foreign relations—
United States.   3. Cold War.   I. Title.

E183.8.F8C74 2006
327.7304409′045—dc22

                                                                          2006043741

Contents

Preface

The Grand Alliance's triumph over the Axis powers in 1945 lifted a grim shadow that had blanketed international life for more than a generation. People everywhere hoped that a new day had arrived in which nations could coexist in a world of peace and stability. This sweet reverie, however, soon turned to bitter rivalry. Ironically, victory in the Second World War spawned one of the most turbulent and dangerous periods in the history of international politics. The policies enacted by the great powers in the extended wake of this conflict wrought unprecedented change, as Europe moved from a fluid constellation of great powers to one seemingly frozen in two antagonistic geopolitical blocs.

Two developments were largely responsible for this change. One was the integration of a rearmed Federal Republic of Germany into the Atlantic Alliance. Germany thus evolved from an international pariah—a symbol of hatred and militarism—to a vital member of the Western community, soldiering loyally in the defense of democracy. A powerful West Germany, however, unnerved the perennially suspicious Josef Stalin, who would not rest easy until he settled the so-called German question to his satisfaction. His efforts to block Germany from rearming and Western leaders' subsequent attempts to resist him ensured a clear political demarcation of continental Europe.

The second and most important development concerned the transformation of America's relations with its European allies. Sharply departing from past policy, the United States went from simply underwriting its allies' defense in peacetime to explicitly committing American blood and iron to the cause of fighting the Cold War. Together, these two events swept aside Europe's traditional geopolitical order and ushered in a new system with a potent American military force as its permanent strategic centerpiece.

Despite its far-reaching consequences, the meaning of this novel arrangement adopted by the Western powers at the end of 1954 has eluded many observers. Claims to the contrary notwithstanding, this arrangement was neither inevitable, nor reached by chance, nor imposed by the United States. Instead, it emerged from a dispute between America and France about one of the central issues of post-1945 international politics—Germany's proper role in the Western world. In this dispute, American officials championed the immediate restoration of German military prowess as an added weapon in their Cold War struggle against Soviet Communism. A rearmed Germany would, in turn, spare the United States from having to assume the role of Europe's permanent night watchman. However, many French officials resisted this plan, convinced that aspects of it compromised France's national interest. Only after the United States reformed its policy to France's liking did the Cold War order in Europe coalesce.

This book seeks to explain how and why this geopolitical system developed by attempting to solve two related puzzles, the first being why the United States did not simply ignore repeated French objections to its desired German policy and rearm the Federal Republic unilaterally. Determined to convert Germany into a political and military rampart against Soviet Communism, American officials possessed a powerful incentive to disregard French objections. Ultimately, other considerations prompted Washington to avoid taking unilateral actions. Leading American officials eventually recognized that the aftereffects of any abrupt move to rearm Germany could imperil the safety and independence of the United States and its allies. A rearmed Germany might prompt the Soviet Union to strike preemptively in order to eliminate a potentially deadly rival. Better to play it safe now, they reasoned, than to rush matters and be sorry later.

The second puzzle involves why France finally yielded and agreed to German rearmament, irrespective of American demands. Perhaps surprisingly, while U.S. pressure played a role in France's decision, it was far less important than other factors. Key French officials concluded that whereas significant drawbacks would attend the remilitarization of the Federal Republic, these disadvantages would pale next to those incurred through France's outright rejection of the plan. Moreover, many French

officials did not see a remilitarized Germany as an unmitigated negative—to the contrary, they believed the French state could benefit if German rearmament were done the right way at the right time.

Despite sometimes heated debate, France and the United States engaged in a genuine political discussion, the fruit of which was an
arrangement that satisfied both sides' most basic needs. This study attempts to lay bare the dynamics of this arrangement, as well as to high-
light its larger consequences. As this account suggests, international
politics is not simply a tug-of-war whose outcome is sealed by the relative power of those nations whose interests and wishes are in conflict.
Rather, this study concludes that while power is an essential ingredient
of international relations, it is merely a tool in the service of diplomacy
and statecraft. Failing such guidance, power alone can achieve little of
lasting value.

The remainder of this book unfolds chronologically and thematically
as a detailed historical narrative. Chapter 1 examines the period from
the end of the Second World War to the summer of 1950, while Chapter 2 treats the remainder of that year. Chapters 3 to 7 cover the years
1951 to 1954.

Acknowledgments

One of my favorite parts of any scholarly book is the acknowledgments, because in those credits you see the depth of the intellectual well the author tapped in order to complete the work. You also get a sense of how much writing a book is a collaborative effort, even though only one name might appear on the cover. Rare is the author who does not accumulate at least a few debts.

For my part, I incurred numerous debts during the course of writing this book, thus I relish the opportunity to publicly thank the following institutions and individuals without whose support this book would have remained unwritten. Financial support is the lifeblood of multiarchival research; therefore, I offer my sincere appreciation to the Committee on Institutional Cooperation, the Institute for the Study of World Politics, and the University of Chicago Council for Advanced Studies on Peace and International Cooperation for providing me the financial resources to do research in Europe, while grants from the Eisenhower World Affairs Institute and the German Historical Institute enabled me to carry out my investigations in the United States. The Florida State University also provided generous financial assistance to do research on both sides of the Atlantic. Equally important was the history department's innovative leave policy that afforded me large blocks of uninterrupted time to complete my labors. It is a model that deserves wide emulation. In addition, the Florida Education Fund was gracious enough to provide me a year of leave time that allowed me to carry out my research free from other responsibilities.

Doing the research for the book required spending many months in several archives sifting through reams of old documents. For making this arduous task easier, I thank Nelson D. Lankford of the Virginia Historical Society; David J. Haight of the Dwight D. Eisenhower Library; David Bilger of the Harry S. Truman Presidential Library; Patrick Facon of the Service historique de l'armée de l'air; Sandrine Einhorn-Heiser, Marie-Annick Hepp, and Hervé Lemoine of the Service historique de l'armée de terre; Jean Luquet of the Mission des Archives nationales auprés du Secrètaire général du governement; the late Marie-Claire Mendès France of the Institut Pierre Mendès France; Françoise Peemans of the Direction des archives, Service public fédéral Affaires étrangères, Commerce éxtèrieur et Coopération au développement; François Gasnault of the Service des Archives du Ministère de l'Économie, des finances et de l'industrie; Monique Constant of the Archives du Ministère des affaires etrangères; Chantal Tourtier-Bonazzi, Elizabeth Ducrot, and Jean Poissel of the Archives nationales; Dominque Parcollet of the Centre d'histoire de Science Po; Henri Rieben and Françoise Nicod of the Fondation Jean Monnet pour l'Europe; and Philippe Vial of the Service historique de la Marine, along with their respective staffs. Let me also express my appreciation to Madame Georges Bidault, Jean Favier, Pierre Milza, and Jean-Noël Jeanneney for granting me permission to consult the private papers of Georges Bidault, René Mayer, Vincent Auriol, and Wilfrid Baumgartner, respectively. Thanks are also in order for the helpful staffs at the British National Archives, the George C. Marshall Museum, the Library of Congress, the National Archives and Records Administration, the Office Universitaire de la recherche socialiste, the Nathan M. Pusey Library, the National Security Archive, the Imperial War Museum, the Liddell Hart Centre for Military Archives, the Bodleian Library, the British Library of Political and Economic Science, the Churchill Archives Centre, the Wren Library, the Seeley Mudd Library, the Sterling Memorial Library at Yale University, and the Air Force Historical Research Agency. Thanks go to Lt. Col. John P. Geis for securing my access to Maxwell Air Force Base.

My peripatetic professional lifestyle constantly leaves me searching for places to stay. At times it means residing in a hotel or a bed and breakfast—expensive propositions. Thankfully, several friends and colleagues spared me from taking up residence in the poor house. I therefore owe a debt to the late Claudine Fitte and especially to Guy Champagne, who each provided me with a comfortable place to stay during several lengthy trips to Paris; to Talbot Imlay, who did likewise during a trip to London; to Andrew Wallace and Ralph Lee DeFalco III, who sheltered me while I was sleuthing in Washington, DC; to Jonathan Ladinski, who put me up while I was doing research in Cambridge, Massachusetts; to Kaye Davis, who opened her home to me during a research trip to Princeton, New Jersey; and to Mark A. O'Neill, who found a place for us to stay while he and I were researching at Maxwell AFB in Montgomery, Alabama.

I readily acknowledge my shortcomings as a writer, so I sought out individuals who are less challenged in this area. Although capable copy editors are in relative short supply, I was fortunate to find some good ones. My sincere thanks, therefore, go to Denise Tanyol, who handled the initial chore of transforming my writing into something more readable; Gwenda Conner and Janice Traflet, who smoothed out the kinks in subsequent revisions; and Gail Farrar, who applied the final brushstrokes. The results of their care and attention to detail appear on every page.

I am also grateful to the many unnamed but unforgotten friends and colleagues who took time to discuss my work and offer me their candid impressions. A few individuals, however, deserve special mention. Ivan Ermakoff, Stacy Bergstrom Haldi, David Holt, Roland Hsu, Craig Koerner, James J. Marquardt, Andrew Moravcsik, Paul M. Pitman, Gail L. Sunderman, Orrin Schwab, Barbara Walter, and Carrington Ward III were kind enough to read and comment on various portions. The following individuals critiqued the version revised for publication: Max Friedman, Nicholas Sarantakes, and Marc Trachtenberg. Anthony Adamthwaite and Tom Schwartz were indefatigable enough to read it twice in its entirety. I am grateful to them all, for without their help this book would have been a shadow of itself.

Several individuals made substantial personal contributions to the present work. I thus extend my gratitude to the Honorable Maurice Faure, the late Honorable Maurice Couve de Murville, and the late Honorable Maurice Schumann for graciously consenting to be interviewed on short notice despite their busy schedules. My thanks to Hélène Erlingson for arranging the interview with Mr. Faure and for sharing some of her research with me.

Special thanks go to Jean Poulard, who not only ensured the accuracy of my translations, but who also introduced me to the subject of international politics while I was an undergraduate, and to Philippe Vial, who tutored me on the European Defense Community, provided me with valuable contacts, and shared with me articles on the French armed forces. I thank, too, Mihaela Bacou of the Graduate Research Institute for cheerfully performing a variety of mundane but important administrative tasks for me while I was doing research in Paris.

A number of young and energetic research assistants helped me out along the way: Daniel Blumlo, Corey Gray, and Kenneth Johnson. Christopher Griffin, a man for all tasks, aided me in compiling the index.

Parts of this manuscript have previously appeared, in slightly altered form, in the journals *Security Studies, Cold War History,* and the *Journal of Cold War Studies.* Michael Creswell, "Between the Bear and the Phoenix: The United States and the European Defense Community, 1950–1954," *Security Studies* 11, no. 4 (Summer 2002): 89–124; Michael Creswell, "With a Little Help From Our Friends: How France Secured an Anglo-American Continental Commitment, 1945–54," *Cold War History* 3, no. 1 (October 2002): 1–28; Michael Creswell and Marc Trachtenberg, "France and the German Question, 1945–1955," *Journal of Cold War Studies* 5, no. 3 (Summer 2003): 5–28. I would like to thank them for permission to include that material here.

I first became interested in the subject of the diplomatic relations between France and the United States during the Cold War as a graduate student. Surprisingly, that interest was greeted not simply with healthy skepticism but rather outright disdain. Such doubts left me unsure how—or whether—to pursue my interest. Luckily, there were two individuals to whom I was able to turn for support.

John Mearsheimer was convinced that I had an excellent topic and possessed the ability to do it justice. Just as important, he provided intellectual inspiration. He taught me to always keep my eye on the big picture and avoid becoming distracted by peripheral matters. Although I have failed to consistently live up to his expectations, his faith in me has been unwavering.

It was John who pointed me in the direction of Marc Trachtenberg. Marc has been extremely supportive, offering generous doses of encouragement and intellectual nourishment. His vast knowledge of the Cold War has saved me from countless mistakes.

Although I can never repay my debt to John and Marc, I hope my efforts here are a start. I alone, however, accept responsibility for the conclusions reached, as well as any omissions or errors in fact, judgment, or interpretation.

One final acknowledgment. As I prepared to put the final touches on the manuscript, I received word that my mother had passed away. Her death dealt me a blow from which I will never recover. Yet in death, as in life, Mom has again given me something valuable—a greater appreciation for all the sacrifices she made to ensure that I would lead a happy life. Therefore I dedicate this book to my mother, Ruby, ever grateful for her love and wishing that she were here to enjoy the fruits of my labor.

Abbreviations

ABC	Atomic, Biological, Chemical
AHC	Allied High Commission (for Germany)
BTO	Brussels Treaty Organization
CDU	Christian Democratic Union
CFM	Council of Foreign Ministers
CGSC	Chiefs of the General Staff Committee
CIA	Central Intelligence Agency
CNIP	Centre national des indépendants et paysans
CSU	Christian Social Union
DC	Defense Committee
ECA	European Cooperation Agency
ECSC	European Coal and Steel Community
EDC	European Defense Community
EDF	European Defense Force
EPU	European Payments Union
FRG	Federal Republic of Germany
GDR	German Democratic Republic
HICOG	High Commissioner for Germany
JCS	Joint Chiefs of Staff
MAAG	Military Assistance and Advisory Group
MC	Military Committee
MDAP	Mutual Defense Assistance Program
MRP	Mouvement républicain populaire
MSA	Mutual Security Agency
MSP	Mutual Security Plan

MTDP   Medium Term Defense Plan
NAC   North Atlantic Council
NAT   North Atlantic Treaty
NATO   North Atlantic Treaty Organization
NDC   National Defense Committee
NIE   National Intelligence Estimate
NSC   National Security Council
PCF   Parti communiste français
PPS   Policy Planning Staff
RCT   Regimental Combat Team
RPF   Rassemblement du peuple français
SACEUR Supreme Allied Commander for Europe
SFIO   Section française de l'Internationale ouvrière
SHAPE   Supreme Headquarters Allied Powers Europe
SPD   Social Democratic Party
TCC   Temporary Council Committee
UN   United Nations
URAS   Union républicaine d'action sociale
WEU   Western European Union

A Question of Balance

Introduction: Who Created the Cold War Order in Europe?

On December 30, 1954, the French National Assembly ratified the Paris Accords, thereby paving the way for the Federal Republic of Germany to take up arms and join the North Atlantic Treaty Organization (NATO) and the Western European Union (WEU). By agreeing to allow Germany to rearm, the National Assembly fulfilled an important objective of American foreign policy. Surprisingly, this vote represented a complete reversal of the French parliament's stance on the same issue just four months earlier.

In rejecting the Treaty of Paris on August 30, 1954, French legislators had demolished America's plans to create a supranational European army led by French and German combat troops, the projected backbone of U.S. national security policy for Western Europe. France's repudiation of this treaty, which would have established the European Defense Community (EDC), seemed to mean that four years of American planning and diplomatic maneuvering had come to naught.[1]

In September 1950, when the United States had demanded that its NATO allies rearm West Germany within the framework of a multinational European defense force, American policy makers had three goals in mind. The first goal was to contain (and even reverse) the spread of Soviet power and influence.[2] In the view of American planners, the addition of West Germany's formidable latent military might to the Allied camp would help to thwart any Soviet designs to expand into Western Europe.[3] America's second goal was to lighten its share of the financial and military burden of defending Europe from Soviet expansionism. Officials in Washington decided that the best way to reduce America's burden would be to make the European allies responsible for maintaining security on the continent, thereby obliging them to unite in order to help themselves. The third goal was to anchor the Federal Republic firmly in the Western sphere of influence. American planners believed that implanting German troops into a European army would guarantee that the remilitarization of Germany remained limited, nonnational, and closely monitored, thus alleviating the apprehensions of countless victims of past German aggression.[4]

Yet after four years of pressuring, prodding, and compromising with French politicians—the Western European lawmakers most skeptical of the plan to rearm Germany—Washington reluctantly faced the prospect of having to rethink its national security policy toward continental Europe. For the United States, France's rejection of the EDC had all the makings of a strategic disaster.

Indeed, the National Assembly's action on August 30 raised several vexing questions for U.S. policy makers. How would a Franco-German entente against Soviet expansion—widely considered the key to peace and prosperity in Europe—be achieved if France were to remain opposed to the plan to remilitarize its neighbor across the Rhine? What policy should the United States adopt if France continued to delay German rearmament: conciliation or coercion? How would Britain react to France's refusal? American decision makers depended on a robust and enduring British military presence on the European continent to ease French fears of a rearmed Germany, to spare the U.S. military establishment from shouldering added burdens, and to advance European unity—a principal objective of American foreign policy. Would the demise of the EDC merely reinforce Britain's traditional skepticism of supranational projects, leading it to remain aloof from continental affairs and thereby halt progress toward the integration of Europe? Moreover, what of Germany? Would it simply end the whole matter, choosing neutrality in exchange for unification, a carrot dangled routinely by the Soviet Union? Or would Germany instead hold its manpower hostage, knowing how highly the Western Alliance valued it, in the expectation of winning extensive political concessions?

American officials' inability to provide ready answers to these and similar questions caused them considerable anxiety in the fall and winter of 1954. However, they averted these potential setbacks when the French parliament ratified the Paris Accords and gave its blessing to German rearmament, freeing the Federal Republic to join in the defense of Western Europe.[5] A grave crisis had been avoided.

Still, two important questions remain. First, why did Washington fail to punish Paris given four years of French delays on the EDC? In light of the high priority that U.S. officials accorded German rearmament, why were they neither willing nor able to coerce French acceptance or to rearm Germany in spite of French objections? This account contends that while strong-arming or bypassing France altogether might have been the most expedient way for America to remilitarize Germany, compelling reasons dictated restraint.[6]

The reasons for the United States' eventual moderation in this matter involved the Soviet Union and Germany as well as France. The potential for conflict with Moscow was the preeminent concern for officials in Washington. Some of them feared that precipitously rearming the Federal Republic might lead the Soviet Union to respond militarily to prevent the revival of a deadly adversary. They surmised that a nuclear-armed Moscow might either retaliate directly against the United States—a conflict for which America believed itself unprepared—or against a region that Washington deemed of vital interest. The Soviet development of thermonuclear weapons further dampened any American desire to carry out a provocative military policy in the very heart of Europe.

American officials additionally worried that Bonn's young and untested democracy might collapse under the strain of remilitarization, a disintegration that could restore authoritarian rule. The United States would then face a rearmed but undemocratic Germany, perhaps one eager to enter the Soviet orbit. Such an outcome, U.S. policy makers feared, would deprive America of an invaluable strategic and economic prize in its Cold War competition with the Soviet Union, a loss of enormous proportions. American planners posited, in by-now-familiar logic, that such a forfeiture would demoralize U.S. allies worldwide, resulting in either the spread of neutralism or a wave of defections to the Communist side.

Washington acknowledged its policy's potential effect not only on Bonn and Moscow, but also on Paris, the designated linchpin in America's national security policy for Western Europe.[7] In the eyes of U.S. planners, America needed French manpower to execute a policy of "dual containment"—keeping the European continent free from domination, whether by Bonn or Moscow. Such heavy responsibilities forced the United States to tread lightly in dealing with France so as to avoid scrambling U.S. defense plans for continental Europe.

American officials also harbored grander designs for France. The United States' view of the Cold War as a global conflict led it to seek France's help in preventing the advance of Communism on several fronts, not just in Europe. In American thinking, France's colonial empire could support U.S. plans in Asia. The United States believed that it was serving its own interests by providing the French massive financial aid to continue their colonial war in Indochina, thus stemming the spread of Communism in that presumably vital region. Many American officials therefore thought it unwise to saddle France with undue burdens in Europe that could weaken French efforts in Indochina.

Turning to the second question, why did the French parliament reverse itself and ratify the Paris Accords? A chorus of scholarly voices indicates that French deputies buckled under American pressure. As Walter LaFeber describes it, "The French had become pawns in a climactic power struggle. They tried to stall the fateful [August 30] vote by following a policy best described as 'keeping the corpse in the closet.' " Finally persuaded to vote, France found that it had "miscalculated. Not fully realizing how they were being acted upon rather than acting in the unfolding diplomacy, the French believed the defeat of the EDC had scotched, perhaps killed, German rearmament."[8]

Frank Ninkovich similarly appraises the French policy turnaround: "Seeing the handwriting on the wall, the French realized at this point [after the defeat of the EDC Treaty] that a completely obstructionist attitude would leave them totally isolated in Europe. Across the Atlantic, American policymakers were already beginning to think of writing off France, likening her hysteria to the nervous collapse she had suffered in 1940. . . . Despite last-minute tantrums, the end result of French policy was acceptance of what it had originally set out to avoid." Echoing this viewpoint, Thomas Schwartz argues, "The strong American stand, coupled with an even stronger British threat to rearm the Germans without the French, led the French Assembly to reverse itself and approve the agreements."[9]

Frank Costigliola states it bluntly: "Although challenged by the French, U.S. hegemony still prevailed: . . . however recalcitrant, France could not block the rearmament of West Germany." Most recently, Mark Sheetz has rejected the notion that France willingly agreed to German rearmament, arguing that "France fought a series of rear-guard actions against Anglo-Saxon policy culminating in resigned acquiescence." This view has long reigned among some prominent French scholars. Pierre Mélandri contends that U.S. policy toward Europe during the early 1950s promoted American imperialism, while the late Jean-Baptiste Duroselle, perhaps the foremost French diplomatic historian of his time, referred to France in this period as an American "satellite."[10]

While these assertions are plausible, this book disputes the notion that America bullied France into accepting the rearmament of Germany. Although U.S. pressure played a part, far more decisive factors—having to do with internal French politics and international French concerns—ultimately led France to sanction, of its own accord, the plan to rearm West Germany.

France's decision resulted from the cumulative effects of several factors. In geopolitical terms, France's determination to deter the Soviet Union militarily is the overriding reason French officials supported the rearming of West Germany despite their lingering concerns. France enacted this decision once Britain and the United States pledged to station large numbers of their ground troops on the European mainland on a long-term basis, thus lessening French concerns over a rearmed Federal Republic. France also embarked on a nuclear weapons program, which would ensure it decisive military superiority over a rearmed, but nonnuclear, Germany. Along this same line, NATO's move to an explicit nuclear strategy offered France the security benefits of extending the Alliance's front line of defense eastward into German territory. This strategy could not be carried out effectively, however, without full German consent and cooperation, an unlikely prospect given continued French delay on the question of German rearmament and the fate of the Saar.[11]

Another reason that Paris proved flexible on the rearmament issue was that it wished to avoid jeopardizing progress toward European integration, a development that it believed could strengthen France's long-term political, economic, and military position in Europe and blunt any potential threat from Germany, be it economic or military. Given France's aspiration to lead the movement to integrate Europe, which would garner it greater influence in the international arena, many French officials thought it wise to include Germany in the "new Europe."[12]

Domestic concerns also played a role in moderating French policy toward Germany, as France's military and industrial leadership roundly endorsed German rearmament. The military leadership adopted this position for geostrategic reasons. They deemed the addition of German manpower essential for the West to deter the Soviet Union effectively, a nation that the French military establishment judged a more immediate security threat than Germany. In fact, members of the French military leadership felt so passionately about this issue that they openly sided against the French government.[13] In view of this dispute, many French parliamentarians believed that the nation needed to appease the military establishment to avoid severe civil-military problems while attempting to meet commitments to NATO and to pacify an increasingly restless French empire. Some legislators also concluded that if the country's military leaders declared German remilitarization indispensable to France's security, lawmakers were in no position to say otherwise.

The French military leadership was not the country's only powerful constituent group in favor of rearming Germany. Due to the strict limits the EDC treaty would have placed on German arms production, high-tech producers in the French arms industry stood to reap substantial economic benefits were Germany to rearm, as they would be called upon to supply the new German defense force. If approved, this clause would have cleared the way for France to depose Germany as the Continent's primary supplier of arms. Conversely, by refusing to come to terms with Germany, some French officials believed they ran the risk that the Allies would unilaterally rearm the Federal Republic anyway. In that event, France would either cede this lucrative market to American and British manufacturers, or ensure that the Ruhr—a resource-rich manufacturing region in northwest Germany—remained the industrial workshop of Western Europe.[14]

This book cuts to the heart of one of the fundamental concerns preoccupying policy makers' attention during the Cold War: how to secure peace and stability throughout Europe. In the wake of two world wars, this issue transcended mere speculation and involved the fate of mankind. The attempt to guarantee the freedom and independence of the European continent took on added complexity with the relative economic and military weakness of the Western European nations, the rising costs of supporting a prostrate West Germany, and the advent of Soviet nuclear capability. Moreover, the United States, especially under the Eisenhower administration, saw America's military presence in Europe as temporary.

America attempted to solve this puzzle by creating a system that would pool the economic and military resources of Western Europe in an effort to deter the Soviet Union. Yet to be effective, such a system would have to enlist the great latent economic and military might of the Federal Republic. From the French standpoint, this system would have to include safeguards that ensured German power would be dedicated not to self-aggrandizement, but to peace. Furthermore, it would have to be constructed in a way that avoided provoking the Soviet Union. The Atlantic Alliance introduced such a system at the end of 1954. Contrary to the conventional interpretations on the subject, this system was not imposed by the United States. Instead, it was the one preferred by France.

CHAPTER ONE

From Hot War to Cold War

For postbellum France, establishing a durable and favorable balance of power in Europe was a matter of bedrock concern. Thrice invaded in seventy years, French officials placed this issue squarely atop the nation's security agenda—yet geographic realities dictated that France could not escape direct involvement should East-West hostilities occur.[1] The specter of a newly ascendant Soviet Union, well positioned to bid for mastery in Europe, exposed France's strategic vulnerability. The country's relative weakness ruled out unilateral deterrence; an alliance with Belgium, Luxembourg, and the Netherlands (collectively known as the Benelux) was insufficient to tip the military balance in France's favor; and the fate of defeated Germany lay in limbo. The inherent limitations on its freedom to maneuver left France little choice but to enlist mightier allies in its defense. To this end, inducing Britain and the United States to provide ironclad military commitments to the European continent was a primary goal of post-1945 French diplomacy. This goal remained elusive, however. Despite France's persistent appeals and despite their shared concern, neither Britain nor the United States agreed to accommodate France's requests.

Neutrality, never an attractive option for France, held even less appeal given the changing international political environment. The onset and intensification of the Cold War heightened French security concerns, as East-West wartime cooperation gave way to peacetime competition. Although France had initially entertained hopes of remaining on cordial terms with Moscow, key events deepened the country's suspicion of

Soviet intentions,[2] leading French officials to pursue closer security ties with Britain and the United States.[3]

Picking up the Pieces

The Second World War was a disaster for France. An early victim of the conflict, France quickly fell under control of the Germans, who were abetted in their rule by the collaborationist Vichy regime. This period both divided and dispirited the French nation, leaving physical and emotional turmoil in its wake. Upon liberation and victory, France put its shoulder to repairing its wounds, reinvigorating its economy, and rebuilding its politics.

France's government also attended to international matters. Aware of the actual and potential power relations on the continent, French officials knew that the country needed help. They therefore decided to improve relations with Britain as a first step toward establishing a formal alliance. Britain also desired an alliance with France partly because British planners had determined that a Western defense bloc intended to contain the Soviet Union and monitor Germany had little credibility unless France took part. Nonetheless, differences between London and Paris over the treatment of Germany, French rule in the Middle East,[4] and Communists in the French government[5] impeded efforts to forge an alliance.

In response to French prime minister Felix Gouin's hints that disagreement over Germany posed no obstacle to an Anglo-French alliance, Sir Oliver Harvey, Britain's under-secretary of state, traveled to Paris in 1947 to discuss the issue. Gouin faced powerful internal opposition, however, as Communist and Christian Democrat members of the French cabinet, who favored an unsparing anti-German policy, rebelled. France consequently adopted a hard-line policy that advocated detaching the Ruhr and the Rhineland, the seedbeds of German military-industrial might, from Germany. Nonetheless, this policy conflicted with British (and American) objectives, which opposed dismembering Germany. In addition, deteriorating East-West relations magnified London's concern over Communist ministers in the French government. Plans for an alliance stalled.[6]

Although one might argue that France's demands prove its overriding fear of Germany, other reasons help explain French policy. Prominent French officials wanted to block the creation of a central German administration because they feared it would eventually lead to Soviet dominance. On September 27, 1945, French Foreign Minister René Mayer met with U.S. ambassador to France Jefferson Caffery. According to Caffery,

Mayer, "repeating what de Gaulle and Bidault have often told me before," told him that the French were worried that a central German government would "eventually be dominated by the Russians" and that they would end up having "the Soviets on their frontiers."[7] French president Charles de Gaulle seconded Mayer. He told Caffery that France rejected the "setting up of any sort of central government in Germany" because they were convinced that any such government "would inevitably" fall into Soviet hands.[8] George Bidault echoed this point: "centralized administrative agencies" would "inevitably lead" to a Soviet-dominated Germany.[9]

Despite their differences over secondary issues Britain, France, and the United States remained close on fundamentals. They strongly believed that they should organize *western* Germany and integrate it into their bloc. The American government adopted such a policy in 1946, and the British soon accorded this plan their support. The French government hesitated, however, largely for domestic political reasons. The French Communist Party held great political influence in France and would immediately block such a move. British officials recognized this point. After a meeting with Bidault, it was noted, "The difficulty of frank discussion with the French government owing to the presence of Communist Ministers was not specifically touched on, but M. Bidault said several times that everything would be easier when the elections were over and if his party won. He implied that he recognized that fundamental questions could not be discused in present circumstances."[10] The political situation changed in 1947 when the government of Paul Ramadier expelled the Communists from his cabinet. From that point France gradually moved toward open acceptance of the "Western strategy" and in 1948 agreed to cosponsor the establishment of a West German state.[11]

Similar motivations explain other aspects of French policy. Although the Soviet Union posed a far greater threat to France than Germany, some scholars disagree with this characterization. According to William Hitchcock, "What made the French security predicament so difficult to manage in 1945–1948 was precisely the dual nature of the threat. As far as the French leadership was concerned, there was both a German problem and a Soviet problem, and both were urgent. We need not privilege one above the other, since the French themselves did not have this luxury."[12]

Yet French foreign policy officials did not share this view. They believed that the Soviet Union represented the primary danger to their security. Beginning to suspect Soviet intentions and clash with Moscow over the future of Germany, French policy makers took refuge in Western collective security arrangements.[13] Their first move was to establish an alliance with Britain. Signed on March 4, 1947, the Treaty of Dunkirk was ostensibly directed against Germany. In truth, however, the anti-German clauses were merely cosmetic—the treaty actually targeted the Soviet Union. The agreement identified Germany as the principal threat because neither Britain nor France wanted to antagonize the Soviet Union given the poor state of Western defenses.[14] In the words of Foreign Minister Bidault, the German threat was a "useful myth."[15] Anti-German language was also useful for internal French politics. The French government included four Communist ministers who rejected any plan that failed to treat Germany harshly. Without the adherence of other European nations, however, the Treaty of Dunkirk's character was more diplomatic and political than strategic.[16]

The collapse of the November–December 1947 Council of Foreign Ministers' (CFM) meeting, at which the Soviets took a hard line on Germany, signaled a definitive rupture between East and West. The Western powers responded by moving ahead with plans to create a West German state. Aware that this move would alarm the Soviets and thus increase the odds of conflict, the West attempted to organize itself to deter Soviet aggression or to repulse it should deterrence fail. Given that their only recourse should the Soviet Union assault Western Europe lay with America's nuclear monopoly, the Western allies moved to construct more ambitious security arrangements to deal with a Soviet attack.[17]

Even before the close of the failed CFM meeting, Ernest Bevin and Georges Bidault, the British and French foreign ministers, decided to hold formal talks on a variety of subjects, including defense. They agreed that America had to affiliate itself with any Anglo-French organization if this body were to have a reasonable chance of success. As Bevin told U.S. secretary of state George C. Marshall, they had to "devise some Western democratic system comprising the Americans, ourselves, France, Italy, &c., and, of course, the Dominions. This would not be a formal alliance, but an understanding backed by power, money and resolute action."[18] In January 1948, Harvey visited Paris to explain a British plan for an organization supported by the Dominions and the United States and committed to defending Western Europe. He suggested first approaching the Benelux and other West European countries to persuade them to join a pact modeled on the Treaty of Dunkirk.[19]

The Europeans Band Together

In early 1948, the Western allies opened talks designed to create a West German state. Not surprisingly, Moscow retaliated by adopting an aggressive tone toward the West. The Soviets began by impeding Western access to Berlin, blockading it completely in June. Although the Benelux countries, Britain, and France bickered over the terms of the proposed successor to the Treaty of Dunkirk, the Communist takeover of Czechoslovakia in February 1948 prompted them to set aside their differences and consider more ambitious defense plans. On March 3, the French cabinet decided to renew its efforts to work out a treaty arrangement with London. The effort soon bore fruit. On March 17, 1948, the Benelux countries, Britain, and France concluded the Brussels Treaty, a mutual assistance pact that bonded its members together for fifty years.[20]

Like the Treaty of Dunkirk, the Brussels Treaty formally identified Germany as the principal threat to European security even though its drafters thought otherwise. Although the Soviet Union was the true target of the treaty, Bevin wanted to refrain from provoking Moscow unnecessarily and Bidault wanted to avoid creating political problems in France.[21] In reality, the Brussels Treaty Organization (BTO) was more symbol than substance. The most the BTO's handful of divisions could accomplish in the face of a Soviet ground attack would be to buy time in hopes that America would eventually intervene[22]—itself an uncertain proposition.[23] Nevertheless, European officials deemed this collective move necessary if they were to overcome the United States' traditional skepticism of continental affairs and persuade it to formally ally with them. The BTO therefore represented a key strategy in drawing the Americans into Europe.[24]

The February Prague Coup especially alarmed French officials, who saw it as the opening move in a Soviet bid for control of Western Europe. In a span of five weeks, beginning on March 4, Bidault dispatched three messages to the United States, urgently requesting a military alliance among London, Washington, and Paris. Although sympathetic to French concerns, U.S. officials did not share the same degree of concern. They suggested instead that Europe should first organize its own defenses before America would act.[25] Soon thereafter, however, Britain, Canada, and the United States held secret talks at the Pentagon. These discussions led to the signing of the North Atlantic Treaty (NAT) on April 4, 1949; the pact was ratified in August.[26]

France greeted the NAT with welcome relief, as Britain, the United States, and other countries joined in a collective security pact. Yet the creation of NATO failed to satisfy all of France's concerns, one of which was the poor state of Western defense. An agreement to create a security pact was one thing; finding the men and materiel to turn the idea into reality was another. Although Article 5 stipulated that "an armed attack against one or more of [the signatories] shall be considered an attack against them all," the agreed-to response to such an attack was vague. The clause provided that each state "will assist the Party or Parties so attacked by taking . . . such action as it deems necessary, including the use of armed force." The United States could thus respond to an attack on France by diplomatic instead of military means and still fulfill its treaty obligations.[27]

In spite of this "out clause," the Europeans—especially the French—pinned their hopes on Article 3, which called for "self-help and mutual aid [in order to] resist armed attack." They expected that U.S. financial and military aid would inevitably link America's interests to those of Europe. Indeed, the request of the Brussels Treaty nations for such aid from the United States came the day after the NAT was signed. France eventually became one of the largest recipients of U.S. aid, which enabled it to rebuild its military might and offset the costs of the Indochina War.[28]

In the months following its creation, NATO formulated its military strategy for Western Europe. In December 1949, NATO defense ministers approved "The Strategic Concept for the Defense of the North Atlantic Area." The European states would provide the ground forces and the United States would contribute an "atomic shield": overwhelming air power and the ability to retaliate massively with atomic weapons. The adoption of NATO Defense Committee paper number 6 (DC-6) codified NATO's reliance on American air power in its war plans.[29]

Despite these positive steps, for France, uncertainties remained. Another French concern centered on rumors that the United States secretly planned to rearm Germany and then bring U.S. troops home, leaving France to deal with the consequences. Giving life to these rumors, the U.S. Joint Chiefs of Staff (JCS) deemed Europe militarily indefensible in the short run. The Joint Chiefs recommended that the United States adopt a peripheral strategy: America's forces would fall back to the Pyrenees and the United Kingdom to later liberate a Soviet-occupied Europe. French and other European officials balked at these plans, unwilling to suffer another occupation. Moreover, because U.S. air power would be the primary means of dislodging enemy forces from Allied soil, European officials found the cost of liberation simply too high. They therefore pressured U.S. officials for reassurance of America's commitment to Europe's defense.[30]

To reassure them, the United States proposed a policy of "forward defense," an outgrowth of the Medium Term Defense Plan (MTDP) developed by NATO's Standing Group in early 1950. NATO planners estimated that in order to carry out MTDP, the Alliance would need 90 ready and reserve divisions, 54 of them located in the Central Region.[31] Revised by NATO's Defense Committee in October 1950 and approved in December as DC 28, the plan called for 95½ divisions, 556 major combat vessels, and more than 9,000 aircraft to be ready for a planning date of July 1, 1954. Under this plan, NATO's Western European Region had the duty of stopping a Soviet attack as far east in Germany as possible.

The German Question

Although NATO was an established fact, one nation was conspicuous by its absence: the Federal Republic of Germany. In light of the growing mistrust between East and West, it seemed clear that Germany would be asked to play some role in Western defense. The potential of German manpower and industrial resources offered a decisive strategic prize for both America and the Soviet Union. For the United States, not only would Germany greatly enhance Soviet power if swallowed up into the Communist sphere, but failing an alliance with Bonn meant forgoing much-needed wealth, resources, and military-industrial potential. In fact, NATO war planners believed that even with additional American and European ground forces, German manpower would still be needed to carry out NATO's strategic plans (DC 6/1 and the MTDP). Thus the United States would realize a great geopolitical advantage if a revived Germany could assist in supporting European defense.[32]

The idea to rearm Germany occurred to some Western officials well before September 1950. They wanted to harness the Federal Republic's potential military-industrial power, but failed to conceive of a politically acceptable way of doing so. Europe's sizable material shortcomings, coupled with the Anglo-American refusal to commit large numbers of ground troops to the continent permanently, made it inevitable that the issue of German remilitarization would arise at the highest governmental levels.

Throughout 1948, U.S. military officials had often raised the topic with their French colleagues. That year a Joint War Plans Branch of the U.S. Army had speculated about Germany's and Japan's place in the postwar strategic balance. In January 1949, U.S. Lieutenant General Matthew Ridgway had broached the subject with General Pierre Billotte, the French delegate to the United Nations. Ridgway argued that it would be impossible to defend against a Soviet ground attack without the Germans, "the best infantry in Europe." Three months later, the secret meetings among Britain, Canada, and the United States led to a report that recommended rapidly creating an Atlantic Pact conducive to including West Germany as a member. In autumn 1949, the U.S. Army General Staff devised a plan to incorporate German forces into NATO. Subsequently, Joint Chiefs of Staff document 2124 of April 30, 1950, urged that "the Western Germans should now be given [a] real and substantial opportunity to participate politically, economically and militarily in Western Europe and North Atlantic region[al] arrangements on a basis of equality and of being integrated rapidly into the North Atlantic Community." Then on May 7, in an interview to the *New York Times,* four-star General Lucius D. Clay, the former U.S. Military Governor in Germany, proposed that Germany contribute a limited force in the context of a European defense force.[33]

Despite the widespread belief among the U.S. top brass, especially the Joint Chiefs of Staff, that German troops were indispensable to Western defense, many American officials believed that the United States needed ironclad precautions. Some U.S. State Department officials, along with their European counterparts, feared that rearming Germany would rekindle German militarism. Other officials counterargued, however, that participating in a European defense force would dampen these militaristic embers by integrating Germany into the West and granting the Federal Republic a constructive role in the larger community of nations on a basis of equality.[34]

Political and financial considerations also underlay the American push for a European army. For example, Allied community forces would promote European integration, a primary goal of U.S. policy. American officials believed that such unity was necessary to ensure the smooth functioning of a market-based international economy. Despair and economic privation, they argued, provided fertile soil for Marxism–Leninism. A prosperous, vigorous, and united Europe would be better able to resist Communist subversion than one still crippled from the war. Additionally, the continued well-being of the U.S. economy required a healthy international environment.[35] The United States wanted desperately to slash its fiscal outlays, and helping to prop up the Europeans presented an inviting target for the federal budgetary ax. Moreover, with a budget-cutting president and a fiscally minded secretary of defense, Louis Johnson, the American military establishment desperately wanted to avoid serving as the lone sentry for European defense.[36]

High-ranking American officials thought that encouraging the Europeans to cooperate militarily would demonstrate to a skeptical U.S.

Congress that the Old World was making a good-faith effort to defend itself. Many Truman administration officials feared that America might return to prewar "isolationism." They believed that a pronounced isolationist sentiment still existed on Capitol Hill, reflecting congressional insistence that the United States direct its concerns inward and let the Europeans fend for themselves. According to this line of argument, America had already done its share prosecuting the Second World War and delivering Marshall Plan aid at great sacrifice.[37] The tide of McCarthyism, which swept the U.S. political spectrum to the right, only encouraged this sentiment. Conversely, evidence of European self-initiative might convince Congress that Europe merited a substantial and enduring American commitment.

Although the question of German rearmament had been quietly discussed for years within the corridors of the Atlantic community, it bubbled to the surface in 1950. The reticence at discussing this issue in public is not surprising; given the tragic events of recent history, the notion of placing arms in the hands of Germany unsettled many. Even Germans themselves were sharply divided over this issue. At a press conference in early January 1950, Kurt Schumacher, the outspoken leader of the German Social Democratic Party (SPD), asserted that the Germans were not "morally, materially, or biologically" able to survive another war. On the subject of rearmament, he advised, "It would be a good idea if all Germans kept their mouths shut."[38]

Yet one prominent German did speak up: Konrad Adenauer, the seventy-three-year-old former mayor of Cologne. Formally elected the West German chancellor in September 1949, Adenauer led the Christian Democratic Union-Christian Social Union (CDU-CSU) coalition.[39] In an interview with the *Cleveland Plain Dealer* a little more than a month before Schumacher's press conference, Adenauer had said that he opposed creating a new *Wehrmacht* but would favor Germany contributing to a European defense force. These remarks triggered a storm of protests both at home and abroad, for they gave the appearance that the Western powers had already discussed the issue with the chancellor (U.S. secretary of state Dean Acheson had visited Adenauer just a few days earlier).[40] These statements also flatly contradicted Adenauer's pledge of November 1949 to "prevent the re-creation of armed forces of any kind."[41]

Understandably, France, which had thrice borne the brunt of German aggression in the previous eighty years, expressed grave concerns. Its sobering experiences meant that French national security policy would rest on France's ability to deny the former Third Reich the capability to wage war. Yet key French officials had already concluded that France needed German manpower and resources to defend against the Soviet Union, which they believed posed a more immediate threat to France's security. These officials knew, however, that attempts to rearm Germany would provoke Moscow and incite intense domestic opposition within France. The direction of the prevailing political winds rendered such considerations vitally important.

The fate of German military might was a key concern for the West's political leadership. Georges Bidault, who played a decisive role in shaping French foreign policy, is often portrayed as a reluctant "European" at best, and a rank nationalist at worst. This image is greatly overdrawn. During 1948 and 1949, he marched steadily toward the European unity idea in order to foster the economic union of the continent as a way to deal with the "German problem." Thus, France wanted Germany to take part in Europe, though with limits on its participation.[42]

Even though Bidault tacitly supported German rearmament, he realized that publicly admitting it would be politically lethal. In a February 24, 1950 speech to the National Assembly, France's lower house of parliament, Bidault, then prime minister, voiced sentiments similar to those SPD leader Schumacher had made a month earlier: "The French Government, to the same extent that it is in favour of the progressive incorporation of Germany in a European whole and in favour of the admission of Germany to the organizations which will form the basis of peaceful cooperation between the countries of Europe, considers that it is quite impossible even to discuss the question of a restoration of Germany's military forces."[43] Not surprisingly, this statement broadly reflected the political currents then coursing through the French body politic. As already noted, however, Bidault considered the German threat a "useful myth." He also told U.S. ambassador to France David Bruce that rearming Germany at present would provoke the Soviets to war. However, he added that "if weapons become more plentiful and it seems safe to rearm the Germans, that is a matter which can be considered at a later date."[44]

Similar efforts at misdirection also occurred outside of France. The fear of Soviet Communism enveloping the continent led many influential individuals to see rearming Germany as a necessary evil. Yet to publicly promote German rearmament posed political risks. For example, on March 16, 1950, Winston Churchill, the leader of Britain's opposition Conservative Party, recommended to the House of Commons incorporating German troops into the framework of a European army.[45]

Twelve days later, in a foreign affairs debate in the parliament, Churchill, under verbal attack, rose to defend his statements: "I said nothing about the re-armament of Germany or about recreating the German Army, but I see no reason why the Germans should not aid in the defense of their own country and of Western Europe. . . ."[46]

Foreign Secretary Ernest Bevin flatly disagreed with the once-and-future prime minister by lecturing him on Teutonic anthropology and present political realities: "The Hitler Revolution did not change the German character very much. It expressed it. . . . Therefore, I must say to the right honourable Gentleman that we have set our face—the United States, France and ourselves—against the rearming of Germany and that, I am afraid, we must adhere to."[47]

Notwithstanding Bevin's public admonition, his actions demonstrate otherwise—that he seemingly favored the rearming of Germany. It was Bevin who negotiated the Treaty of Dunkirk and the Brussels Treaty, both of which created alliances directed against the Soviet Union, not against Germany.

Across the Atlantic, Dean Acheson's thinking on the German question steadily evolved. Although the U.S. secretary of state had not long before been highly dubious of German trustworthiness, at the end of March 1950 he telegrammed John J. McCloy, the U.S. high commissioner for Germany (HICOG), expressing his revised thinking on the subject. Acheson now wrote that the State Department wanted a "strengthened Western organization both economically, politically and militarily." By incorporating Germany into such an organization, "the main outline of our Ger[man] policy will be fixed." According to Acheson, the State Department also thought that from the standpoint of public relations, it would be a good idea to play down such considerations.[48]

In response, a Policy Planning Staff (PPS) report offered a rationale for making use of Germany:

> The main stake in the struggle is Germany, whose future remains in doubt. The Soviet Union holds important cards but the West's are probably better, the former is better able to bid its hand, and both are vulnerable. What is not in doubt is the absolutely critical importance of Western Germany's orientation.
>
> In an important measure, this orientation depends on the wisdom and daring of American policy. Western Europe has not demonstrated a capacity to organize itself in such a way as to enlist Western Germany's resources and to ensure its Western ties. If

there is to be an effective organization of Europe, it will have to be set in a framework which assures continuous and responsible leadership by the United States.[49]

The PPS report underscored a sentiment that would recur frequently during the rearmament affair: the Western nations needed Germany to buttress their defense but must take care not leave it to its own devices; Germany had to be irrevocably tied to the West. If not, it might once more lash out, and the Western world might once again face world war.

Although France claimed to be flexible on the subject of German rearmament, John Foster Dulles, the recently appointed consultant to the secretary of state, voiced doubts: "I do not think that the French will at any predictable date admit Germany to membership in the North Atlantic Treaty. Schuman[50] told me last June that he thought the French would never agree to this because they look upon the Treaty as a defense against Germany as well as against Russia." Appreciative of the NAT's legal structure, however, Dulles added that "the French have, of course, a veto in this matter." This point is key: despite their many disagreements over a variety of issues, the Allies respected the Alliance's legal structure. As such, the United States made no attempt to abrogate France's legal rights, despite what it believed to be French obstructionism.[51]

In the late spring of 1950, the idea of remilitarizing Germany received a public airing. In a speech in early May, General Clay recommended that the Germans again take up arms—but this time under the banner of a European army. Sensitive to public opinion, French president Vincent Auriol quickly responded to Clay's remarks. That same day, Auriol publicly asserted that after having paid the "blood price," France could not accept any trace of German rearmament and would block all efforts to accomplish this goal. French defense minister René Pleven declared that if such a policy were adopted, he would resign on the spot.[52]

The Schuman Plan

An influential figure then offered a proposal that would alter the political landscape: Jean Monnet, a French-born brandy salesman turned international financier and government official.[53] Named in 1946 by General de Gaulle as the commissioner general of the plan for modernization and equipment, France's first postwar five-year plan, Monnet had long labored to expand the nation's economy and enhance its security. Recently, however, he had begun to champion greater international economic cooperation, of both the Atlantic and European varieties. Keenly attuned to the attitudes of U.S. officials, Monnet realized that France, saddled with its negative attitude toward the rehabilitation of West Germany, was gradually losing influence within the North Atlantic Council (NAC). He therefore attempted, successfully, to persuade the French government to take action. The resulting proposal took the form of a high authority that would administer the pooled coal and steel production of France and Germany. The Benelux countries and Italy would also take part.

Aware of the controversial nature of this binational economic arrangement, Schuman sought to line up support before going public. On May 7, 1950, Acheson stopped in Paris before heading to London for upcoming tripartite talks between Britain, France, and the United States. Meeting with Acheson, Schuman attempted to secure America's blessing for France's new European initiative: the European Coal and Steel Community (ECSC). Better known as the Schuman Plan, this supranational organization was designed to end Franco-German hostility by internationalizing the resource-rich Ruhr.[54] Although initially skeptical, Acheson soon came around after being assured that the project would not degenerate into an out-and-out cartel.

The next day, Acheson and Schuman discussed the situation in Europe and in Indochina. Although they decided to defer specific questions on Germany for the upcoming tripartite meeting, the two men did agree that military occupation would be effective only for a limited time and that Germany must be tied to the West. Accordingly, the Federal Republic had to be offered two things: security from foreign aggression and a bright economic future. These two goals could be accomplished by strengthening NATO ("not [by] building up German military forces") and by incorporating Germany in international economic organizations.[55]

The theme of integrating Germany into the community of Europe was subsequently taken up at the meetings in London. On May 9, France publicly announced the Schuman Plan. Schuman insisted from the beginning on the nature of France's intentions: "I hope that the work to which we will devote ourselves will offer our desired cooperation to all of Europe, including cooperation with Germany."[56]

Schuman, who had confided in Adenauer about the plan on May 7, received the chancellor's full support. In a confidential letter to Schuman, Adenauer praised the French foreign minister and predicted that the German public would support the idea "because for the first time since the catastrophe of 1945, Germany and France shall work together as equals."[57]

The U.S. government embraced the plan enthusiastically, viewing it as a welcome sign of flexibility on the part of France. Acheson told Dulles: "[It is] important that [the] French be given credit for making a conscious and far reaching effort to advance Franco-German rapprochement and European integration generally." Dulles was equally euphoric, saying that the plan was "brilliantly creative and could go far to resolve the most dangerous problem of our time, namely the relationship of Germany's industrial power to France and the West."[58]

The Truman administration soon accorded the plan its official support. The following month, in response to a query from Senator Alexander Wiley, the Wisconsin Republican on the Senate Foreign Relations Committee, as to whether the Schuman Plan was a force for war or peace, Paul Hoffman, the U.S. administrator for Marshall Plan aid, replied: "I think that everyone who has studied this European problem comes up with the same answer. If Western Germany is not integrated into the community of Western Europe, you have a dangerous spot that may, sooner or later, once more bring war to Europe."[59]

The French government, in contrast, had to contend with domestic critics. In a speech to the Council of Europe, Guy Mollet, the secretary general of the French Socialist Party, expressed deep opposition to the Schuman Plan.[60] Mollet said that he opposed a Europe of the Six.[61] In this Europe, France's "Third Force"—a centrist parliamentary coalition of the Socialist Party, the Radical Socialists, and the Mouvement Républicain Populaire (MRP)—would wither and die. Without London, the ECSC would divide Europe even further, for if Britain did not join, neither would the Scandinavian countries. If they did not join, the Benelux countries might not do so either, thus leaving a Europe composed of France, Germany, Italy, and perhaps Greece and Turkey. According to this scenario, "Europe" might very well be a conservative entity, possibly dominated by the Federal Republic. Mollet feared that in such an environment his cherished Third Force ideal would soon fade into memory.[62]

The Truman administration did not share these concerns. It wanted to establish European unity, a goal that would be reached only when France and Germany set aside their differences. American officials believed that the ECSC signaled a step in that direction. So did the Europeans, as the Benelux countries, France, Germany, and Italy began negotiations on the project in June. The U.S. administration also took heart at the creation of another supranational European organization: the European Payments Union (EPU). Devised in the waning weeks of 1949 and set up by the seventeen European Marshall Plan countries in

1950, the EPU's mission was to ensure Western Europe's smooth transition from bilateralism to full currency convertibility, a goal it eventually achieved.[63]

The U.S. government believed that, together, the ECSC and the EPU would foster European unity and French flexibility on the German question, thus laying the groundwork for a peaceful and prosperous Europe. Yet U.S. officials continued to worry about Europe. They also feared that growing German impatience would, in connection with the continued presence of large Communist parties in France and Italy, incite hypernationalism.[64] Hopes for the economic integration of Germany would yield to a military solution by early summer.

CHAPTER TWO

A Year of Living Dangerously

The beginning of the Cold War ended America's plans for extended cooperation with the Soviet Union. Although the onset of this conflict led the United States and its European allies to craft security arrangements intended to protect Europe from Soviet aggression, they judged these measures unsatisfactory in the long run.[1] Given that Moscow was solidifying its rule over Eastern Europe and possessed greater numbers of men under arms than the West,[2] Allied officials decided that Western Europe would have to improve its defense to deter Soviet aggression over the long haul. In the meantime, the Soviet Union's substantial lead in conventional military forces was offset by two factors: America's superior mobilization capability and its nuclear monopoly.[3]

The first pillar of U.S. deterrence was the inviolability of the American mobilization network, a vast industrial base that would enable America to prevail in a protracted conflict. The second pillar was the United States' nuclear monopoly, a strike force able to visit devastating retribution on any potential attacker. As long as its war-making capability and its nuclear arsenal remained untouched, U.S. officials believed that America could either deter a Soviet invasion of Western Europe, or defeat Moscow militarily should deterrence fail.[4]

Grave New World

Three events jolted American decision makers from their relative confidence: the Soviet detonation of an atomic device in August 1949, the

Communist victory in China later that year, and North Korea's attack on South Korea in June 1950. These sobering events compelled a seemingly complacent U.S. leadership to rethink America's national security policy.[5]

The grave political and military implications of Soviet nuclear capability alarmed U.S. officials. The belief that the odds for war with the Soviet Union had increased took hold among many American civilian and military planners, as Soviet detonation of the bomb, much sooner than expected, deepened apprehensions about America's professed unpreparedness for war. The United States' prodigious mobilization potential, supported by its atomic monopoly, would have been the trump card in the event of a U.S.-Soviet armed clash. An atomic-armed Soviet Union altered that equation. American officials subsequently determined that the relative size of each side's nuclear arsenal carried less importance than the ratio of warheads to military-industrial targets. Therefore, the greater size of America's nuclear stockpile meant nothing if the Soviets were able, in one massive strike, to lay waste the United States' ability to retaliate and a significant degree of its war-making potential. The Soviet Union's conventional military superiority would then allow it to quickly overrun Western Europe and the Middle East, leaving America powerless to oust the Red Army or to destroy Soviet war-making capability.[6] The projected growth of the Soviet nuclear arsenal led U.S. planners to see America at a crucial economic, military, and political disadvantage should the Soviets strike first.[7]

The Chinese Communist Party's victory over nationalist Chinese forces and the subsequent creation of the People's Republic of China in October 1949 deepened America's worries. For U.S. officials, these events signaled not just the birth of another client regime for Moscow, but one controlling untold millions of people and a vast swath of vital territory. The Chinese Communists posed a serious potential military threat to U.S. allies in the region and confronted the United States with a formidable political challenge as well. American policy makers feared that Japan might be intimidated into renewing its traditional trade ties with the Middle Kingdom, thereby vitiating the United States' effort at rehabilitating the former Axis power. A Communist-led China could also provide aid and comfort to the forces opposing Syngman Rhee, the U.S. ally in Korea, and could do likewise in Indochina, where French forces were embroiled in a bloody confrontation with forces loyal to Ho Chi Minh.[8]

The outbreak of the Korean War heightened American anxieties and altered the course of the Cold War.[9] American officials believed that the

Kremlin orchestrated North Korea's invasion of South Korea in order to divert Alliance attention and resources from Western Europe as a prelude to a Soviet attack in that region.[10] President Harry S. Truman responded by renouncing plans to reduce defense spending below $15 billion for fiscal year 1951 and instead increased defense outlays fourfold. The Truman administration now saw fiscal austerity as entirely unacceptable in the worsening international security environment.[11]

The Korean War also refocused attention on NSC 68, a National Security Council (NSC) document drafted months earlier by a joint State-Defense committee.[12] NSC 68 urged the United States to renew its conventional military might and to enlist the support of powerful allies to halt the spread of Soviet power and influence. Predicting that the Soviet Union would increase its nuclear stockpile significantly from 1950 to 1954, warning against an overreliance on strategic air power, and raising serious doubts about the effectiveness of U.S. air defenses against a Soviet nuclear attack, the NSC draft added the weight of its concerns to those of the spreading conflict in Asia.[13]

Subsequent reports in the NSC 68 series indicated that the Korean War, and the threat of other conflicts in Asia, jeopardized America's military buildup. The United States intended this buildup to redress the global balance of power and to prevent a "one shot" Soviet victory by 1954—not to fight smaller and limited conflicts such as the Korean War. For example, one month after China intervened in the Korean War, NSC 68/4 approved America's mobilization plan. According to the document, "It should be realized that the forces recommended herein will not be adequate to defeat aggressive Soviet or Soviet-directed actions in Soviet-selected areas around the periphery of the USSR, although they will act as a deterrent to further Soviet-inspired aggression."[14]

Soviet nuclear capability destroyed a world of certainties. America was no longer safe from direct enemy attack. Moreover, the country's role as the "arsenal of democracy" was no longer sufficient. American officials determined that the United States had to take active steps to ensure its survival. Spurred by the Communist world's challenge, U.S. officials began to recast America's national security policy.

To meet the Truman administration's goal of rolling back Soviet Communism, NSC 68 evaluated four alternative courses of action: first, "continuation of current policies, with current and currently projected programs for carrying out these policies"; second, adopting a policy of "isolation"; third, launching a "preventive" war against the Soviet Union; and fourth, rapidly building up Western political, economic, and military strength. NSC 68 ruled out the first option, for continuing current policies would simply perpetuate the present unfavorable situation and do nothing to reverse this trend. It also rejected the second option, for a policy of isolation would allow the Soviet Union to "quickly dominate most of Eurasia, probably without meeting armed resistance." Moscow would then acquire superior military-industrial potential that could be turned against the United States.

NSC 68 also discarded option three. Beyond moral qualms about initiating an attack, U.S. planners determined that such "operations alone would not force or induce the Kremlin to capitulate and that the Kremlin would still be able to use the forces under its control to dominate most or all of Eurasia." By a process of elimination, the United States chose the fourth option, which called for "a rapid and sustained buildup of the political, economic, and military strength of the free world."[15]

Adopting this option had far-reaching implications for America's grand strategy. It required the United States to undertake a massive military expansion that included strengthening Europe's defenses.[16] It also required the United States to conduct an all-out global economic and political offensive against the Soviet Union. Yet American policy makers saw this option as a temporary arrangement. Unwilling to station large numbers of its own armed forces on European soil indefinitely, the United States wanted Europe to increase its own military strength to the point where American troops were no longer needed there. America could then embrace the second option—isolation—without fear of serious repercussions.[17]

Nonetheless, a stumbling block existed. Given that Soviet nuclear capability raised the specter of a war-winning first strike that would decimate America's industrial base, NSC 68 mandated a shift from mobilization potential to forces-in-being. The United States' refusal to establish a long-term military presence in Europe made it imperative to enlist other military resources to make up the difference. Another document, NSC 82, offered a solution: it formally approved the deployment of additional U.S. combat forces to Europe and called for a German military contribution "without delay."[18]

From America's standpoint, Germany's potential military and industrial assets, combined with its central European location, made German participation in Western defense arrangements highly attractive. Yet rearming Germany would not only engender considerable controversy, but—given the uncertainty surrounding Germany's future political complexion and the Soviet Union's possible reaction—perhaps pose a danger as well. Two concerns, that of a devastating Soviet attack and the possible withering of German democracy, weighed heavily on U.S. officials. The past ravages of German political and military extremism and the shroud of Moscow's iron curtain blanketing Eastern and Central Europe confronted American policy makers with a daunting task: crafting a strategy that would erect a firewall between two nations hostile to the geopolitical status quo and to one other. The Korean War further complicated this task, as this conflict drained U.S. resources to a region of limited strategic value.

Despite reservations within the U.S. government about rearming Germany,[19] the accumulated weight of other considerations tipped the scales in favor of a German military contribution. By July 1950, the Truman administration subordinated reservations about remilitarizing the Federal Republic to *realpolitik* thinking. This change in thinking was codified by NSC 82.[20] American policy makers believed that creating a European defense force would enable the United States to meet its goals of containing Communism and sharing the costs of doing so. In their opinion, such an army would help to unify Europe by obliging the Europeans to band together in their own defense and thus reduce the need for a substantial U.S. military and financial contribution. American officials further believed whatever the hesitations of the NATO allies, the compelling logic of German-assisted collective security would eventually overcome their resistance to a remilitarized German state.[21]

French Opposition

The Truman administration, however, overestimated its ability to command assent. Its plan immediately encountered Allied opposition. The main critic was France: it refused to countenance a massive revival of German military power without receiving sufficient financial and military guarantees—guarantees the United States was unwilling to provide.[22] French objections surfaced at an NAC meeting in September 1950. The U.S. secretary of state, Dean Acheson, demanded that the Allies agree immediately and publicly to create a European defense force that had to include several German ground divisions or they would not receive additional American financial and military assistance.[23]

Most historians portray France, represented at the talks by Foreign Minister Robert Schuman, as bitterly opposing any move to rearm Germany. Irwin Wall, for example, writes that "Schuman remained obstinately against any idea of German rearmament." Likewise, Frank

Ninkovich contends that "Schuman was completely unmovable" on the issue. David Clay Large and Robert Gildea concur. Large asserts that "Schuman, for his part, refused to budge from France's categorical rejection of any German rearmament," while Gildea maintains that "Schuman was vehemently opposed to the rearming of Germany." Finally, William Hitchcock proclaims that Schuman refused to accept even "the principle of German participation" in an integrated force.[24]

The records of these meetings paint a different picture. These documents show that Schuman did not object to rearming Germany. Rather, his primary concern was to keep the idea secret. At a preliminary meeting, the American, British, and French delegations discussed ways to strengthen the defense of Western Europe. This conversation led to a discussion of the role Germany should play. Acheson then presented his "package proposal": in exchange for sending additional American troops in Europe and the appointing of an American as the Supreme Allied Commander for Europe (SACEUR), the European allies had to construct a European defense force that would include twelve German ground divisions. Although wanting to set limits on the growth of German power and independence, Schuman accepted the need for Germany to contribute to Western defense. He said that while he favored consulting the Benelux countries on this matter, such talks had to remain strictly confidential. Enlarging the audience to include other NATO countries would jeopardize this confidentiality.[25]

Later, in a private meeting of the three foreign ministers, accompanied only by their assistants and an interpreter, Schuman was more to the point. He admitted that it made no sense to attempt to defend Western Europe without German help. Rearming Germany would, however, pose psychological problems in France. Forcing the French government to take a position on the subject too quickly would be very unwise. NATO must first bolster its own defenses; only then could the French government take up the issue. He then expressed hope that the other NAC foreign ministers would be patient.[26]

Despite Schuman's pleas for secrecy, Acheson announced to the entire NAC his intent to rearm Germany. Forced to confront the matter in this larger forum, Schuman stated his concerns. He explained that while anti-German sentiment in France was waning, the proposal to rearm Germany had to be presented to the French public in the right way. Moreover, a premature announcement might cause repercussions. One also had to consider the Soviet reaction. According to Schuman, ties between the Soviet Union and its satellites were weakening as of late.

Rearming Germany might strengthen these ties because political refugees from these countries would be among the first groups to join German units. Thus although the West had to run the risk of inciting Soviet aggression by rearming itself, there was no reason to incur an additional risk.

Schuman said, "What I cannot do at the present time and under present circumstances, is to reach a premature decision on this problem. Such a decision might, besides, be fatal if it were to become known. We are all in agreement in considering that there is no time to [be] lost." Schuman closed by assuring his colleagues that while France did not oppose to plans to rearm Germany, he believed that making such a move would be untimely and that announcing the decision now would do more harm than good.[27]

Acheson knew that Schuman was as forthcoming as he could be on the question of German rearmament. The secretary of state informed President Truman that French officials indicated that domestic politics presented the major obstacle to agreement. The French Socialist Party (SFIO), which steadfastly opposed rearming Germany, controlled 99 of 622 seats in France's parliament. The party wielded considerable influence because French prime minister René Pleven, a member of the Union démocratique et socialiste de la Résistance, owed his position to SFIO support.[28] As a result, nine Socialists participated in the thirty-three-man coalition government, including Minister of Defense Jules Moch, an archenemy of any move to empower Germany.[29] This political arithmetic prevented frank discussion of this incendiary topic. Acheson warned that Moch, a leading member of the SFIO, would soon arrive in New York and "will be hard to deal with." Acheson therefore advised that "we should clearly differentiate in our minds what we can get the French to agree to in extreme secrecy and what we can say about the situation both in the supposed secrecy of the Atlantic Council and in the communiqué."[30]

The talks in New York continued at the September 22–23 foreign and defense ministers' meetings. At one of the sessions, Moch, whose son had been strangled by the Nazis, erupted: "Never will the French government accept a rearmament limited to Germany alone." Then, while the Frenchman was imploring his audience to consider the memories of the still-living victims of Nazism, Bevin cut him off, saying that although he was aware of the fate of Moch's late son, many English had suffered a similar tragedy—it was not an argument for condemning Europe. If France were to persist in its present course, Bevin warned, it would find itself alone. "Well, gentlemen," Moch retorted, "France will be alone once more, as in 1870, as in 1914, and as in 1939."[31]

These passionate emotions eventually subsided. In fact, that evening Moch, though still opposed to German rearmament, admitted that rearming the Germans was "rational on political grounds." He also conceded that the actual Soviet threat was greater than a still hypothetical German threat.[32] At the final meeting of the NAC, convened on September 26, the conferees agreed to an integrated force established within NATO under an American SACEUR. At that meeting, Schuman did not reject the German rearmament proposal in principle.[33]

Yet as the sole NAC member to object publicly to the plan to immediately rearm Germany, France came under critical fire from its Atlantic partners. France's international position deteriorated further due to events in Indochina. After suffering a historic defeat in October at Lang-Son,[34] the French government decided to prosecute the war in Indochina with even greater vigor, according it "absolute priority."[35] Yet adopting this policy would require France to augment its military presence in Southeast Asia at the expense of its military posture in Europe. The powerful French Chiefs of the General Staff Committee balked at the government's reordering of priorities: "France cannot abandon Europe because no system of security can be constructed without the French Army." The French military establishment now had orders to meet two contradictory objectives simultaneously without being given the necessary resources. For senior French military officials, the government's decision made a German military contribution to deter the Soviets even more urgent. They would eventually find this situation untenable.[36]

Nonetheless, the political damage had already been done. On October 6, the French cabinet examined the U.S. plan and unanimously delayed making any decision. At this point, Monnet stepped forward again, this time advising Prime Minister Pleven: "Our attitude must be extremely firm, and we must resolutely oppose America's present policy. But we have no hope of succeeding unless we give our opposition a positive content inspired by an overall policy for Europe."[37] Meeting with Pleven and Schuman on October 16, Monnet counseled the two men on how to make the best of the situation.[38]

The fruit of Monnet's counsel was the "Pleven Plan," a rearmament initiative that envisaged a 100,000-man supranational European army powered by divisional units from Belgium, France, Germany, Italy, Luxembourg, and the Netherlands integrated "at the level of the smallest possible unit." Modeled after the Schuman Plan, it was designed to keep the French Army intact while dividing German troops into small units, thus avoiding the creation of a German national army, a stipulation necessary to ensure French parliamentary approval. German units would depend on the other member countries for logistical support, further limiting their independence. Not least important, it was also designed to bolster the Schuman Plan, which was then floundering.[39] On October 21, the French cabinet agreed to the Pleven Plan; five days later the National Assembly gave its consent, 343 votes to 225.[40]

Although many French civilian leaders expressed deep skepticism about the idea, the French high command had long argued for some measure of German rearmament to offset numerically superior Soviet ground forces. By 1950, the question of remilitarizing the Federal Republic occasioned little wrenching debate in French high military circles. During the negotiations for the 1948 Brussels Treaty, General Paul Ely and Colonel Paul Stehlin had sent notes to the prime minister giving their views on the subject, writing that it would be inconceivable that the Germans not also pay the "blood price" for their own safety. Stehlin concluded that "a Germany that remained neutralized and demilitarized would soon fall under Soviet dependence and the frontier of the Western world would be on the Rhine."[41] This rift between French civilian and military leaders over how and when to rearm Germany would widen with time.

Although in favor of rearming Germany, French military leaders condemned the Pleven Plan, which had been crafted by a team of civilians—Monnet and his staff—without once consulting them. The military leadership believed that unmodified, the Pleven Plan was militarily inefficient and would undermine French security by placing unacceptable limitations on the French Army's freedom of action. The limitations levied by the plan's supranational character would prevent France from freely withdrawing its soldiers from the European army for use in the French Union, France's colonial empire. They also thought that the Pleven Plan failed to make effective use of German military potential. Unable to block the plan, military leaders tried to mitigate what they judged to be its serious flaws. Thus on the night of October 24–25, a group of officers directed by Ely and Stehlin vainly attempted to imbue the plan with a greater military character before Defense Minister Moch departed for an upcoming NAC Defense Committee meeting.[42]

The following day, Foreign Minister Schuman met with his Belgian counterpart, Paul van Zeeland, to discuss, among other things, France's position on German rearmament. Schuman explained that the French government found itself in an extremely difficult position because a large portion of its parliamentary majority, the Socialist bloc, rejected any sort of German rearmament. Yet France recognized that if were it to reject America's condition for financial aid—accepting German rearmament—Western Europe's defense arrangements could unravel. Schuman then detailed the plan for van Zeeland, saying that he did not yet know precisely how Bonn, London, or Washington would react. Schuman also expressed regrets that Moch would have to defend the Pleven Plan at the talks in New York, given that he was one of its most implacable enemies.[43]

Contrary to the common belief both then and now, the Pleven government designed the Pleven Plan not to prevent Germany from rearming; rather, it attempted to delay rearmament until a more opportune moment. As evidenced by Schuman's statements, a basic French concern about remilitarizing the Federal Republic stemmed not from fear of a German attack on France, but worry that such a move might provoke the Soviets to retaliate. Moscow stoked these anxieties by sending notes to America, Britain, and France soon after the New York conference, protesting their intention to rearm the Federal Republic. Soviet leader Josef Stalin proclaimed that he "would not accept the renaissance in western Germany of a regular German army," and on October 19 the Kremlin declared that it "would not tolerate" the rearmament of Germany.[44]

France took such threats seriously. For this reason, and for reasons of domestic politics, France's leadership proceeded with extreme caution. The main point to bear in mind, as Foreign Secretary Bevin noted, was that the French had "agreed to the principle of a German contribution."[45]

Even Moch, the French cabinet minister most hostile to German rearmament, agreed that Germany needed to contribute to Western defense. At the NAC meeting, which opened in New York on October 26, Moch seemed ready to compromise. Despite some differences, he did not outrightly reject German rearmament. He argued instead that France would accept only integrated battalions of 1,000 men.[46] Two days later, Emanuel Shinwell, Moch's British counterpart, asked him, "Do we now understand the French Government accepts the principle of the creation of German military units?" Moch responded, "The answer is: yes, but only under the condition that the creation of these units be not or tend not to become a risk which might be mortal to the democracies. In other words, that these units be not large units, but be integrated into European Divisions."[47]

One of Monnet's goals in crafting the Pleven Plan was not to prevent Germany from rearming; rather, he wanted to lessen the repercussions that might result from such a move by taking the initiative. Monnet feared that rearming Germany would doom the Schuman Plan, his blueprint for creating a foundation for European integration by pooling, under a supranational authority, the coal and steel of France and Germany. He noted, however, that the Germans had hardened their tone in ECSC negotiations once they learned that NATO wanted to rearm them. Realizing that the West now needed Germany, Bonn used its newfound leverage to make far-reaching demands. Monnet, who deemed the Schuman Plan essential to French security, insisted that France make no decisions on German rearmament until the ECSC Treaty was signed. As he told one of his associates, Paul Reuter, in October, "You well understand, dear friend, that if we rearm, there is no longer a Schuman Plan."[48]

Although known as the "father of Europe," Monnet did not intend to create a unified, stand-alone Europe. He instead wanted to construct an Atlantic system comprised of America, Britain and the Dominions, and the nations of Western Europe. His Atlanticism derived not from cultural or personal sympathies with the United States, but from his belief that only the United States had the necessary financial and military muscle to provide France with both butter and guns. Nonetheless, Monnet envisaged an equal relationship with the United States. He foresaw France contributing as much to the Atlantic world as America or Britain. The latter, with its Dominions, would contribute an international flavor while the former would be instrumental in helping Europe to rebuild. A France-led Western Europe would round out this politically integrated Atlantic world. These two conceptions, Atlantic and European integration, obeyed the same logic and hence complemented each other.[49]

Yet while Monnet and other French officials wanted "atlanticist" defense arrangements—in other words, strong American involvement— the Pleven Plan became a European plan by default. Monnet thought that the problem of German rearmament could be resolved only in an Atlantic framework, not a European one. America, however, rejected this view. When on July 22 Dean Acheson asked all the NATO countries to report the nature and extent of the increased defense effort they proposed to undertake,[50] France responded on August 5 with a memorandum that outlined a three-year plan committing France to a supplementary defense program of $5.7 billion, activating fifteen new divisions by the end of the third year.[51] This effort, the memorandum noted, would be ineffective unless there were greater organization among the Allies. France therefore said that this "New defense effort must be a collective enterprise of the Atlantic nations." The plan additionally required substantial aid from the United States and the other members of NATO.

The August 5 memorandum indicated that France would spend $1.4 billion in 1950, about 8.2 percent of the country's total revenue. It also contained a recommendation for the United States to increase the number of its armed forces in Germany. On August 15, France published a second memorandum that proposed almost total Atlantic integration (a common diplomacy, a single army, a common Atlantic defense budget, and an armaments pool in which the United States would participate).[52]

The two memoranda contained nothing, however, about rearming Germany. Instead, they called for Germany to contribute to Western defense financially and materially. The French proposals displeased the United States because they appeared to U.S. officials yet another transparent attempt to revive the French NATO directorate plan. France, fearful of Anglo-American domination of NATO, regularly proposed that the organization be led by a triumvirate of America, Britain, and France. It was also a way for France to have the United States underwrite French expenditures on the Indochina War.[53] American officials also failed to see how sending more U.S. troops to Germany related to the rearming of France. Moreover, U.S. officials thought that efforts to create this plan would lose valuable time. America's decision to reject these proposals thus forced Monnet to renounce his intentions to create an Atlantic army and instead to favor a European one.[54]

The Pleven Plan prompted a variety of responses within the Alliance. French officials tried in part to delay German rearmament until Europe had sufficiently rearmed and the French public had been psychologically prepared. German officials meanwhile fought any proposal that failed to ensure complete equality among the members of the proposed European army, including the Federal Republic. Finally, although the official American reaction to the Pleven Plan was cautiously favorable, Truman administration officials in private expressed strong reservations, referring to the plan several times as "unsound."[55] These disagreements over when and how to rearm Germany would continue for four years.

This delay raises an important question: why did the United States not simply ignore French objections and rearm the Federal Republic unilaterally? While the importance of turning Germany into a military and political bulwark against Soviet Communism provided U.S. officials with powerful motivations to ignore French opposition, ultimately, other considerations prompted Washington to renounce unilateral initiatives.

Many American policy makers agreed with French officials that rearming the Federal Republic might provoke Soviet retaliation.[56] Given immense Soviet losses at the hands of Germany in two world wars, such worries had considerable merit.[57] In addition, U.S. studies comparing American and Soviet military capabilities at the time stated that armed conflict with the Soviet Union would in no way guarantee an American victory. American intelligence sources in 1949 and 1950 indicated that Moscow was positioning itself to take advantage of this window of opportunity.[58] Some U.S. officials therefore believed that moving cautiously with German rearmament would not only avoid provoking the Soviet Union, but also buy time for America and its allies to improve their position and strength relative to Soviet capabilities.[59]

Lingering doubts about the strength of German democracy provided another reason for caution. Many American decision makers worried that rearming the Federal Republic so soon after the Second World War might stoke the embers of militarist and nationalist sentiments still smoldering in the ashes of German defeat. Yet proceeding methodically with rearmament might allow time to smother any rekindling of antidemocratic politics in Germany and thus avert an outcome inimical to the interests of the United States and its European allies.[60]

President Truman thought the idea to rearm Germany unwise and ultimately dangerous. Although he later changed his mind, when recommendations to remilitarize Germany first reached his desk, the President dispatched memos to Acheson deriding the plan as "decidedly militaristic and . . . not realistic [under] present conditions." While he agreed that a West German police force was needed to ensure local order, Truman warned that such a force should "not be allowed to develop into a training ground for a military machine that can combine with Russia and ruin the rest of the world."[61]

This last point resonated among U.S. officials. They feared that an independent Germany might, in return for reunification, embrace the Soviet Union. Were Moscow to harness the abundant mineral resources of the Ruhr, it would vastly increase the war-making potential of the Soviet bloc and consequently undermine the confidence of the West Europeans. Denying the Kremlin the opportunity to control all of Germany was a cornerstone of U.S. foreign policy.[62]

The United States also assigned great value to maintaining good relations with France. Thanks to France's geographic location, U.S. planners expected that country to contribute the lion's share of Europe's ground defense. French manpower would not only assist in deterring a Soviet land assault on Western Europe, but also act as an insurance policy against German revanchism. Peaceful Franco-German relations were a central pillar of U.S. policy because American officials believed that a Europe divided against itself would surely fall.[63]

American planners further expected to derive valuable benefits from France in areas other than Europe. They believed that by successfully prosecuting the war in Indochina, France would aid in arresting the spread of Communism in Asia, another region of great importance to the United States, especially in light of China's intervention in the Korean War in October 1950. Given these larger aims, antagonizing France with unilateral action regarding Germany would, in the eyes of U.S. policy makers, be plainly counterproductive.[64]

American planners also wanted to avoid applying too much pressure on Paris lest the United States topple its centrist coalition government and possibly bring to power either the rightist Rassemblement du peuple français (RPF), founded by Charles de Gaulle, or the French Communist Party (Parti communiste français, PCF). Due to their vehement opposition to the EDC, among other reasons, Washington officials would have welcomed neither party's accession to power.[65] In addition, membership in postwar multinational organizations conferred on France legal standing in many important international economic, military, and political matters. America refrained from trampling on these rights not because of qualms about flouting international "norms," but because their violation would doubtless anger French legislators, who might respond in ways counter to U.S. interests.[66]

Bidault, Monnet, Schuman, and several other top French officials agreed that the West had to rearm Germany in order to redress the conventional military balance in Europe.[67] These officials wanted, however, to slow the pace of German rearmament until the region had sufficiently recovered, America and Britain had provided long-term security guarantees, and French public opinion could be prepared for this move. Four years under the yoke of German occupation left the French public understandably wary of any revival of German power and independence. Yet French officials dared not reject America's demand outright lest it make good on Acheson's "threat."[68]

American Gears, German Sand

France was not alone in wanting to slow down things: Germany wanted to put a break on U.S. plans, too. On the one hand, Chancellor of the

Federal Republic Konrad Adenauer also feared Moscow's potential response to the rearming of his country. In April 1950, he had demanded the creation of a 25,000-man mobile police force to balance the Soviet-established *Volkspolitzei* in East Germany. According to Adenauer, the East German paramilitary force had the makings of an army, clear evidence of the Soviet Union's aggressive intentions.[69] On the other hand, rejecting America's demands altogether would risk precipitating a withdrawal of U.S. military forces from Europe and antagonize his supporters who strongly favored rearming Germany.[70]

Soon after the New York conference, Armand Bérard, France's deputy HICOG, reported to his government that Bonn was in no hurry to rearm. Herbert Blankenhorn, Adenauer's chief aide, confirmed to Bérard that although America was pressuring Germany to rearm, Germans refused to serve in an "American army." Blankenhorn also lamented the "Prussian spirit" that still infected many former German generals. To cure this infection, one needed a new generation of German soldier instructed in American, British, or French military schools. The chancellor suggested instead that France grasp the initiative by proposing the creation of a European army under Allied command, a solution the Federal Republic would then support.[71]

Bérard echoed this theme in a later communication. He noted that despite the escalating German demands since the September NAC meeting, French and German interests ran parallel. Both countries wanted to avoid having their territory serve as a battlefield, both wanted to avoid having their militaries serve as "shock troops" for America's anti-Communist offensive, and both wanted to avoid provoking the Soviet Union before Western military might had been rebuilt. Furthermore, neither side disputed the principle that French rearmament took priority over German rearmament. According to Bérard, Adenauer believed that a Franco-German solution would solve the economic and military problems facing Western Europe. Bérard closed by renewing his call for France to propose the creation of an integrated European army.[72]

Besides desiring to avoid provoking the Soviets while Western defense was unprepared, Adenauer had domestic political reasons for wanting to slow down America's drive for immediate rearmament. The main opposition party in Germany, the SPD, rejected outright U.S. demands to rearm. Moreover, a December 1950 poll indicated that almost 70 percent of the German public opposed rearming their country. In addition, the CDU lost November *Landtag* elections in Hesse, Württemburg-Baden, and Bavaria, a drubbing Adenauer attributed in part to public dissatisfaction with the discriminatory features of the Pleven Plan. Finally, Interior Minister Gustav Heinemann, who opposed German rearmament and disliked Adeanuer's "authoritarian" style of governing, threatened to quit the cabinet. A prominent Protestant leader, Heinemann's departure would hurt Adenauer politically.[73]

In light of these developments, the chancellor soon began criticizing the French proposal and raising demands that could not be met immediately. Adenauer was taking advantage of the Federal Republic's increased strategic value by demanding as many concessions as possible, and in tacit concert with the French he delayed U.S. plans. Added to America's own concerns about Germany and the need to accommodate the NATO allies, moves to rearm the Federal Republic slowed considerably.[74]

Westbindung

Adenauer's actions in the international arena derived from his policy of *Westbindung:* aligning the Federal Republic with the Western bloc. This policy would enable Germany to bury its recent past and play a prominent role internationally. More than just a foreign policy, *Westbindung* was a domestic policy, too. As Adenauer once noted, "Everything depends on foreign policy . . . the entire economy, what we accomplish in social policy." The new Federal Republic's identity was tied to its relations with the United States.[75]

In addition to seeking close ties with the West, the policy of *Westbindung* rejected plans to neutralize Germany and dealing with the Soviet bloc. Although Adenauer chose to ally with the West, this choice engendered much domestic criticism because continuing the Cold War ruled out German unification, at least in the short run. Adenauer conceded this point, saying that *Westbindung* would, over the long haul, lead to national unification. In the meantime, he had to fend off countless domestic critics who longed to heal the division of Germany.[76]

Moreover, Adenuer's political followers held no common understanding of the "West." Similar to the situation in France, disagreement arose over how to balance relations between France, Germany, and the United States. Germany wanted American support, European integration, and political autonomy. Finding the proper balance among these goals would prove difficult.[77]

Adenauer was not a naïve statesman. He put Germany's interests first and took for granted that his allies also put their own interests first. He recognized that no other country would sacrifice its own interests for the sake of the Federal Republic: "I believe we should understand that the Americans . . . follow an American policy, not a French or German policy." Adenauer therefore moved closer to the United States when conditions dictated it, and he moved nearer to France when he thought that America was taking actions that harmed Germany's interest.[78]

Predictably, announcing publicly the decision to rearm Germany triggered Moscow's vehement protests. The Soviet government argued that the accords the Grand Alliance had signed at Potsdam in July 1945 mandated German *de*militarization. Sensing an opportunity to stymie Western initiatives to remilitarize the Federal Republic by sowing disunity in NATO, the Soviets proposed on November 3 quadripartite talks on German demilitarization.[79] In deference to public opinion in Europe, the Atlantic Alliance now had to prove that it was making every effort to cooperate with the Soviet Union.[80]

Opinion among France's military and political elite about German rearmament was far from uniform. The French military command advocated rearming Germany in order to contain the Soviet threat. Differences between French civilian and military leaders over this issue would eventually poison their relations.[81] Despite this rift, many top French civilian officials quickly accepted the idea that Germany must contribute militarily to Western defense arrangements. Their primary concern was how to control German rearmament, not how to prevent it.

This attitude meant that differences with the United States on this issue concerned timing and procedure, not ultimate objectives. A November 4 foreign ministry memorandum underscored the common ground between Paris and Washington. "The points on which agreement now exists," the author pointed out, were "of capital importance":

> Because it has been decided that the defense of Europe requires establishing a line as far east as possible, the two plans draw from this the logical conclusion that Germany is called upon to benefit from a system of security resulting from the application of this strategic concept, and that it is only fair that Germany furnish its contribution to enable a defense of Western Europe. There exists, then, an agreement in principle of "German rearmament."[82]

This point was born out at an important December 16 meeting of French high officials summoned to discuss the issue. In the meeting, Defense Minister Moch merely insisted that "the error to be avoided" was to accept German rearmament "while Western forces are still not ready." His implication is clear: German rearmament would be acceptable once the Western bloc had built up its own power. The tone of the meeting, moreover, was rather moderate. No one was saying, "We must stop Germany from rearming at all costs." Instead, the French leadership sought to manage German rearmament, not to sabotage it. Once again, the Soviet factor loomed large. As the record of this meeting shows, French leaders worried that a decision to rearm Germany right away might incite a sharp Soviet reaction. This possibility, in their minds, was particularly dangerous while the West as a whole was still too weak to withstand the shock. It was for this reason that the West needed to move slowly.[83]

Compromise

Although the Allies had agreed to create a European defense force, they deadlocked over the details. In late November 1950, they reached a compromise—the Spofford Plan—that called for the creation a transition or interim period during which German ground forces would be limited to Regimental Combat Teams of 5,000 to 6,000 men, approximately one-third of a division, and would not exceed 20 percent of NATO forces serving in the European army. France would be exempt from these conditions.[84]

At the December 18–19 meetings of the NAC and of its Defense Committee, the Allies formally adopted the Spofford Plan and planned two sets of negotiations. The Allied High Commission would conduct the negotiations at the Petersburg, a former hotel that lay across the Rhine River from Bonn. There the Allies would discuss the question of securing a German military contribution to NATO. France would conduct the other set of negotiations in Paris on the question of forming a European army. Belgium, Germany, Italy, and Luxembourg would also take part in the latter set of talks. This two-track approach would allow the United States to move forward on strengthening NATO irrespective of what transpired in the talks in Paris. For his part, Schuman obtained assurances that the negotiations on revising the Occupation Statute would not lead to the complete return of German sovereignty and that the option to negotiate with the Soviets over the German question would be left open.[85] NATO also agreed on a forward defense strategy that ensured German participation (MC 30), an integrated NATO force, a supreme allied commander for Europe (SACEUR) for all NATO forces, and the naming of Dwight D. Eisenhower as the first SACEUR, decisions that would have important consequences in the United States.[86]

Despite these agreements, important questions remained unanswered. How would the French government handle domestic opposition? Memories of Nazi Germany's murderous behavior in the Second World War remained fresh. Appeasing such concerns would pose special difficulties. How would the Soviet Union react to the remilitarization of Germany? It had suffered greatly at the hands of the German state. Perhaps such a move might spur the Soviet Union to war, a conflict for which the West thought itself unprepared.

The year 1950 marked a turning point in the Cold War, as German rearmament became the stated objective of the Atlantic Alliance. This policy presented a compelling challenge to the Soviet Union and forced the Allies themselves to come to grips with several important issues. Increasingly, this debate would be carried on between France and the United States, for they had to reconcile their differences over how to rearm Germany before they could move forward with other common defense plans. France would also debate this issue internally, as powerful French groups clashed over this controversial topic.

In this debate, some observers have praised the United States for proposing to rearm Germany. Such a move, they argue, was necessary given the immediacy of the Soviet threat. They also assert that an irrational France frustrated such plans due to its absolute opposition to any hint of German rearmament. Yet this interpretation distorts the situation. Several high-ranking French officials accepted German rearmament in principle; they simply had their own ideas as to how and when this should be done. They worried about Moscow's possible reaction to such a move as well as about creating a potential power imbalance within the bosom of the European army itself. Debate over these issues would extend into 1951 and beyond.

CHAPTER THREE

Washington Pulls, London Follows, Paris Accepts, Bonn Hesitates

At the start of 1951, one of the preeminent issues facing the Atlantic Alliance—determining the conditions under which Germany would contribute militarily to Western defense—remained unresolved. The Alliance wanted to settle this issue quickly because its defense posture depended on having extensive German military might at its disposal.

American policy makers were especially concerned because U.S. national security policy toward Western Europe required a rearmed Federal Republic. Only if it were militarily revived could Germany play a leading role in containing Soviet Communism, thus sparing the United States from having to play that role itself. Under the whip hand of Dean Acheson, U.S. policy in late 1950 and early 1951 focused on rearming Germany as rapidly as possible. At first glance it might appear that the United States faced few obstacles in this regard, as France already had agreed to the Spofford Plan and accepted German rearmament in principle. Truman administration officials hoped that the upcoming Petersberg and Paris talks, scheduled to begin in January and February, respectively, would allow the Alliance to promptly work out any remaining disagreements and then move to consolidate Western defense plans.

Unexpectedly, however, the Federal Republic insisted on several political conditions before it would rearm, the most important being an immediate end to the occupation regime and the transformation of its political status. As the political status of Germany had to be determined before rearmament could even begin within the framework of the interim agreements foreseen by the Spofford Plan, German demands effectively halted U.S. plans.

It was no accident that German demands arose at this point. In contrast to the Americans, Adenauer and his colleagues wanted to take their time. As Adenauer understood, the international political environment in December 1950 and January 1951 markedly differed from what it had been during the previous summer. In the summer of 1950, Allied officials on both sides of the Atlantic assumed that a conflict with the Soviet Union was not imminent and that they had at least until 1952 to prepare for it. Consequently, they thought that a German defense contribution, which presumably could be brought into being by this date, would make a significant difference.

This assumption fell flat. The downturn in the international political environment in late 1950 convinced European officials that a clash with Moscow was much less remote than they had assumed. Many European officials therefore believed that moving to rearm Germany might trigger a crisis with Moscow, possibly even prompting the Soviets to invade Western Europe. Although the Europeans thought that Washington was running a risk by trying to rearm Germany so quickly, some members of the NAC, in their weakened condition, ultimately capitulated to U.S. demands. Adenauer then seized the initiative by raising demands with the implicit goal of avoiding a clash with the Soviet Union while the West was so weak.[1] This chapter examines this intra-Alliance dispute.

America Responds

The belief that the West's strategic position relative to the Soviet Union was deteriorating led the Truman administration to accord rearmament top priority.[2] The administration concluded that it had to rapidly increase the West's collective military and economic might.[3] The Europeans, however, wanted the United States to assume most of the responsibility for defending Europe, and for obvious reasons they wanted the front line of defense extended as far east on the continent as possible. Yet the American Joint Chiefs of Staff insisted that U.S. military forces in their present condition could not carry out such a task. The Joint Chiefs instead recommended adopting a peripheral strategy. Understandably, the Europeans resisted these plans.

To reassure them, the United States proposed a policy of "forward defense." According to this plan, an outgrowth of the MTDP, NATO's Western European Region was responsible for stopping a Soviet attack as far east in Germany as possible. A January 1951 study by the JCS sanctioned the MTDP when it concluded that the Korean War possibly represented the opening salvo in a global conflict that could neither be negotiated away nor lessened in severity. According to this study, due to the relative weakness of Western military forces, the only action for deterring Soviet activity that might "involve the risk of global war or for thwarting . . . Soviet piecemeal aggression is to continue, pending [the] build-up, the tactic of containment but more vigorously implemented and including the use of armed forces as appropriate and available. The present world situation is fraught with danger but it can be satisfactorily resolved if faced with resolution and action."

The study also accorded a special role to the French:

> France is the key to continental Western European policy. France is still afraid of antagonizing the USSR by strong policies and at the same time is afraid of a resurgent militaristic Germany. While France is fearful of her weak position, her leaders are unwilling to face up to the harsh and dangerous realities of the situation. As a result, France has not only failed to take effective measures for the strengthening of her own military defenses but has also made it difficult for [NATO] to take all of the actions which are imperative for an effective collective defense of Western Europe. If France continues to vacillate and does not rapidly build up her military strength in being, the United States may be forced to review its strategic policy toward continental Europe.[4]

From the American standpoint, France should play a crucial role in continental security arrangements because its army was the largest in Western Europe and should, as a result, provide the lion's share of Europe's ground defense. This role involved two missions: deterring a Soviet ground attack and monitoring a remilitarized Federal Republic. By fulfilling these tasks, France would unwittingly allow the United States to withdraw American military forces from the continent, confident that relative peace and stability would prevail in their absence.

Yet the Joint Chiefs ignored mitigating factors. For example, the study made no mention of simple geographic reality: the French government was being asked to countenance the rearming of a geographically contiguous—and much potentially stronger—traditional enemy. France was also still financially and militarily exhausted by the Second World War and the ongoing Indochina War. In short, France was being asked to shoulder a burden arguably greater than any of its allies. Its army would be the one both to endure the brunt of a Soviet ground attack and to keep an eye on a perhaps vengeful Federal Republic.

From the French standpoint, rearming Germany also posed an immediate danger: Soviet retribution. Over the longer term, the Federal Republic's vast economic potential could enable it to grow so strong as to upend power relations in Western Europe. To prevent such unwanted outcomes, France needed Britain and the United States to commit their forces to the continent to help offset any economic, political, and military advantages that a remilitarized Federal Republic might accrue. Yet after nearly two years of French entreaties, London and Washington still declined to make precise formal engagements. Anglo-American reluctance on this issue would help to prolong this affair until late 1954.

French Finances

Financial concerns also shaped French foreign policy. French officials believed that German rearmament could not occur without a concurrent and superior French effort—a point with which Adenauer agreed. France, however, had several responsibilities, both at home and abroad, that stretched its already thin resources. The most costly overseas responsibility was the Indochina War. At home, divisions within the French government made it increasingly difficult to close the gap between means and ends.

For instance, a gaping chasm existed between the Finance Ministry and the Socialist defense minister, Jules Moch. While the former stressed fiscal restraint, the latter, an uncompromising advocate of greater defense spending, often pursued his goals with abandon. After an acrimonious session with Moch in late December 1950, the finance and budget ministers wrote to Prime Minister Pleven to register a formal protest against Moch, who they accused of introducing chaos into the budget procedure. Moch responded by assuring Pleven that thanks to his (Moch's) efforts, France had achieved its first coherent national defense plan since liberation. Despite opposition, he vowed to fight on: "In their eyes the real struggle seems to be . . . a bureaucratic battle. I can assure you that, despite the ambushes, despite the opposition or objections of the financial ministers, I will continue to give every effort to carry out the plan for French rearmament in the time foreseen."[5]

These disputes would ultimately reach the floor of the French parliament. The National Assembly debated the fiscal year 1951 defense budget in an extraordinary session from the second until the eighth of January, on which date the budget passed by 333 votes to 181. The government agreed to spend $3.2 billion on defense. This total included $2.11 billion for ordinary military charges, of which $630 million was earmarked for Indochina and $1.1 billion for material for rearmament. To finance this special rearmament budget, France authorized a loan of $14.3 million and a tax increase of $400 million. It also counted on U.S. aid of $400 million. France also committed itself, within the limits of these amounts, to add twenty army divisions before the end of 1953.[6] France had set a difficult task for itself.

East-West Talks

Many Western officials feared that rearming Germany might trigger Soviet military retaliation. These fears were not without foundation. In a highly secret January 1951 conference between Soviet and East European leaders, the Soviet chief of staff, General S. M. Shtemenko, gave a speech highlighting the gathering threat posed by a rearming NATO. He recommended that the Soviet camp respond in similar fashion. Ignoring dissent from members of the Eastern bloc, the Soviet Union ordered them to set and meet specific targets within five years. The Soviet Union did not exempt itself. It focused on advancing its atomic weapons program, constructing military bases, building up the Soviet Navy, and instituting other steps to strengthen itself militarily.

Then on January 16, the Politburo resolved to create a bureau to handle military-industrial and military matters for the Council of Ministers. This new body would coordinate the efforts of the various Soviet agencies in order to impart greater coherence to issues such as mobilization plans, weapons production, and similar issues.[7]

NATO's plan to build up its military power clearly spurred the Soviet Union to respond. Yet rather than resort to physical confrontation as it did when it blockaded Berlin in 1948, the Soviet Union instead first initiated a war of diplomatic notes with the Western powers, offering to settle the German question through discussions.

Although several U.S. officials doubted the sincerity of these offers, they nonetheless went through the motions of negotiating in hopes of proving the futility of such talks. They believed that the exchange of these notes would mute domestic critics in the Allied countries, who argued that the Alliance favored a military rather than a political solution to the East-West conflict. The German problem, these critics argued, could be solved only on the basis of a negotiated settlement, a sentiment that the Soviet Union actively encouraged. Although many Western officials did believe it possible to hold fruitful discussions with Moscow, they cautioned that the West should enter such talks only from a basis of preponderant power.

The Soviets said they wanted to "discuss first of all the question of demilitarization of Germany as the most acute question for Europe." Eventually, the two sides agreed to hold a four-power CFM meeting to discuss carrying out the Potsdam agreements on German demilitarization.[8]

French officials anticipated the possible consequences of four-power talks. According to an internal document, the "fundamental principle" of French policy must be to prevent war and avert the "rebirth of American isolationism." Yet regardless of whether the negotiations "do not take place or if they end in complete failure, there is no doubt that Germany will recover its sovereignty and will be shortly called upon to play the role of a continental great power. No juridical or political-juridical arguments will halt this fatal evolution." The note suggested simply that France accommodate itself to a powerful Germany.[9] France therefore kept a close eye on the changes in German politics. If the revival of German power seemed inevitable, it was crucial to get the right kind of Germany.

Initially, things seemed to go well. On January 5, French HICOG André François-Poncet reported that the Pleven Plan was gaining popularity in Bonn as German politicians began to better understand the interesting future possibilities that it offered to Germany.[10] He soon backtracked from this view after SPD leader Kurt Schumacher savaged the French plan in a late January speech in Heidelberg. Schumacher charged that the Pleven Plan discriminated against Germany: "Whoever wishes to be taken seriously in political matters knows that the Pleven Plan cannot be a serious base of discussion for examining the problem of European defense." Schumacher concluded that the plan must be "quickly abandoned if one wants to arrive at concrete results."[11]

Schumacher's caustic remarks underscored to French officials that their best bet was to support Adenauer. The chancellor had actually suggested to France that it propose a European army. Unlike Schumacher, many of Adenauer's criticisms were merely tactical. Adenauer, as head of government, had to placate several domestic constituencies or face consequences. Schumacher's role as opposition leader, however, was to criticize, not applaud.

Like the French, the Americans also eyed the course of German domestic politics, which would play a key role in Allied negotiations with the Federal Republic. On January 5, U.S. HICOG John McCloy outlined his concerns to Acheson. He wrote that, "U.S. policy in Germany clearly enters 1951 facing extremely difficult problems in [the] implementation of [the] Brussels decisions, both [in] obtaining [a] German defense contribution and [the] negotiation of [a] new partnership status for [the] Fed[eral] Rep[ublic] vis-à-vis [the] Western occupation powers." The reasons for these difficulties, McCloy explained, lay within the bosom of German domestic politics. Schumacher had said recently that he might accept neutrality in exchange for unity. Moreover, the bitter Adenauer-Schumacher rivalry prevented the country from forming a grand coalition necessary to create a bipartisan foreign policy. Finally, McCloy opined, the German people also suffered from "uncertainty, apathy, and defeatism." They feared, as did many American and European officials, that rearming their country could provoke a Soviet attack.[12]

Although both France and the United States were correct to closely observe German politics, they often misread. In fall 1950, Adenauer received overwhelming support from his party on the question of a German defense contribution. Yet rearming was simply a means to an end. For many of Adenauer's followers, European integration was the primary objective and they believed contributing militarily to Western defense would help them to reach this goal. Adenauer's main goal, however, was sovereignty, which would enable Germany to obtain respect and influence in the international arena. Rearming, he thought, was just the best way to reach this objective. Yet rearming Germany without offering it adequate protection from the Soviet Union forced Adenauer to delay U.S. plans until Europe could rebuild its strength and the United States extended a continental military commitment.[13]

Adenauer's personal tendencies contributed to the complexity of the challenges facing him. He thought that time was working against him. The chancellor harbored powerful fears of a conference similar to that of the 1945 Potsdam Conference, at which the great powers called for German demilitarization. He worried that the allies would forge an agreement with the Soviets at Germany's expense. He therefore sought to cement ties with the West—a goal of *Westbindung*—before it was too late.[14] However, the inability of the Americans, the British, and the French to understand the complexities of German politics often led them to blunder.

The Petersberg Talks

At Brussels in late 1950, the Allies had committed to holding two sets of talks, one of which, the Petersberg talks, would begin on January 9 and last until June 4. These talks were designed to examine how Germany would contribute to NATO.[15] The negotiators included the three Allied Deputy HICOGs: John G. Ward (U.K.); Major General George P. Hays (U.S.); and Armand Bérard (France). State-Secretary for Defense Theodor Blank, a close advisor to Adenauer, Lieutenant General Hans Speidel, and Lieutenant General Adolf von Heusinger represented Germany.

The talks started slowly start because the Allies viewed them as simply a forum for the Germans to make proposals on the level of forces that they intended to make available. The Allies thus declined to inform the Germans of the force structure they were being asked to provide. The Germans replied that they needed to know the general extent of their expected military contribution so that Adenauer could tell the Bundestag how much other NATO countries would supply. The Allies countered that these figures would be provided by each country only after General Eisenhower had devised a defense plan, which was still in the planning stage. Actually, even if the Allies had known the precise figures, they could not be revealed for reasons of secrecy. In consequence, the Allies' stance forced the Germans to negotiate with a handicap. Not surprisingly, the talks broke down on the first day, forcing the Allied delegates to confer with their home governments.[16]

On January 16, the second meeting convened, at which time Chairman Ward told the Germans that although the Allies were still unable to provide a precise figure, the Federal Republic should prepare plans to raise 100,000 ground troops by the end of 1951. He emphasized that the Allies based this figure on a transition period that would permit Germany to begin immediately recruiting, training, and organizing such a force "without prejudicing later agreements which may result from the conference on the European Army."[17] Ward also said that the Allies were prepared to agree on the size of these units, which would correspond to the British reinforced brigades or American reinforced combat teams, and which would be "self-sustaining in combat."[18]

Proving to be a tough negotiator, Blank insisted on five preconditions before committing any German contributions:

1. The Allies must station land and air forces in the Federal Republic so as to provide security to Germany while it rearmed.
2. The Occupation Statute must be replaced by a contractual agreement.
3. The Allied High Commission must be replaced by a Conference of Ambassadors.

4. German military units should be accorded full equality with the other powers.
5. Financial assistance must be provided to the Federal Republic.[19]

The Allied representatives responded that these preconditions exceeded their competence. Blank replied that once the Bundestag had agreed to allow Germany to contribute to a European defense force, the country would need a minimum delay of three to four months to set up a federal office and to pass the appropriate legislation.

Speidel then noted that because of the great effectiveness of Allied demilitarization policies in Germany and the absence of detailed statistical records from which to draw, the Federal Republic had no basis for organizing and equipping its troops other than relying upon old *Wehrmacht* records. Even though Germany intended to rely on a volunteer force, its need for skilled specialists would require a certain level of conscription. Speidel, along with Heusinger, then presented a plan for creating these initial units, a plan containing three phases that encompassed the training of the proposed forces. If the Bundestag approved this plan by May 1, units would be available for combat by the autumn of 1952.

In view of the German plan, the Allied representatives realized that the Federal Republic would need to know how many troops it would be expected to provide in 1952 to allow it to calculate the size of units to be created in 1951. They then agreed to seek the information for the next meeting, which was scheduled for January 26. For their part, the Germans agreed to present proposals concerning the size, organization, and armament of German units under the brigade or combat team formula.[20]

As the Petersburg Conference resumed on January 26, the Federal Republic continued its demands for equality and sovereignty. Germany claimed that because it was operating under the Occupation Statute, it was independent of international law and thus not able to wage war legally. Moreover, the laws passed by the Allied Control Council could impose the death penalty on any German found in violation of them. For Germany to be legally entitled to wage war, there must be an end to the Occupation Regime; the return of German sovereignty in foreign affairs; and the creation of German armed forces once certain laws regarding demilitarization had been eliminated.

The Germans also presented proposals on the size, organization, and composition of its units under the brigade or combat team formula. These proposals were based on Germany's experience in its Soviet campaigns. Taking into account current Soviet military doctrine, which stressed armored warfare, Speidel said that Soviet armored units had to be countered with Allied armored units. Believing the tank to be the decisive arm in land warfare, Speidel argued that "the most effective unit . . . is a division with a competent allotment of armor which is given appropriate infantry and artillery support." Given that NATO would be fighting at a numerical disadvantage in open country, it had to counter with mobility and equality. This consideration would, in turn, determine the size, organization, and composition of German units.

To add weight to his argument, Speidel then quoted from a U.S. Army field manual, which stated that a division was the only U.S. Army unit organized to act independently. Speidel also quoted General Eisenhower as saying that he could not command units that were both forced into serving and discontented. In short, the Germans considered that any independent unit smaller than a division possessed little military value.

General Heusinger then set forth the German delegation's view of the smallest combat unit able to act independently. It would comprise twelve battalion size units along with a staff and signal unit, bringing the total strength to approximately 10,000 combat troops. Heusinger remarked that when one considered that an equivalent Soviet division was comprised of around 11,500 fighting troops, the German proposal was the minimum size acceptable. Heusinger also commented on the need for a coastal navy and a tactical air force that spoke the same language as the ground troops, along with a clear, easily understood chain of command for all Allied troops.

Aware of the limitations on the Allied delegation's authority, Blank requested that at the next meeting the Allied representatives be prepared to comment on the proposals the German delegation had advanced during the first three meetings. In asking for advice, General Hays anticipated that if the Allies told the Germans that the proposals were unacceptable, the Germans would merely throw the ball back in the other court and demand that the Allies come up with an alternative plan for German rearmament. Acheson told the AHC, however, to inform Germany that it could not comment on overall troop strength pending studies by the military chiefs of the occupation powers along with NATO members.[21]

The fourth meeting, commencing on February 2, concerned mostly technical matters such as the question of a German arms industry. In response to Blank's request at the end of the previous meeting, the Allied delegation also informed the Germans that their proposals on the size, organization, and composition of their units were being forwarded to the Allied governments.[22]

Blank took offense at the Allied delegation's refusal to share with the German delegation the decisions agreed to at Brussels about a German military contribution.[23] He told Henry Byroade, the State Department's director of the Bureau of German Affairs, that in view of the negative silence with which German proposals were greeted, they apparently far exceeded that to which the Allies had agreed. Attempting to mollify Blank, Byroade responded that the Germans were under the mistaken impression that the Allies had detailed plans. In fact, they had dealt with the issue only in a general way, and the primary aspects had already been given to Adenauer. Byroade then recommended that the Germans be less concerned about knowing the final product and instead concentrate on all the necessary preliminary work involved.[24]

At the fifth meeting of the Petersburg Conference on February 16, General Heusinger presented a tentative plan because he did not know the final size of the European army. It assumed that Germany would contribute a total of 250,000 men, composing twelve combat units of 10,000 men, a tactical air force and coastal force of 65,000, reinforcement troops of 20,000, and 15,000 men in staff work.

Asked by Chairman Hays whether Germany had any proposals concerning the component part of a division, Blank realized that the German proposals were valid only if other participating units were organized in the same fashion. Without knowing how other NATO units were organized, he chose to remain silent. Blank later agreed to present ideas on how divisions could be formed using multination combat units operating on a basis of equality. He continued to insist, however, that it would be wise to agree on the final form of the European army before they began forming and training small units.[25]

The Indochina War

While the French government had its hands full with European affairs, events in Southeast Asia forced it into a juggling act. January 13–17 marked the battle of Vinh Yen, the first of a series of French military victories in Indochina. Although these triumphs in the field improved the military situation there, they cost large numbers of reinforcements, which in turn placed the French Army in a bind at the very moment it was required to rearm in Europe. The inability of the French government to provide the military establishment with the resources to carry out national policies fueled a growing estrangement between the French civilian and military leadership. This dispute would plague France throughout this affair.[26]

The Indochina War and how it affected European defense were the topics at the January 19 meeting of the National Defense Committee (NDC), the heart of French military and political power since 1947. At the meeting, Defense Minister Moch drew a direct connection between French commitments in the European and Asian theaters. As he said, if war erupted in Europe, "The defense of Indochina appears, therefore, as very secondary: we cannot in prosecuting operations in this theater sacrifice the means necessary for the defense of Europe." Yet if one ruled out war in Europe, one could run the risk of "retarding dangerously the mobilization of our divisions in Europe by sending more aid to Indochina. In this hypothesis, it would be equally easy to consider that in holding our engagements in Europe, we would stem the current of America's isolationist sentiment."

Nonetheless, Moch concluded that France could not "reinforce our Expeditionary Corps and form the ten divisions as announced in our rearmament program in the recommended time frame. This insufficiency of our troops . . . will not permit us to contemplate this dual task." President Auriol agreed with Moch: Europe remained France's priority.[27]

Franco-American Talks

In addition to negotiations between the "big three" and the Federal Republic, France and the United States also planned talks. Prime Minister Pleven planned to visit Washington January 29–31 for talks on U.S. aid to France and American support for the Pleven Plan. In anticipation of his arrival, U.S. ambassador to France David Bruce met with top French officials to discuss the agenda for the upcoming visit. Pleven wished to discuss the Indochina War, the Pleven and Schuman Plans, and France's stand vis-à-vis a four-power conference. Bruce also said that the French were "very anxious" to know what the United States would do if the Red Army marched through France and Germany. They wanted to be informed whether, in the event the United States declared war on the Soviet Union, America would be in position to intervene rapidly and drop atomic and conventional bombs on individual Soviet targets. Pleven insisted that France should be included as a full partner along with Britain and the United States in Atlantic Pact decisions. Pleven also wanted to discuss how to combat inflation and talk about the status of France's military and rearmament programs. He said that he would not, however, request additional aid.[28]

On January 29, the U.S.-French summit opened. After dealing with Indochina in the first meeting, the two sides discussed European questions in the second session. The French delegation said that to solve the German problem, one must integrate Germany into Europe, exactly the goal of the Schuman and Pleven plans. Pleven also pledged that France would do its utmost to ensure that it carried out the October 5, 1950 rearmament program on time. Pleven then raised a concern. He said that when asked by the French public whether Western rearmament would provoke Soviet retaliation, the government always replied that Europe was protected by America's nuclear umbrella. Yet recent reports led him to wonder if America still maintained its lead over the Soviets in atomic weapons. Acheson replied that it did, and that America's counterstrike capability was the first deterrent to Soviet aggression while its military potential was the second. Nonetheless, power relations between East and West were so unsatisfactory as to render the situation unstable. Lastly, they discussed four-power talks with the Soviets.

Economic questions claimed center stage at the third major meeting. Pleven said that inflation, triggered by America's great productive power, remained a terrible problem for Europe. American diplomats said that they recognized this problem and were taking steps to correct it. Pleven also complained that the United States was too rigid to meet changing needs. Again, the U.S. delegation agreed and indicated that America was making efforts to ensure that its responses were more flexible. Finally, Pleven said that the German question should remain open before holding a four-power meeting. Acheson replied that Allied progress on Germany should occur independently of upcoming talks. Moreover, he continued, any Soviet proposal should be greeted with suspicion. Pleven replied that he was more concerned with European and French public opinion than with the possibility of genuine Soviet concessions. Both sides agreed that the Soviets would attempt to sow discord among the Western powers. Yet when Pleven said that one could not rule out an acceptable Soviet proposal a priori, Acheson retorted that it was difficult to imagine an acceptable Soviet proposal.[29]

Having questioned the Americans, Pleven's government faced tough questions itself. Although the Pleven Plan remained official policy, the French military leadership still leveled severe criticisms against it. On February 3, 1951, the uniformed leaders received directives from the minister of defense that laid out French policy for the upcoming Paris

Conference. Three days later, the Chiefs of the General Staff Committee responded: "[The] European army should be a military instrument of an economically and politically unified Europe. Placed at the disposition of a European federal government, this army would find its moral force and its cohesion in an enlarged patriotism and in the conviction that the interests of each state are better guaranteed by a complete association." It should have begun, they continued, by creating institutions, "the European army coming at the end of the project, crowning the economic and political edifice already in place." The European army, the Chiefs argued, should have been put in place progressively and in successive stages. The French government, however, had placed the "cart before the horse."[30]

The Chiefs also argued that the French government would reduce the effectiveness of Western defense by creating a supranational European army integrated to the smallest unit. They believed that in proposing this unwieldy polyglot fighting force, France had isolated itself from the other members of the Alliance, who saw French policy as obstructionist. According to the Chiefs, the government attempted to use the Pleven Plan to resolve the question of German rearmament and to advance its European policy. Yet in doing so it risked entering into an impasse due to the difficulties inherent in defining an entire organization that would reconcile military effectiveness with the political conditions that it imposed on German participation. With its principal goal to prevent the rebirth of a German national army, the French government directed all its energies toward reducing the German organization to a strict minimum. It was necessary, the Chiefs affirmed, that the outcome of negotiations disrupt French forces as little as possible and ensure a rapid and effective German military contribution to Western defense. Notwithstanding the Chiefs of the General Staff Committee perspective, the French government adhered to this policy.[31]

The Paris Conference

The Paris Conference, the second track of Alliance policy, opened on February 15.[32] Its goal was to consider how to form a European army based on European political institutions and within the framework of NATO. Although the talks would continue throughout the rest of the year, the first phase of the conference lasted until July 24.

Opening the conference, Foreign Minister Schuman outlined the political and military aspects of the French plan, presenting arguments in favor of it and responding to objections. He acknowledged that some people believed that the European army would harm the Alliance. He denied that this was the case, but said that if it were true, France would postpone its plans.[33] France's delegation then circulated a memorandum that presented a reworked Pleven Plan. It contained three primary aspects: military—creating a European army with a homogenous unity, structure, and administration; integrative—training leading to a fusion of European divisions and reserves, accompanied by central recruitment and basic training; and political—a plan to advance European federation. France, however, remained opposed to any German military unit larger than the existing regimental combat team (RCT). French officials believed that forming German divisions would inevitably lead to the creation of a German national army and general staff, both intolerable outcomes.[34]

At the outset, the French and German delegations quarreled over the size and the level of integration of the German units in the proposed army. The German delegation asked its French counterpart to define precisely the basic European army unit. The French delegates replied that RCTs of 5,000 to 6,000 men would be the largest national unit of mixed European divisions; they additionally called for the European army to be consummated in stages. Yet this proposal, the sole aim of which seemed designed to prevent Germany from rearming, ran counter to what had been accepted at the Bonn Conference. Consequently, discussion between the French and German delegations ground to a halt. The issue finally had to be set aside so that progress could be made on other fronts.[35]

Indochina: Hold or Fold?

The EDC affair did not occur in a geopolitical vacuum; rather, it was closely linked to the Indochina War. As long as the latter raged, the former would continue because the war drained precious French men and materiel that could otherwise be devoted to Europe. This juggling act posed severe economic, military, and political difficulties for France. The French government's unwillingness or inability to devote sufficient resources to the European army meant that a rearmed Germany would dominate this force and hence demand commensurate political power. French policy seemed adrift.

On February 20, the NDC discussed the war in Asia. At the meeting, General Jean de Lattre de Tassigny, France's high commissioner for Indochina and its commander-in-chief for the Far East, indicated that the Indochina War "was about holding," and that he "would hold" if given supplemental means. De Lattre's demands, however, had to be weighed against responsibilities in Europe and the French protectorates in North Africa. Schuman said that the crucial question was whether if in fulfilling de Lattre's requests, France would compromise European defense: "On this point, we are formally committed to our Allies to have ten divisions in Europe by 1951. This obligation must be kept; even a delay could have serious consequences by placing us in a very difficult position vis-à-vis our Allies." Schuman further remarked that it was essential to undertake a political analysis of all the questions raised by the war in Indochina and responsibilities in Europe. In any event, President Auriol said that a way had to be found to raise new units for Indochina without compromising France's ten-division commitment.[36]

Meeting again on March 17, the NDC continued the discussion. At the meeting, de Lattre professed that he understood the burden his requests for more help in Indochina had placed on the French Army. Yet, he argued, given additional means, he could resolve the crisis in Indochina. The campaign there was not an overseas adventure but a "test of France's capacity to transform its Empire into the French Union, namely a political and economic unit adapted to modern life. . . . As long as we hold in Indochina, we will remain a great power. . . . On the contrary, if we lose, we will be the 'sick man' of the second half of the twentieth century." For de Lattre, Indochina represented the "frontier of liberty," where France was stemming the tide of Communism. It was there, not Europe, where France contributed most to the Western allies. France merely had to hold until the armies of the "Associated States" were up to par.

General Alphonse Juin, then the inspector general of the armed forces, agreed with de Lattre about Indochina's importance. He contended that France could not keep its commitment in Indochina forever, only until the Vietnamese Army was in condition to relieve the French Expeditionary Corps. Juin also disputed the views of General Clement Blanc, the chief of staff of the French Army. According to Juin, although it would be difficult to honor de Lattre's request for more troops given France's commitment to provide ten divisions for Europe in 1951, the nation had to expend the maximum effort to meet this request, which de Lattre believed would enable him to successfully complete his mission within a year. This request must be honored, Juin asserted, even if it set back France's plan to field ten divisions in Europe. After a general exchange of views, opinion rallied around de Lattre. They agreed that France would prove its military worth to the Allies by "holding" in Indochina.[37]

American Impatience

French concerns were well founded. Disappointed with the pace of European rearmament, U.S. officials questioned France's effort. On February 19, the Joint Chiefs of Staff commented disparagingly on France's position toward German rearmament: "The French government apparently is willing to proceed with West German rearmament only as fast as is consistent with an avoidance of a political upheaval in France as a result of such rearmament. The French Communist Party is currently refraining from tactics of such extreme aggressiveness as would invite the risk of being outlawed but the large number of Communists in France continues to constitute a menace to the defense program."[38]

An April Joint Chiefs' study mirrored these doubts:

The military power of France, as well as that of the other continental NATO nations, has not increased as rapidly as expected. . . . France has been intransigent with respect to the rearmament of Western Germany and to certain details of United States collaboration with the United Kingdom. There is evidence that France regards the United States and the United Kingdom with some distrust.

Concluding that "the solidarity among the Western World had lessened," the report recommended that the United States increase the "will and determination" of its Allies to increase their mobilization readiness so as to meet the requirements of the MTDP.[39]

In addition to supporting the EDC, the Truman administration heavily endorsed the creation of the ECSC, hoping it might end permanently Franco-German enmity and create a peaceful and united Europe sufficiently powerful to withstand Soviet pressure without American aid. This goal began to appear closer, as on March 14 Germany finally accepted the Allied decartelization plan, which permitted the negotiations on the Schuman Plan to close successfully. On April 18, the Benelux countries, France, and Germany signed the Treaty of Paris, which established the ECSC. Two weeks later, the Council of Europe offered membership to Germany. With the Schuman Plan Treaty signed, Monnet could devote himself to relaunching his other project, the stalled Pleven Plan. The problem, according to Monnet, was that even though the civilian officials disagreed for political reasons, the military officials involved in planning the European army agreed on technical matters. Months would pass before this impasse would be broken.[40]

The principal problem for France was that it simply lacked the resources needed to carry out its international responsibilities. In lieu of shedding some of its commitments, France looked to Washington for support. Although the United States provided it aid, France expressed qualms about how much, when, and how the aid was given. On April 2, meetings began between the U.S. Embassy, the European Cooperation Agency (ECA), the Military Assistance and Advisory Group (MAAG), and French economic and military officials.[41]

Disagreements between the two sides soon arose. On April 18, David Bruce told Acheson that tension between the two sides over the level and method of U.S. assistance to France had reached the breaking point. Bruce feared that further strain on Franco-American relations could trigger a crisis. He said that Schuman had told him that the French cabinet was puzzled and resentful over the situation and that it would take up the subject at future meetings. Gaullist attacks that portrayed the French government as capitulating to the United States only fueled the resentment.

According to Bruce, Franco-American difficulties stemmed from divergent interpretations of the agreements reached in Washington the previous October and mutual misunderstandings on the part of Paris and Washington about the terms of that agreement.[42] Among these misunderstandings were the following: First, France substantially reduced its defense budget without informing the United States; second, the French reductions diverged from the pattern of priorities established at the October talks, contradicting oral promises France had given; third, Washington's shift to a new method of financing created another misunderstanding and the French interpreted this shift to mean that the Americans were imposing new, unforeseen restrictions; fourth, France believed that the United States had set a $240 million cap on aid for the first half of 1951 rather than determining the amount on the basis of current needs, which the French thought had been agreed on; and, finally, France believed that the United States was considering making the aid contingent on immediate changes in the French budget and military program.

Bruce feared that these misunderstandings might wreck rearmament discussions and "bog down in a morass of misunderstandings and mutual ill-will." He further asserted that the United States needed France's full support and confidence, for without it, "it would be a failure of United States diplomacy." Bruce asked the administration for permission to assure French officials that the remaining $129 million of the original $240 million would be dispersed immediately and without any conditions.[43]

Once the relevant U.S. agencies agreed to adopt Bruce's recommendations, Acheson then authorized Bruce to inform France that the aid would be forthcoming. Acheson also emphasized that the United States was *not* trying to make France conform with the changes in the October agreements: "What we are basically interested in, of course, is getting Fr[ance] to carry out [the] present program rapidly and to increase it as soon as possible. Our goal is not conformance with [the] October presentation but a program adequate to [the] requirements of MTDP."[44]

Although this particular episode portrays the extent of U.S. influence on France, it also illustrates the limits of that influence. America predicated its fundamental strategic plans on a militarily and economically strong France. Yet because the Truman administration was politically weakened at home and soon had to stand for elections, it could not propose large-scale overseas aid, a move guaranteed to provoke the Republicans, who would surely exploit it for political gain.

On May 24, the Truman administration submitted a new Mutual Security Program (MSP) to Congress. The administration designed MSP with three major characteristics of the Soviet threat in mind: that it was worldwide; that it was total; and that it was of indefinite duration. The MSP consolidated several foreign aid programs including military aid under MDAP and economic aid to underdeveloped countries as outlined under the Point IV concept. Under the program, the United States would send arms and aid in support of noncommunist allies.

The U.S. government earmarked the bulk of the assistance for NAT countries ($1.65 billion in economic assistance; $5.24 billion for military assistance). In the message, Truman noted that "the loss of Europe to the Soviet Union would not only be tragic in itself; it would also result in a tremendous shift of world power. It would compel us to convert the United States into a garrison state." The administration asked Congress to approve $6.25 billion in military assistance and $2.25 billion in economic assistance to other nations for the fiscal year ending June 30, 1952, an increase of $5.3 billion and $3.0 billion from the current fiscal year.[45]

France Compromises

Regardless of the amount of U.S. assistance provided, the Allies had yet to resolve their internal differences. On March 8, the Paris Conference held its first plenary session since February 22. Fundamental disagreement on the size of the basic unit of the European army divided France and Germany. The German delegation proposed to match the Soviet

Union's edge in quantity through quality. The Germans insisted that all operating units be entirely motorized, possess modern combat arms, and be of the same nationality and national command. Based on their experience during the war, the Germans argued that the units proposed by the French memorandum would be ineffective.[46] The representative from Bonn questioned the military effectiveness of mixed divisions of 16,000 to 17,000 combat troops, condemning them as too unwieldy and unable to confront an adversary possessing superiority in numbers and boasting powerful armored units. Moreover, the Germans asserted that combining two operating units should result in a self-sufficient fighting force of 10,000 to 12,000 men. France's Hervé Alphand, the president of the conference, immediately declared the proposal unacceptable because it conflicted with the principle of integration.[47]

The differences between the two sides centered on the question of the basic size of each unit: between 5,000–6,000 or 10,000–12,000 comprising homogenous operating units. The French delegation hesitated in part due to the upcoming French parliamentary elections in mid-June. Under pressure from the other participants, however, France compromised, and on May 6, it accepted the principle of an 8,000-man unit as the basic military grouping of the European army. Two days later, in a memorandum to Schuman, Monnet brought the foreign minister up to date on the state of the Franco-German talks. He confirmed the evolution of the French position. On May 18, France further compromised, indicating that it was ready to accept 10,000-man "groupements."[48]

These compromises were unsatisfactory to U.S. HICOG John McCloy. Frustrated with the lack of progress on the European army, McCloy increased the political pressure. In June, he delivered two speeches that set off political tremors in France. On June 11, relying on the conclusions issuing from a meeting between American and German military experts, he called for the creation of twelve German divisions—three of which would be armored. These units would be integrated in the Atlantic army at the level of army corps, contrary to the dictates of the Pleven Plan. Then on June 26, McCloy certified that Germany would indeed participate in NATO. The next day the French government, headed by Henri Queuille, reaffirmed that Germany would participate in Western defense only in the framework of a European army. It seemed that the EDC quarrel had finally come to a head. Two events, however, would alter substantially the political context of the debate: the June 1951 French legislative elections and the Eisenhower "conversion."[49]

June 1951 Election

The composition of the French parliament colored Europe's plans to integrate militarily. The political fortunes of the PCF and the Gaullist Rassemblement du peuple français (RPF) posed a dilemma for France's moderate political class. If a right- or left-wing party assumed power, it would alter France's political complexion substantially. Thus far, the so-called Third Force, a centrist coalition of SFIO, Radical Socialists, Modérés, and MRP deputies, had governed the Fourth Republic. However, the rising fortunes of both the PCF and the RPF threatened to end its parliamentary dominance and endanger the health of the French parliamentary system. Under the proportional electoral system then in place, the Third Force believed that the PCF and the RPF could win enough seats to make it impossible to form a cabinet and thus throw the political system into chaos. In an attempt to withstand the challenge from both the left and the right, the government tried to design an electoral law that would prevent either party from coming to power. Under the proposed law, when a coalition captured an absolute majority of votes in one of France's 183 constituencies, it became a winner-take-all proposition.[50]

The June 1951 elections placed many staunch EDC opponents in the National Assembly. The hard-core foes of the EDC—the Communists and the Gaullists—lay claim to 222 seats out of 627, more than one-third of the chamber. The elections also saw the centrist MRP plummet from 169 deputies to 96; the PCF drop to 101 seats, and the Gaullist RPF shoot up to 121, while the SFIO was left with 107. The Third Force failed to gain an absolute majority of 314. Yet due to the new electoral law, the PCF, which won 26 percent of the votes, received only 16 percent of the seats. Likewise, the RPF, despite winning 22 percent of the votes, controlled only 19 percent of the seats.[51] In the short term, this parliamentary shakeup allowed the new Pleven coalition government (Queuille had resigned on July 10) to make progress on the plan that bore his name. In the long term, however, this new political arithmetic in the National Assembly worked against the European army.[52]

The Eisenhower Conversion

The "Eisenhower conversion" marked the second great impact on the EDC affair in 1951. Dwight Eisenhower, like most military officials in the Allied community, disliked the Pleven Plan. He opposed the early incorporation of German troops under his command. His position created a formidable obstacle for those who supported the EDC.[53] Yet on June 27, at the urging of McCloy, Eisenhower met with Monnet, who tried to convince him of the dire need for a European defense force. Monnet's pleadings succeeded, as Eisenhower turned into a steadfast supporter of the plan, later testifying on its behalf before the Senate Foreign Relations Committee. Given the great respect Eisenhower commanded among civilian and military leaders, others found it exceedingly difficult to oppose him on issues of national security.[54] NSC-115 made support of the EDC official U.S. policy, as America pinned its hopes on the success of the Paris Conference.[55]

The Interim Report

In late June, McCloy met with Adenauer in an effort to secure the chancellor's blessing for the Pleven Plan. Adenauer used the opportunity to raise the price for a German military contribution. Pointing out that over a year had passed since the Korean War had begun, Adenauer questioned whether the West still wanted a German military force. If so, he expected the Western powers to offer more extensive concessions than they had the year before. Consistent with *Westbindung*, he later publicly announced that "if we are to be included in Western defense, it can only be if we are granted the same rights and equality with everyone else." He also told the French that "we don't intend to be mercenaries," while telling the Americans and the British, "Of course we belong to Western Europe."[56]

On July 7, Adenauer announced that Theodor Blank, his defense advisor and former negotiator at the Petersberg, would head the German delegation at the Paris Conference. Blank soon made his presence felt. Issued three weeks later, on July 24, the conference's preliminary report—"the Interim Report"—bore his fingerprints. In this nonbinding preliminary statement, the French recommended creating "European divisions" composed of three nationally homogenous *Groupements de combat* of roughly 5,000 men. The Germans noted that creating divisions comprised of *Groupements de combat* from different nations would create military inefficiencies. Blank made a number of demands:

1. A 250,000-man *Wehrmacht*.
2. Twelve German ground divisions.
3. A German air force composed of 2,000 aircraft.
4. A German general staff overseen by a German civilian defense minister.

The report, which remained silent on limitations on the size of German units and the question of a German general staff, aroused stiff French opposition, as the numbers suggested exceeded those contemplated in the Spofford Plan. Unable to bridge the difference, the report indicated that the Conference would solicit the opinions of the governments themselves.[57]

In short, the French wanted a division of 18,000–20,000 men while the Germans wanted operating units of 10,000–13,000 men. According to the report, "The General Staff of the Army Corps will be, according to these two conceptions, a composite: support units, including tactical and logistical support, will be divided among different nationalities. Each basic unit (regiment or battalion) will remain homogenous, and the division among nationalities will be fixed according to the percentages outlined in the Treaty."[58]

French Policy Shifts

French policy soon shifted. In mid-August, Hervé Alphand, the French deputy representative to the NAC, drafted a detailed report that analyzed the talks in Paris and Petersburg. Despite some drawbacks, Alphand saw advantages in adopting the Interim Report. He believed that the European army would forestall a revival of German militarism by tying the Federal Republic firmly to the Western camp. Coupled with the Schuman Plan, this defense force would deny the Federal Republic the opportunity to act as an arbiter between East and West and stop it from making common cause with the Soviet Union in a bid for world domination. A "European" solution also would confer other advantages. It would enable France to take leadership of the European army as well as its general staff; prevent direct ties between the American and German military organizations; inhibit close ties between the military establishments of Germany and the United States; and provoke Moscow less than a national German army.[59]

Although Schuman shared Alphand's point of view, he needed additional guarantees because of opposition from some quarters of the foreign ministry. This anti-EDC sentiment contrasted with U.S. policy. On July 30, Truman approved America's new pro-EDC policy, which Acheson followed up on August 9 by telling Schuman and Britain's Foreign Minister Herbert Morrison to move forward. Schuman replied on August 25, saying that it was necessary to take precautions against a German army "subject to rapid and unforeseen changes," avoiding the creation of a nationalist German army. France, he continued, "ardently wishes that Great Britain could participate in these arrangements or be associated with them."[60] McCloy then intervened and persuaded Acheson to drop his insistence on adopting a timetable and the interim concept.[61]

France's Top Brass Responds

The French military leadership, though unenthusiastic about the EDC, agreed to support it—that is, provided the government took certain precautions. On August 23, the Chiefs of the General Staff Committee examined the Interim Report and the Alphand report. At the French government's request, the Chiefs paid particular attention to the military questions posed by the latter document. In response, the Chiefs informed the NDC that they conditionally approved creating a European army, noting the points where the government should stand firm at the Paris Conference.

They recommended that Germany be deprived of the Ruhr, the taproot of its military-industrial power; that all German regulars must be assigned to the European army—to that end, all of Germany must be included in the combat zone area—France should allow only its forces designated to NATO to be under EDC command, keeping enough forces under national control to meet its responsibilities in the French Empire and metropolitan France; France must also be allowed to freely redeploy its EDC forces from Europe in case of major difficulties in the French Union because of its extra-European responsibilities; the French Navy must remain national; France must have greater numbers of ground forces in the European army than did Germany, while the European Commander-in-Chief "can only be French"; and each basic German unit must be placed under the command of an integrated European command and depend on integrated European logistical organs for its maintenance.[62]

On August 27, the NDC adopted the Chiefs of the General Staff Committee's recommendations along with the requirement that Britain participate. The Chiefs looked to their civilian bosses to champion these demands at the Paris Conference.[63] In a September 10, 1951 note, however, the military leadership identified two contradictory requirements concerning the level of German units to integrate and the number of units to be included in the European army. If one adopted too large a volume and at too high a level, "it would give Germany, which will integrate all of its forces, a preponderance of power, and it would allow

Germany to demand leadership. On the contrary, adopting too low a level would risk fashioning a European army comprised of incompatible units without any real operational value."[64]

Eventually, the Paris Conference set the German contribution at twelve U.S.-sized divisions, or 240,000 men; it was therefore crucial that France furnish at least the same number so as to obtain a rough parity with Germany. Yet according to the Chief of Staff of the Combined Armed Forces, such a figure signified "an effort incompatible with our [present] international burden." Finally, twelve "light divisions" (180,000 men) were adopted. The Chiefs of the General Staff Committee, however, strongly opposed Germany's suggestion to increase its contribution to eighteen divisions.[65]

In late August, the Allied High Commission (AHC) and the Federal Republic reopened the Petersburg negotiations over the logistics of German rearmament and the repercussions on Germany. Bonn's insistence on the condition that contractual agreements based on complete reciprocity replace the Occupation Statute threatened to hold up the discussion. In addition, Bonn wanted twelve divisions, a defense minister, and the right to participate on a basis of full equality in all political and military institutions.

From September 10 to 14, the three Western foreign ministers met in Washington, DC, to examine these demands. Although Britain's Herbert Morrison suggested giving the Petersburg report to NATO, Acheson rejected this suggestion. Schuman's conciliatory attitude, however, allowed them to avoid a breakdown, and the AHC received the green light to negotiate on a contractual basis as large as possible. It agreed to establish a "Tripartite Group on Germany," which would study the Federal Republic's financial contribution. Schuman's attitude grew from the belief that paper agreements offered no guarantee against German militarism. The only guarantee was a Germany integrated into a European community.[66]

The Temporary Council Committee

At the September 15–20, 1951, meeting of the NAC, financial problems relating to Western rearmament came to the fore. Disagreement over each country's respective contribution to the rearmament effort led the NAC to create on September 19 the Temporary Council Committee (TCC).[67] The NAC gave this body the task of studying the financial problems facing the Alliance—specifically, closing the gap between the MTDP goals and the financial constraints of the NATO countries.[68]

One particular problem Monnet detected was the extreme difficulty in achieving equilibrium between the amount France and Germany would contribute to defense, even after taking into account France's expenses for the Indochina War. Simply put, France would not meet the financial requirements of the EDC.[69] General Paul Stehlin shared Monnet's concerns about the financial problems confronting the Paris Conference. Stehlin said two reasons justified the principle that France and Germany should contribute equally to the European army. First, there were technical reasons:

If France's national revenue exceeded that of Germany's, the difference would decrease rapidly and could change in the other direction near 1954–55. If, conforming to the Interim Report approved by the government, these expenditures on the European Army were shared according to the criteria derived from the economic capabilities of each state, one could admit the equality of the contributions for the three coming years.

Second, there was a political reason:

If Germany were required to pay more than France, it would not be at all surprising that it might use this fact to demand greater authority within the Community, and most certainly a greater number of troops than France.

Germany would derive from this argument the fact that its contribution would already serve as part of the upkeep of non-German European troops and it would have great reticence to pay a supplementary contribution at such a level. It would not, moreover, miss the opportunity to emphasize this disproportion between German and French expenditures in order to demand a more important place within the Community, or—what could be equally dangerous—the creation of purely German services administering these sums.

The impossibility for the French delegation to respond to the question posed by the London Conference[70] leads the British and American delegations to think that the European army problem hinders, or at least compromises, the negotiations to be undertaken with the German government.

It is therefore appropriate that the [French] government examine if the conclusions presented above must remain unchanged or be revised.[71]

France wanted Germany to spend as much as possible but not more than France because Bonn would then demand greater authority. Yet the rapid growth of the German economy and the growing costs of the Indochina War made this goal increasingly remote. France was in a bind.[72]

The French military leadership underlined France's difficulties. At its meetings of November 7 and 13, 1951, the Chiefs of the General Staff Committee asserted that current French policy would doom the Paris Conference: "It no longer appears possible to assert the principle of equality of rights, nondiscrimination, and effectiveness without inciting the Germans and Americans to take positions incompatible with our basic plans, our financial possibilities, and our desire to avoid a revival of German militarism."[73] Then on November 15, the Chiefs of the General Staff Committee, headed by General Alphonse Juin, informed the government that the negotiations were headed toward an impasse that could be avoided only if France increased its defense budget. Yet France could ensure its own rearmament program neither militarily nor financially while the Indochina War devoured precious resources. This fact, the Chiefs of the General Staff Committee argued, made German rearmament even more urgent.[74]

That same day, Juin warned Defense Minister Georges Bidault that the Paris Conference verged on collapse, the effects of which would present extremely grave consequences for France. According to Juin, "It is therefore indispensable that the conditions imposed do not lead to militarily unacceptable solutions."[75] Juin advised the government to obtain a transition period and to ensure the progressive implementation of the EDC. He was convinced the EDC would throw the French Army into disarray, rendering it unable to meet its missions in Europe and elsewhere. Juin believed that until these international hot spots cooled, the EDC should be postponed.[76]

In late November, the three allies agreed that Germany should contribute $3.1 billion for 1952 to 1953, an amount that Bonn found excessive. Negotiations proved fruitless, so the Allies turned to the TCC in order to arrive at a figure.[77] Due to the slow pace in carrying out the EDC and German rearmament, no action took place. As a result, Acheson pressured France to make progress by the upcoming NAC meeting in Lisbon, Portugal.

The French government wanted to set its defense budget for the following year at $2.7 billion. On December 1, Finance Minister René Mayer told the cabinet that France could expect $600 million in U.S. aid for 1951 to 1952, $200 million of which would be counterpart funds. This amount failed to resolve France's budgetary difficulties. The government's figure fell far short of what Bidault, who considered an increase in U.S. aid indispensable, deemed necessary. The French military leadership expected the budget to be $4.3 billion. The difference between the two was $1.6 billion. On December 10, the French cabinet agreed to maintain its original figure of $2.7 billion.[78]

Approved on December 17, the TCC report presented a tentative plan for a defense buildup, proposing national defense expenditures necessary to implement this plan up to mid-1954. The TCC asked the majority of NATO countries to increase defense spending substantially, by approximately one-sixth of their December 1951 programs. Although the report recognized the dollar deficits its recommendations would produce, it contained no solution. Averell Harriman, the chairman of the TCC and the U.S. director for Mutual Security, did not hide the fact that a $5–7 billion U.S. budget deficit for fiscal year 1953 would, in an election year, be political suicide. As Harriman proclaimed, the United States could not increase defense outlays; moreover, it could not commit to any aid at all after 1954.[79]

The TCC recommended that France increase its defense budget by 5 percent. Although this figure was below what the French military proposed, Prime Minister Pleven complained to Eisenhower that the TCC report still exceeded France's ability. Pleven said that without an additional $285 million for the calendar year, his government would collapse. That same day, he informed Bruce and Harriman that he had passed legislation to raise $200 million and had placed his program before parliament for an additional $571 million. Pleven told them it would be politically impossible to raise more than $770,000 in 1952 by taxes due to the opposition of most deputies. He also said that after frequent postponements, the government would have to submit its 1952 defense budget to the Finance Committee the next day.

The prime minister said that from a military standpoint, if his 1952 budget failed to approximate $3.7 billion, his government would fall. The French military leadership said that it could not meet the bare minimum of its commitments on a lesser amount—and even this figure would mean cutting defense production already underway. He thought that Bidault would resign rather than accept a smaller amount ($3.7 billion surpassed the figure the TCC thought appropriate for France). Given the gap between revenues and expenditures, submitting a budget of $3.36 billion would topple his government.

Pleven noted that the way in which the United States planned to give the aid offended the National Assembly. The American plan for $300 million in military expenditures for American use would not generate counterpart funds. Importantly, Paul Reynaud, the chairman of the Finance Committee of the French parliament, opposed any budget that would produce an uncovered gap.

Pleven admitted that the United States could do no more than the $600 million already discussed for the fiscal year ending June 30, 1952. The United States, however, should be prepared for his government to fall and for its possible effect on NATO. The prime minister also claimed that he could not reduce the portion of the budget devoted to investment and reconstruction if he were to obtain the Socialists' support for the Schuman Plan. Besides, the amount allocated for investment was the bare minimum. The next day, Pleven repeated his concern over the budget gap and proclaimed that the Indochina War was primarily responsible. Harriman stated that the United States could not exceed $600 million for the first six months of 1952. Over the weekend, the French government indicated that it would present a defense budget of $3.7 billion. In exchange, the French wanted the U.S. administration to ask Congress to transfer $100 million from aid for the Indochina War toward the $600 million. In light of this situation, Bruce and Harriman decided that the administration should approach Congress to seek some adjustment of U.S. aid to France.[80]

On December 18, Finance Minister René Mayer testified to the Finance Committee. Although the TCC considered a defense budget of $3.022 billion necessary, he proposed a provisional budget of $3 billion of which $257,000 would comprise U.S. aid. The military leadership, along with several deputies, disliked this budget; they argued that France would not be able to carry out its tasks at the same pace as in 1951. The Finance Committee indicated that the government would be asked to testify again.

As he had promised, Bidault resigned following Mayer's testimony. In his resignation letter to Pleven, he wrote that Mayer's remarks indicated the impossibility for those charged with France's defense to continue in the country's "indispensable effort."[81]

On December 26, Henry Labouisse, the chief of the ECA Mission in France, sent a draft memo of an understanding to William Foster that he proposed be initialed by France as well as serve as a record for the recent set of bilateral Franco-American talks.[82] Labouisse said that the two sides had agreed to the allocation of $35.7 million in counterpart funds but that the United States first required a list of productivity uses. He also indicated that France still had to submit a comprehensive statement of its economic and financial policies before the United States would agree to the plan.

In general, however, Labouisse thought that the "major objective" of Franco-American bilateral talks—French agreement to meet the TCC recommendations for defense—had been achieved. He saw progress in other areas as well and believed that the French were willing to continue moving forward. Nonetheless, the United States needed to work closely with France. It was along these lines that the memo would be useful, Labouisse thought, serving as a base for the United States to examine closely French programs such as the military budget and others.

The memo itself merely stated that the primary goal of the recent Franco-American talks was to work with France to help it achieve its maximum defense effort within its economic and financial capabilities. In addition, France needed to maintain an adequate level of dollar imports. France estimated that a dollar import program of $825 million for fiscal year 1951 (July 1, 1951) through June 30, 1952, was the minimum necessary. The United States disagreed, however, and set the level at $600 million for the same period, which the United States would provide through various means. In response, France promised to increase productivity and restrain inflation.[83]

The Soviet Response

The Western bloc's resolve to fund a military buildup attracted critical attention. In August 1951, V. Starovskii, the head of the Soviet Union's Central Statistical Administration, alerted the Soviet leadership that the United States and its allies had decided to markedly increase spending on defense. Starovskii asserted that the United States intended to spend twice as much on defense in 1951–1952 than it had spent in 1949–1950. According to a document drafted by the Cominform, the Truman administration planned to exceed the estimate provided by Starovskii. Impressed by these figures, the Soviet leadership responded by vastly increasing its own defense spending.[84]

Britain's Role

Since the end of the Second World War, a primary French concern had been enlisting closer British cooperation in European affairs. Despite strenuous efforts, France had failed to overcome traditional British skepticism toward continental arrangements. Near the end of 1951, however, Britain's new prime minister, Winston Churchill, and his foreign minister, Anthony Eden, arrived in Paris for two days of talks.[85]

In advance of the visit, Eden sent to Churchill on December 15 a minute concerning British policy toward the continent. Among its salient points were the following:

> 4. But as you yourself said in the Defence Debate we cannot merge ourselves in schemes like the . . . European Defence Community.[86] We can only associate ourselves with them as closely as possible.
> 5. We can merge ourselves wholeheartedly in associations for common purposes among European governments, when control remains in the hands of governments. We have done this in the O.E.E.C. We have done it in NATO.
> 7. I would define our policy as follows:
> First, we want a united Europe. There is no doubt about that, or our sincerity.
> Second, there are two ways in which His Majesty's government can foster and strengthen the uniting of Europe:
> (i) we can and will continue to play an active part in plans for uniting national efforts on an intergovernmental basis;
> (ii) we will also give all help and encouragement to the continental European countries when they wish to form federal organs among themselves. And though we cannot merge ourselves in such federal organs, we will always try to find the most practicable and useful means of establishing close relations with them. This is what we are doing in the case of the Schuman Pool, and may do on behalf of the Pleven Plan.[87]

In their December 17 meeting, the two sides discussed the Schuman Plan. Churchill announced that he welcomed the plan because it might cut short the historic animosity between France and Germany and it might also return Germany to the family of European nations. While London supported the plan, the British could not take part. Eden did state that Britain would maintain forces in Europe at the disposition of the SACEUR, but they would be closely tied to the EDC.

Yet a degree of ambiguity remained over the proposed ties between Britain and the EDC. London clearly wanted to avoid being bound by a restrictive agreement. British inaction thus frustrated French plans, for when parliamentary debates over the EDC began in February, the French government, once again left empty-handed by Britain, would have nothing to present to the National Assembly. This rebuff would, in turn, fuel French legislative resistance to the project.[88]

French fears concerning the progress of France's rearmament program were confirmed by the December 28 defense budget debate. Bidault conceded that France would fall three divisions short of its objective of fifteen combat-ready divisions by 1952.[89] In light of these developments, the French Chiefs of the General Staff Committee could only reiterate in January 1952 its request for a transition period, along with a demand that the government declare its position on this point.[90]

Given the American stance in January, the year ended badly for the United States. Washington had overcome French objections to German rearmament and wanted to complete the process as quickly as possible. Yet because he feared that Moscow might attack if his country rearmed too quickly, Adenauer raised several political demands, thus slowing matters to a crawl. Other European officials, loath to antagonize the United States, quietly applauded this move because they shared Adenauer's fears of Soviet retaliation.

These points relate to the interpretation of this entire affair. To begin, Acheson emerges as a major obstacle to resolving this matter, not the French: his hard-line diplomacy caused Alliance division on this issue. Nonetheless, some might ask did it really matter that he took such a bold—some might say reckless—line with the Europeans? After all, he did not get his way, and the Soviets, though poised on the brink of war in the terrible winter of 1950–1951, did not attack. Still, U.S. pressure had enduring consequences. First, it helped create the sense that the United States saw NATO as its own fiefdom, where Washington would run matters by strong-arming its more cautious allies. Second, it helped to foster a common Franco-German interest in resisting America and avoiding East–West conflict. Both Adenauer and the French leaders came to see that French and German interests ran parallel and diverged from those of the United States.

The third point concerns Britain. For continental officials, London's "true colors" in this affair emerged with greater clarity. Although London shared the same sentiments as Bonn and Paris, it nonetheless sided with Washington. London also refused to join either the ECSC or the EDC. In the eyes of continental officials, therefore, the British were not "real" Europeans—their loyalty had been tested and they had failed. London was seen as Washington's second hand, and thus could not be trusted in any truly European policy. This conclusion was not set in stone, but the impression had been made, and both the French and the Germans began to see Britain as in thrall to the United States. Such beliefs influenced the resolution of the German question and a host of other issues of long-term importance.

CHAPTER FOUR

Progress, Promises, and Problems

The primary hurdle facing the Atlantic Alliance in 1952 remained unchanged: achieving consensus on how Germany could participate in Western security arrangements safely and effectively. During 1951, U.S. secretary of state Dean Acheson had pressured the Allies to forge ahead with plans to rearm Germany and augment their own rearmament programs. Much progress had occurred. In April, the treaty creating the European Coal and Steel Community was signed. Then, in September, the foreign ministers of Britain, France, and the United States agreed that the Allies should change the contractual status of the Federal Republic, opening the door to German sovereignty. Two months later, Adenauer and the Allied foreign ministers signed the draft of the Contractual Agreements on German Sovereignty. Finally, France dropped its opposition to the creation of German ground divisions, eliminating another source of dispute.

Obstacles remained, though. Relying on U.S. assessments, Acheson insisted that the Alliance's rearmament program continue without pause. The Allies balked, however, citing the financial and political difficulties that would attend such an effort. To ease their concerns, Acheson agreed to the creation of a committee of experts that would decide what level of defense spending was both politically feasible and militarily effective.

Along with his attempts to meet Allied objections, Acheson continued to rely on diplomatic pressure to speed matters along. Although at times successful, this tactic also entailed costs, one of which was to fuel the

Allies' resentment over U.S. interference in their internal affairs. This sentiment ran strong in the Federal Republic, where Chancellor Konrad Adenauer fell under extreme pressure to seek greater freedom from Allied restrictions as well as more German influence in the international arena. This domestic pressure, coupled with fears of Soviet retaliation, led Adenauer to present a series of demands to the Allies, which slowed considerably America's drive to rearm Germany.[1]

The stridency with which Germany presented its demands vexed Washington and fueled French anxieties. The United States soon found itself in an increasingly tenuous position, for it not only had to somehow meet German calls for equality, territorial revisions, and entry into NATO, but do so in a way acceptable to France—no small task indeed. Adenauer knew that the Allies viewed him as the most responsible political figure in Germany, so he bargained from a position of strength.[2]

The United States wanted the Alliance to attain preponderant power in Europe. Although American planners worried little about an immediate Soviet attack, miscalculation could easily cause armed conflict between East and West. Accordingly, U.S. officials deemed that a German military contribution was of even greater necessity in order to increase the West's chance of prevailing should such a conflict occur. It was imperative that the Alliance quickly agree on a way to make effective use of Germany's substantial military potential. The Alliance hoped to resolve this issue within the framework of the Paris Conference. These talks were intended to reach Allied agreement on the establishment of a European army that would include German ground units.

Although much had been accomplished since the conference opened in February 1951, progress slowed in January 1952 due to German demands. Highly displeased with certain Allied policies, Bonn signaled its displeasure by stiffening its negotiating stance. Its public discontent centered on three issues: the political disposition of the Saar; German admission to NATO; and continued Allied limitations on German sovereignty.[3]

The Saar

The Saarland has long sparked passionate emotions in both France and Germany. Although traditionally German territory, the Big Three in 1947 declared the region semiautonomous but economically tied to France.[4] Despite this stricture, the French soon began to dominate the Saar politically. France attached great importance to controlling the Saar, for without access to the region's abundant coal deposits, it could never hope to compete on equal terms with Germany either industrially or militarily. In response, the German government negotiated strenuously for its return, claiming that under the Allied Declaration of June 5, 1945, the German state (as of its December 31, 1937, frontiers) remained in existence. German officials therefore argued that the Saar mines were still state property. They further contended that under legally binding agreements, no action could be taken on the Saar except under the terms of a peace treaty, a document that did not yet exist. Although the Federal Republic previously had little clout, the Allied request to rearm now enabled it to press its claims with much greater authority.[5]

In late January 1952, the French government announced that its high commissioner in the Saar, Gilbert Grandval, military governor of the region from 1945 to 1948, would assume the post of ambassador to Saarbrücken. Appointing someone at the rank of ambassador normally confers recognition of the host country's statehood. This appointment outraged the Germans. Adenauer exclaimed, "We can go no further in the European Defense Community if Germans of all parties have misgivings about French aims in the Saar. In all frankness, let me say that I find it full of danger that at a moment when negotiations are in progress for E.D.C. trust and confidence should be destroyed in this way."[6]

Admission to NATO

Germany also became increasingly unequivocal in expecting membership in NATO. At the January 26–27 EDC foreign ministers conference, a Bonn representative dropped a political bombshell by reiterating the Federal Republic's unwillingness to enter the EDC unless it also entered NATO, or unless the EDC were somehow brought into NATO.[7]

During a January 28 press conference, Professor Walter Hallstein, the Federal Republic's secretary of state for foreign affairs and a personal advisor to Adenauer, announced that many problems would result if the Alliance refused to admit Germany into NATO. Hallstein contended that excluding it would reduce the number of EDC countries' votes in the NAC because Germany was the sole EDC nation not also a member of NATO. This situation would conflict with the Federal Republic's unconditional demand for equality of rights. Moreover, Hallstein asserted that it was inaccurate to say that the United States fundamentally opposed Germany's accession to NATO, noting that the January 4 issues of the *Frankfurter Zeitung* and *Le Monde* confirmed this point.[8]

Given that German entry into NATO would contradict Allied policy, Hallstein's assertions drew fire. French officials, in particular, reacted forcefully to his remarks. In a question and answer session before his legislature's Foreign Affairs Committee, Foreign Minister Schuman responded to Hallstein's declarations. He assured the committee that he had made clear to Bonn on several occasions that France would never allow Germany to enter the Atlantic Pact.[9]

As high-placed observers noted, the Quai d'Orsay, France's foreign ministry, objected to German membership in NATO on three levels: juridical, political, and timing. Juridically, the Quai argued that such a move would imply recognizing the full sovereignty of the Federal Republic. Formally recognizing Bonn would call into question the Occupation Statute and therefore permit Germany to challenge the legality of Allied Occupation forces stationed on German soil. Accepting these arguments would spell the end of the quadripartite system in Berlin and all hopes of solving the German problem on a political, rather than a military, basis.

The Quai's political objections centered on the Federal Republic's putative revanchist tendencies. It feared that adopting the NATO option would fundamentally alter the defensive character of the Atlantic Pact, as Germany would find it difficult to resist using force in pursuit of territorial revisions in the East. This scenario raised the specter of a German-Soviet war, which had the potential to engulf the rest of the Continent. The West wanted to avoid such a war, especially given its continuing economic and military weakness in the face of Soviet atomic capability.

Finally, the Quai rejected the timing of such a move. It believed that early 1952 was the wrong moment even to raise the issue of Germany entering NATO. Taking note of the cautious mood that prevailed in certain national parliaments, the foreign ministry thought that such a plan would be soundly rejected in any event.[10]

Some American officials took a different line. Gontran Begougne de Juniac, the counselor at the French embassy in Washington, questioned Geoffrey Lewis, the U.S. State Department's deputy director of the bureau for German affairs, about the accuracy of the December 25, 1951 *Le Monde* article that claimed the United States would welcome the Federal Republic's entry in NATO. According to a French report, "Mr. Lewis declared that the American government, as we already knew, had no intention of insisting that Germany immediately become part of the Atlantic Pact, but that German participation in NATO would constitute a logical and practically inevitable development of the policy now followed by the Western Powers and by the Bonn government." When de Juniac countered that France would raise serious objections, Lewis replied that these objections had been considered and were found inconclusive. Indeed, he said that the NATO solution would actually solve a number of problems.[11]

Given the stakes involved in this debate, both Bonn and Paris tried to influence Washington. On the eve of meetings in London between the Big Three and Germany, Hallstein met with General Eisenhower to discuss the European defense force. He told Eisenhower that France's actions regarding the Saar impeded progress on the European army and the Schuman Plan Treaty, which the Bundesrat, Germany's upper house of parliament, still had to approve. Eisenhower replied that this dispute was essentially a political matter to be worked out by the civilian leadership, a proposition with which Hallstein agreed.

Hallstein then raised the question of the European army's relations with NATO. He contended that his government would find it difficult to refute parliamentary claims that the West was asking Germany to commit troops to the defense of Western Europe without granting it a part in NATO decisions governing the use of these forces. Noting that objections to the Federal Republic were "largely on the part of France," Hallstein implied that his government might be willing to accept a theoretical rather than substantive solution so as to avoid giving the German parliament the impression that the Federal Republic would have no voice in decisions concerning the use of force. Eisenhower admitted that because the future of German-NATO relations was a political, rather than a military, question, it was a decision for the NAC. As a result, the Supreme Headquarters Allied Powers Europe (SHAPE) could not take a stand. Hallstein said that unless a formula could be devised to give Germany knowledge of NATO's strategic plans, Adenauer would face legislative resistance. Eisenhower stated that this issue was a variation of the question of German relations with NATO, and thus a political question. He argued, however, that as a practical matter, Germany would have intimate knowledge about strategic plans by virtue of its membership in the EDC structure, which would support the European army in carrying out its plans.[12]

France Responds

France then pled its case. On January 29, Schuman expressed to Acheson his concern about the evolution of the Petersburg negotiations on the contractual agreements. The French foreign minister reiterated that a German military contribution must conform to a European defense force, not lead to the creation of a German national army. He then expressed optimism that the Paris talks would lead to this outcome. Yet because the proposed European army treaty would contain no discriminatory clauses, precautions against "the latent danger which would result from a Germany freed from every restriction" must come within the framework of the "agreements defining the future relations between the allies and Germany." Bonn would be asked to make "special commitments." If not, it would be difficult to persuade France's parliament to accept a treaty from which Germany could simply withdraw, free from all restrictions.

From this standpoint, Schuman wrote, the slow pace in the Petersburg negotiations was a matter of great seriousness. He contended that the discussions on the annexed conventions, which would contain the safeguards France required, had come to a standstill. Bonn wanted to limit all such discussions to the general convention, where its few limitations represented what the Germans claimed were the bearable maximum. Regarding arms manufacture, Bonn would reject clauses aimed solely at Germany, foreclosing the limitations the Big Three deemed necessary. Concerning the costs of maintaining occupation troops, Bonn wanted the EDC to pay, a plan that would never pass the French parliament. Schuman warned that the stridency with which Germany advanced its demands could prompt a powerful French counterreaction. One of France's main concerns was to prevent an imbalance within Europe. According to Schuman, "France's outside obligations, the demographic superiority of West Germany, the rapid recovery of the Ruhr industries and of the German economy as a whole are in different degrees, elements of an unbalance, to which we must apply correcting factors. That is why we agreed at Brussels in December 1950 on a clause limiting German forces to one-fifth of the forces of the Atlantic Army."

Similar worries led Schuman to defend French actions toward the Saar. He insisted that uniting the economies of France and the Saar comprised "an essential element of economic balance inside the European community." He also insisted that creating a diplomatic mission was not incompatible with the Saar's present status; it was simply "an evolution parallel to that envisaged for Federal Germany where our high commissioners are to be replaced by ambassadors." Schuman concluded by saying that although a solution to the problem of EDC-NATO relations could be found, bringing Germany into NATO would raise a host of difficulties—it could, for example, alter the defensive nature of the

Alliance. For these reasons, he argued, Hallstein's words demanded a response.[13]

Although Acheson tried to calm his French counterpart, he refused to backtrack. He told Schuman that they had to take risks: "We have put our hands to the plow and we cannot look back."[14] For the United States, too much was at stake to turn back now. Yet the United States was not the only Allied nation that would benefit from this project. One should not discount the importance of a European defense force to the Allied community as a whole. It would provide America a way to achieve European unity—particularly between France and Germany, the foundation of a strong European defense—thus sparing the United States from carrying the entire load. It would also lift Germany out of international purgatory and into the community of nations. A European army would prevent the unregulated growth of German military might while permitting France to assume the leadership of Europe. Agreement therefore existed on the goal; debate centered on how and when one arrived there.

Chafing under Allied limitations on its sovereignty, the Federal Republic yearned to shed the fetters of occupation. The touchstone of Adenauer's policy was to attain full equality and to reject all discriminatory measures, a position the chancellor's personal beliefs and domestic politics reinforced. Given that the Allies premised their defense policy on Germany's full participation in Western defense, Adenauer wielded considerable leverage with which to advance his claims. Nonetheless, the forcefulness of German demands clouded the atmosphere at the Paris Conference. Yet because America wanted to achieve results in time for the February NAC session, it liberally applied pressure on the participants, a move that brought progress.[15] Anticipating the debates by national parliaments before the Alliance opened the summit, the Allies published an initial draft of the treaty on February 1.[16]

As noted above, a significant development in the French parliament would powerfully influence Western defense arrangements. The outcome of the June 1951 elections changed significantly the political hue of the National Assembly. Afterwards there sat a large number of French deputies who demanded an end to the conflict in Indochina, and who loathed what they judged to be America's dominance and France's weakness in the Atlantic Alliance. The charismatic Radical Socialist Pierre Mendès France emerged as the chief spokesman for this bloc. The combination of political division, the weight of the costly and increasingly unpopular war in Indochina, and a serious budget pinch fueled anxieties on both sides of the Atlantic.[17]

French parliamentarians were not the only group skeptical of the EDC; France's military leaders also voiced their displeasure with the project. One of the most important considerations for the country's top brass was how the EDC would affect France's armed forces. Convinced that the EDC would disrupt the French Army, the Chiefs of the General Staff Committee recommended at its January 7 and January 19, 1952 meetings that the government adopt a transition period. The government's inability or unwillingness to satisfy the military leadership's wishes, however, would alter the political landscape drastically in 1952. Differences between the two sides would eventually lead France's uniformed leadership to rebel openly.[18]

Budget Woes

Although year-end budget debates in France had long occasioned much tumult, deep concerns over the nation's economy, as well as persistent worries over foreign policy, rendered the debate ending 1951 even more frenzied than usual. To balance the budget, the Pleven government proposed raising $457 million in taxes along with cutting certain public services. The Finance Committee rejected these measures. Unable to agree on an appropriations bill, the dispute forced the National Assembly to approve stopgap measures to keep the government running in the interim.[19]

Inflationary pressures brought on by rearming and the Korean War battered the French economy. Forced to import many raw materials that drove up the price of its exports, France recorded a trade deficit of $262 million for the first ten months of 1951, a figure that would balloon to $500 million for 1952. In fact, since 1950, exports as a percentage of imports fell steadily from 87 percent in 1950 to 73 percent in 1951 to 66 percent in 1952.[20]

As France's economy plummeted, its international responsibilities skyrocketed. To meet its obligations to NATO, the French government pledged to spend an estimated $2.7 billion for defense in 1952, up from $2.1 billion in 1951. Defense Minister Bidault, however, determined that a minimum of $4.3 billion was needed. According to Bidault, "The Government is unable to propose a military budget based on the continuation of this plan without any of the additional assets foreseen at the time, and without any assurance as to the size, or even the form, of the aid she will receive." The final clause of Bidault's statement directly implicated the United States. France's primary problem was the absence of dollars; yet the U.S. Congress had still to vote on an aid package, so the French defense budget had to remain on hold.[21]

Economic woes caused the already weakened Pleven government to fall on January 7, ending its five-month-old cabinet. Pleven had previously attracted intense fire for discussing a record $9.62 billion 1952 defense budget, narrowly losing a vote of confidence.[22] Next on the political chopping block was Edgar Faure, a forty-three-year-old Radical Socialist. Although the National Assembly confirmed Faure on January 18, 401 votes to 101, the Gaullists and the Communists, parliament's largest and third-largest groupings, opposed Faure, forcing him to rely on the Socialists' support, which they gave reluctantly. Faure took over finance himself, Schuman remained as foreign minister, and Bidault kept his post as defense minister. Such turmoil came at a particularly bad time for France because officials would have difficulty concentrating on two important conferences taking place in Paris and in Petersberg, as well as a third scheduled to begin in Lisbon in late February.[23]

Economic problems plagued not just France, but the entire Atlantic Alliance because it had to give serious concern to determining the level of spending that each member should devote to defense. Although the members agreed that much work remained, fear of domestic political repercussions prevented them from taking bold action. For this reason the Alliance created the TCC, a body designed to reconcile the Alliance's collective defense needs with the political and economic realities of the member states.

On January 18, the TCC delivered the official summary of its report to the NAC on the policies and plans for building up defense forces in the NAT area during 1952. Despite the TCC's understanding of the political and financial concerns of NATO's European members, serious difficulties remained. In addition to its chronic dollar deficiencies and unstable currencies, Europe was also short on coal supplies, placing a heavy drag on its economy and hence its efforts to rearm.

The United States recognized France's financial woes. In late January, U.S. ambassador David Bruce reported that top French officials had been telling him all week that France's $3.4 billion budget would not allow it to make an adequate defense contribution to NATO; instead, France could field only seven divisions instead of fourteen, with no increase in subsequent years. Furthermore, France would produce only 600 planes instead of 1,800, and the duration of military service would have to be reduced from eighteen to twelve months. Operations in Indochina, however, remained a priority and would not be cut. Bruce asserted that none of this was a surprise: "We have, of course, known for many months that [French] force goals were far too high for their own financial resources combined with scheduled U.S. aid."[24]

The French government faced additional concerns. Robert Schuman appeared before the National Assembly's Foreign Affairs Committee to defend the Pleven Plan. Schuman focused on the guarantees that the European army would offer France, while reiterating his firm opposition to Bonn's entry into NATO. "We would," he warned, "introduce in the character of the Atlantic Pact a new element incompatible with its defensive character, and risk being pulled into conflicts which, one day or another, would risk giving rise to territorial claims."[25]

Despite its concerns, France decided to compromise. In early January, negotiators at the Paris Conference agreed to adopt divisions of 12,500 men, and that the German contribution be about one-third of the total force instead of the one-fifth that France had requested. Germany was forbidden, however, to employ a defense minister or a general staff, thus satisfying two key French demands.[26]

Although the French government's opposition to the Federal Republic's entry into NATO heartened many French deputies, the military leadership balked. On February 8, the French Chiefs of the General Staff Committee (CGSC) met and determined that, given the nature of the problems that cropped up at the Paris Conference concerning EDC-NATO relations, accepting the Federal Republic in NATO remained the only solution.[27]

The French government still had to assure the French military leadership of the correctness of its policy. Although the military chiefs had conditionally approved the EDC in 1951, several events shook their confidence about whether the conditions they had outlined to the government would be met. In November 1951, the top brass had highlighted two problems that it insisted the government rectify. First, France had to increase its rearmament effort so as to ensure its dominance of the European army and to prevent America from providing more aid to Bonn. Second, France should drop its opposition to a transition period that would allow all the European army participants—except Germany—to retain national forces and thereby avoid undermining the Paris Conference. In short, the military leadership wanted the EDC formed in stages.[28]

On February 9, 1952, the NDC discussed NATO's upcoming Lisbon Conference. Defense Minister Bidault remarked that France found itself at a dangerous turning point regarding its military effort. Pinched between the cost of the Indochina War and endemic financial limitations,

France could not, he argued, produce more than eight viable divisions without outside aid, even though France had already announced fourteen divisions, including two for North Africa, for the same period. For Bidault, the answer was clear: to receive the help it so badly needed, France had to endure new sacrifices so as to underscore the country's commitment to defense. He further stated that France's reputation was suffering in the eyes of its allies. Accordingly, he recommended that "we must keep our commitments, even reduced, without cutting the length of military service."[29]

Before the NATO conference in Lisbon opened, France's National Assembly had to vote on the European army. Debate over rearming Germany caused powerful waves of emotion to wash over parliament, as speaker after speaker climbed the rostrum to warn of the dangers in rearming the successor to the Third Reich. Georges Heuillard, a deputy crippled by two years in a Nazi concentration camp, spoke movingly against the project: "I am dying because of the German army. I would not want my sons or my grandsons to be enlisted alongside the tyrants and executioners of their father." It fell to Schuman to argue the government's case: "Don't you think that the U.S. and all countries which feel threatened will turn to other solutions holding for us the gravest dangers? Germany will take the place of France and the discouragement of our allies will be heavy with fearful consequences."[30]

In the end, the National Assembly watered down the final bill, merely agreeing to plans for creating a European army, but not approving the army itself. The government prevailed on February 19, 327 votes to 287, as the National Assembly voted confidence and adopted a resolution on the European defense force and German participation in the EDC. The deputies had now given Schuman strict marching orders for his upcoming meeting in London. Yet they had also given approval to creating a European defense force. Now France could go to Lisbon bearing if not good tidings, then at least not bad news.[31]

The Lisbon Conference

A number of pressing issues required close attention in Lisbon; among the most important were the NATO force requirement goals. The TCC, created to reconcile NATO's defense needs with the politico-economic constraints of each of the member states, delivered a report recommending that the Europeans adopt extensive rearmament programs in order to meet specified force goals.[32] The TCC had asked Germany to spend

$3.1 billion, but Bonn had insisted that it could pay only $2.5 billion for fiscal year 1952–1953. They finally agreed on $2.5 billion, measured in October 1951 prices. Having settled these issues, the four nations paved the way for considering NATO's relations with the future EDC.[33] The TCC also asked Belgium and Canada to contribute more. Overall, the TCC recommended that NATO's European members and the Federal Republic spend $73.9 billion over four years, $41.8 in fiscal year 1952–1954.[34]

From February 20 to 25, the NAC met in Lisbon. Despite the potential for a diplomatic breakthrough, U.S. officials expressed pessimism in the weeks before the conference opened. Frustrated by France's outright rejection of any proposal designed to bring the Federal Republic directly into NATO—an option that the Germans had already suggested—Acheson feared that the Lisbon meeting might be a waste of time. The NATO option, even if agreed to, could not be exercised without changing Germany's contractual status. The United States, therefore, wanted to restore German sovereignty through "contractual arrangements." Yet this move required that the EDC be consummated. Consequently, America then tried to pressure its allies to accept a May 1952 deadline.[35]

The NAC also adopted the TCC's plan of action, bringing the committee's work to an end.[36] Finally, the NAC agreed to provide over fifty combat-ready divisions by the end of the year and over one hundred divisions further down the road. The United States, which had struggled to persuade the Allies to increase their military efforts despite their financial constraints, welcomed this agreement.

The Lisbon conferees also endorsed German rearmament and the European army and adopted reciprocal security agreements between NATO and the EDC. Although the United States did not sign the EDC Treaty, it did initial the related conventions and protocol. It remained for the six EDC members to negotiate and approve ratification of the treaty.[37]

Lisbon Fallout

Nevertheless, even though the Alliance considered the force goals indispensable for carrying out NATO's forward defense policy, doubts about the feasibility of meeting them surfaced among the Allies soon after the close of the conference. Aware of a U.S. study of force requirements that took into account recent advances in nuclear weaponry, the Europeans hesitated before undertaking politically and financially costly rearmament programs, fearful of voter backlash. In addition, the deployment of tactical or battlefield nuclear weapons might even preclude the need for large numbers of ground forces in Western Europe. Not surprisingly, with the prospect of a new administration in Washington a few months hence, the Europeans increasingly viewed the ambitious goals set at Lisbon as less and less urgent.[38]

Some of the initial consequences of the June 1951 parliamentary shakeup in France followed the Lisbon Conference. At that meeting, Prime Minister Faure pledged to increase French defense spending by $1.51 billion for 1952. Faure counted on the United States to pay for part of this increase while France would shoulder the rest of the burden. Faure attempted to comply with the recommendations made by the TCC. He asked the National Assembly to increase taxes by 15 percent to fund its $4 billion rearmament program and put the issue to a vote of confidence. Aided by defections from the prime minister's own party, opposition lawmakers reversed the government on this question, forcing Faure to resign on February 28.[39]

This vote marked France's first governmental crisis over the EDC: the French government refused to increase its contribution to Atlantic defense. Although deputies approved overwhelmingly $370 million for the Indochina War, that conflict's burdensome cost made increases elsewhere in the defense budget political suicide. By week's end, the government, out of money, had to ask the Bank of France for a $142 million loan. Nonetheless, bank governor Wilfrid Baumgartner approved only $71 million. "The state," he lectured, "like its citizens, is living beyond its means." Baumgartner did not exaggerate France's economic ailments. Among the symptoms were rising inflation, a $660 million trade deficit in the dollar zone, $400 million owed to the EPU, gold reserves of only $550 million, and a daily spending-revenue gap of $2.8 million. Indeed, the Indochina War alone cost $2.85 million a day, soaking up most of France's U.S. dollar aid.[40]

French economic woes greatly concerned the Truman administration, for France played a key role in Western defense. On March 3, Acheson briefed the Senate Foreign Relations Committee on the Lisbon talks, mentioning that bilateral Franco-American meetings took place during the conference.[41] The United States recognized that France needed additional aid to support its efforts in Indochina and Europe. America therefore agreed that, under certain conditions, it would modify its assistance program for 1952 out of fiscal year 1952 Mutual Security Agency (MSA) funds.[42] Yet the amount of this aid sparked many disputes. Acheson said that the

United States would give France $300 million in economic aid and place offshore purchases of $200 million. This aid was not new, he pointed out; it would come out of funds that had already been appropriated.[43]

Aware that many of the Allies held it responsible for weakening European defense, France tried to put its situation in the most favorable light. The French government took pains to point out the heroic effort France was putting forth in Indochina. When the foreign ministers of the NAC met in a special committee on February 21 to examine the international situation, Schuman offered a brief exposé on France's effort in Indochina, insisting that it was making great sacrifices to fight Communism.[44] Such declarations proved useful to France's civilian officials for political reasons. Yet when placed in a military equation, fighting the Indochina War while trying to achieve a balance of power in Europe simply failed to add up. As a result, the situation in Indochina continued to worsen. The government's failure to secure the guarantees in the Paris Conference that the French military leadership deemed necessary led uniformed opposition to the EDC to grow apace.

In a March 4 letter to President Auriol, General Juin put the problem starkly: "Two months after the beginning of the fiscal year, we have plunged into great uncertainty concerning our plans for 1952, which closely affect those of 1953." He contended that the resources France needed to dominate the future EDC equaled the amount devoted to the Indochina War. Juin predicted that France and Germany were going to find themselves in the EDC "head to head, quickly vying for predominance." The Paris treaty needed guarantees, "and to take for ourselves the best assurances, those that consist of making the French force the majority in the Community." But, lacking the means necessary, France could not support "the number of divisions needed in Europe." As Juin argued on April 24, the solution was to extend military service to two years and send the contingents to Indochina so that a part of the active army there could return and instruct, train, and form the new units to be placed in Europe. The government, however, disagreed. The CGSC responded by trying to block the treaty's application to prevent Germany from dominating the EDC.[45]

France's brief but intense governmental crisis soon appeared over. On March 6, sixty-year-old Independent Republican Antoine Pinay, with the help of rebel Gaullist deputies, formed a government. Soon thereafter, Piany addressed the National Assembly on the state of France's finances. Concerning France's foreign exchange: "There can be no dishonoring of [France's] signature." Regarding the bankrupt treasury: "A new loan will have to be negotiated." And on the budget: "We must settle a deficit of $1.1 billion." Prudently, he made no mention of taxes, the downfall of Faure.[46]

In international matters, the conservative Pinay also gave wide latitude to French negotiators at the Paris Conference where talks on the European army continued.[47] From this point things moved quickly, so much so that the conferees reached agreement on Germany's financial contribution.[48] Nonetheless, the Pinay government searched in vain throughout the year to find a majority to approve ratification of the EDC Treaty.

The Stalin Note

Despite the many legal, economic, and political obstacles that the Alliance had to surmount before the Federal Republic could rearm, the Kremlin chose not to leave events to chance. In early 1952, a Soviet Foreign Ministry official had convinced forty-three-year-old Deputy Foreign Minister Andrei Gromyko, a protogé of the hard-line Molotov, that the Soviet Union needed a new German policy. Gromyko then approached Stalin. He explained to the *Generalissimo* that sending a diplomatic note to the Western Powers "would have great political meaning for the reinforcement of the fight for peace and against the remilitarization of West Germany and would help the proponents of German unity and peace to dissect the aggressive objectives of the three Western powers that are connected with the 'General Treaty.' "[49]

Gromyko further contended that such a note would help "to provide political circles in the GDR and West Germany [the means] to wage a similar campaign in the press and among the German population against the aggressive policy of the three powers toward West Germany . . . aiming for its integration with the aggressive plans of the Atlantic bloc." In short, Moscow intended the note to spearhead an information campaign that would engender resistance to Allied plans to rearm the Federal Republic.

On March 10, Soviet foreign minister Vishinsky delivered a diplomatic note to the three Western Powers that called for early negotiations of a German peace treaty. A four-power conference would then meet to establish a neutral but united Germany that would possess an army and an arms industry and be able to develop its own economy.

Germany would not, however, be allowed to take part in any alliance or military coalition directed at any nation that had fought Germany during the Second World War.[50]

Although Acheson rejected the note as crude propaganda designed to undermine the Bonn and Paris treaties, he nonetheless agreed with British and French demands that they test the Kremlin's intentions. Thus on March 25, Britain, France, and the United States replied to the Soviet note. In their similar replies, they said that Moscow should allow United Nations (UN) inspectors into East Germany to determine if free elections could be held there; should pronounce whether a united Germany could conduct an independent foreign policy and join international organizations; and should explain why it invoked the Potsdam accord that granted the Soviets German territory east of the Oder and Neisse rivers, yet ignored the Potsdam agreements that prohibited German rearmament. Rearming Germany in the framework of a European army was one thing; allowing it to rearm on its own was quite another.[51]

On April 19, the Soviet Union responded to the Western notes by suggesting that instead of having the UN supervise elections in all of Germany, let the Big Four be responsible. This move would, of course, give the Kremlin a veto at every step of the way. Fearful that Stalin's sweet music might resonate in the ears of Germans longing for reunification, the Western Allies, prodded by Acheson, worked diligently to complete a peace treaty with West Germany that would end the Allied occupation.[52]

As stated at the outset, one of France's primary goals in this whole affair was to prevent German equality, not German rearmament. For example, when the deputy HICOG General George P. Hays, at the April 18 meeting of SHAPE's Security Committee, said that SHAPE had to treat the Federal Republic just like any other ally—without discrimination and on a basis of equality—the French representative said that his country's General Staff rejected this suggestion: "The three allies must respect responsibilities, rights, and specific powers. As long as large-scale German contingents are not yet in a state to participate effectively in the common defense, one cannot claim that Germany's position is equal to those powers who actually defend." The French CGSC noted on February 8, however, that accepting the Federal Republic in NATO seemed the only solution given difficulties surrounding EDC-NATO relations at the Paris Conference.[53]

On March 20 to 21, the French CGSC met and again underscored the necessity for a transition period characterized by vast decentralization. The committee also recommended that forces be free to switch from national to European ones but not vice versa.[54] Then on March 29, it brought to the government's attention the inconvenience the French Army would suffer if forced to take part in a nine-member supranational organization.[55]

Britain Relents

Another chief concern for France was Britain's role in Western defense arrangements. So far, London had refused to make a continental commitment, a fact that would soon come to the fore in Allied negotiations. Following the Lisbon meeting, the Paris Conference hit an obstacle. The EDC Treaty would provide a mutual guarantee of its member states, each member in regard to the others. Germany proposed, however, that EDC forces automatically resist an attack on any member. The Netherlands, conversely, wanted to reproduce Article 5 of the NATO Treaty. This article would give the member states of the EDC, in the event of an armed attack against one of them, the power to respond as they deemed appropriate. Deadlocked, Hervé Alphand, the president of the Paris conference, asked Sir William Hayter, the British observer, to inquire of his government its intentions on the matter.[56]

British foreign minister Anthony Eden, who feared the conferees would blame Britain if the talks were to fail, flew to Paris where he explained that his government objected to extending the Brussels Treaty guarantee to another organization—the EDC—and for fifty years. After returning from Paris, however, Eden convinced his government that France would never agree to the EDC without a British commitment. On April 15, therefore, Britain publicly announced that it intended to establish relations with the EDC. London indicated that it would, in principle, accept a treaty of mutual assistance in case of aggression in Europe against the six EDC nations.[57]

While the French government welcomed Britain's declaration, it did not satisfy French critics of the EDC, for it merely extended by twenty years the automatic guarantees already available to the Federal Republic under NATO and failed to respond to concerns about a rebirth of German militarism. Although the French wanted an Anglo-American guarantee protecting France should Germany one day quit the European army, neither London nor Washington would countenance an anti-German alliance within an existing alliance. To add fuel to the fire, Eden declared a week later that in case East and West Germany reunited, the treaty would no longer apply to the resulting German state. Britain once again refused to provide France an unambiguous continental commitment, continuing to frustrate French demands and the Alliance's efforts to create a European defense force.[58]

The French Military Leadership Speaks

April 1952 marked a turning point for French civil-military relations, as many French military and civilian officials began to question the wisdom of continuing the Indochina War. One anonymous general even published an article in the influential Parisian daily, *Le Monde*, demanding an end to this debilitating war so that France could buttress its position in Europe.[59] As for Juin, he argued throughout the month in favor of extending military service so that the government could provide to the French Army the means to simultaneously rearm in Europe and to fight in Indochina.[60]

Despite loathing the EDC Treaty, Juin altered his position at the April 24 meeting of the National Defense Committee. Although initially not "hot" about the European army, he now said he supported it "because it is imperative to reinforce immediately the defense of Western Europe, and a negative position would lead to the reconstitution of a German army with the complicity of the United States." Juin contended that although it was necessary to create German ground divisions, France had to avoid recreating a German army. Juin continued, saying it was important to ensure that the number of French contingents in the European army outnumbered the German contingents. To meet this goal, France had to solve the Indochina problem and, in the meantime, ensure that its recruits would be instructed and appointed officers. He proposed to achieve this task by sending young soldiers to the Far East and by extending military service to two years.[61]

Thus after being initially hostile to the European army, Juin and the rest of the French military leadership appeared ready to give the EDC their tentative blessing—that is, provided the government took certain steps. These steps included adding a protocol to the EDC Treaty that would delay its application until the Indochina War ended. Notwithstanding the European army's putative defects, the military chiefs still deemed it necessary to augment Western defenses.

Signing the Treaties

On May 26, 1952—almost two years after Washington had proposed a European defense force and Paris had unveiled the Pleven Plan—France initialed the tripartite Contractual Agreements in Bonn. The 400-page Treaty of Bonn that Acheson, Adenauer, Eden, and Schuman signed ended the occupation regime and the Allied High Commission, and reestablished the international sovereignty of the Federal Republic. There were, however, certain limits: the Convention forbade Bonn to expel Western troops, change its borders, conclude a peace treaty with the Soviet Union, or undermine Western access to Berlin. Furthermore, its application was subordinate to the Treaty of Paris.[62]

On May 27, the foreign ministers of the Benelux countries, France, Germany, and Italy signed the Paris Treaty, which established on paper the European Defense Community—a proposed two-million-man army wearing the same uniform, using the same weapons, and serving under the same commander, General Alphonse Juin of France. This force would comprise forty-three combat *groupements*, 6,000 planes, and a navy. It would also possess several administrative bodies: a Council of Ministers, a nine-member Commissariat, a Court of Justice, and an Assembly. This last body was the most ambitious, for if all went as planned, it would develop into a European congress with jurisdiction over the ECSC, the EDC, and all of Europe.[63]

Although theoretically the treaty did not discriminate against Germany, restrictions remained. As a "strategically exposed area," the Federal Republic would be prevented from manufacturing atomic, biological, or chemical weapons. Bonn could manufacture guided missiles, but only short-range ones. While Germany could raise an 85,000-man air force, it could not build planes. Although the eight non-EDC members of NATO would consider an attack on the EDC a threat to their own security, France wanted greater guarantees. As a result, at France's insistence, both London and Washington warned Bonn that they would keep their forces in Germany until the EDC was up and running, and they would treat a threat "from whatever quarter" to the "integrity or unity" of the EDC as a threat to their own security. And to remove all doubt, German misbehavior would constitute such a threat.[64]

Under great domestic pressure, Adenauer had struggled to get the best deal possible.[65] Although he failed to get all he wanted, the Allies did make certain concessions. Under the treaty, the West would continue to station sixteen divisions and support units in Germany, but as invited protectors, not occupiers. There were other concessions as well: If the two Germanys were to reunite, the contract would be subject to renegotiation; the Allied powers would intervene to protect threats to Germany's freedom only if Bonn and the European army were clearly unable to do so; Allied anticartel laws would remain in force only until West Germany passed its own laws; an Allied all-German board would review applications of convicted war criminals and would be competent to grant amnesty; and Bonn would be able to tax Allied business firms in Germany after two years had passed. Despite this progress, obstacles remained. Although the Western powers agreed that Germany would contribute to Western defense, Bonn wanted all the money to go toward its own effort, while London wanted the money to pay for the costs of British forces.[66]

Hopes for French parliamentary approval of the treaty, which were never bright to begin with, dimmed considerably. One reason is that the political center of France's parliament had shifted to the right, a development that weakened the pro-European forces and strengthened those forces opposed to European solutions.[67] Another reason is that France's military leadership believed that the question of relations between NATO and the EDC remained unresolved. The French military leadership thought that the government had not met their most important recommendation. The government and the Chiefs of the General Staff Committee collided over NATO membership for Germany. For the civilian leadership, the task of the Interim Committee was to ensure the rapid application of the treaty. For the Chiefs of the General Staff Committee, implementing the treaty had as its predicate a profound modification of the document.[68]

Keenly aware of the Chiefs of the General Staff Committee's fury, the government attempted to weaken it by asking, as of July, that France's military negotiator at the Paris Conference, General Edgard de Larminat, an avowed partisan of the EDC Treaty, henceforth sit in the Chiefs of the General Staff Committee with voting rights. In response, General Clement Blanc retorted on July 26 that if this decision were carried out, he himself would no longer appear before the committee. Juin, who in July had reached the rank of marshal, wrote to Prime Minister Pleven the same day expressing his concern over this issue. The Chiefs of the General Staff Committee's resolute opposition obliged the government to renounce the project. This incident marked the first open conflict over the EDC between the civilian and military leadership.[69]

Jean Monnet, the architect of the European army, disliked the current model of the EDC because it bore little resemblance to his other project, the Schuman Plan. Monnet retained, however, his duties as President of the High Authority, and was required to move to Luxemburg. Although he telephoned, sent letters, and frequently visited Paris, he proved unable to devote himself to the EDC, a contradiction of the "Monnet method." More importantly, Monnet's distance from Paris diminished his influence on the EDC negotiations.[70]

Unlike America or Germany, France was in no hurry to ratify the Bonn agreements or the EDC Treaty. Signing the treaties was merely a first step—they now had to be approved. Paris intended to use this fact to its advantage to obtain concessions. As French President Auriol reminded, "signing is not ratifying."[71] Schuman appeared before the Foreign Affairs Committee on June 4 to defend the government's actions. He said the agreements would end in "a normalization of our relations with Germany." French policy, he explained, consisted of placing Germany in "a European framework where she will no longer have the possibility of practicing an expansionist policy that has so often threatened us."[72]

Yet Bonn harmed its own cause in France, as German demands riled French critics. In mid-June, Theodore Blank, an unofficial personal adviser to Chancellor Adenauer, announced that at the beginning of 1953, the Federal Republic would recruit 100,000 volunteers that would provide the framework of German divisions. By the end of 1953, however, they would number between 500,000 and 520,000, a number larger than the 400,000 anticipated by the treaty.[73] Given the conditions that would result if Blank's words became reality, the French Army, which now saw its fears of a dominant German military force in the EDC realized, could only be comforted in its opposition to the treaty such as it was, as the Chief of Staff wrote in a note dated July 5.[74]

Events like these ratcheted up tensions between the government and the military leadership. In the eyes of the French military, the question of relations between NATO and the EDC remained unresolved. On July 23, Marshal Juin appeared before the Chiefs of the General Staff Committee to discuss the problems related to deploying German forces. He insisted that it was impossible to integrate all twelve members into the EDC, because this would diverge from SHAPE's needs. Only seven at most could be integrated—two to Central Europe and three to the command north of the Elbe.[75] On August 5, Juin admitted that problems over EDC-NATO relations lingered. He insisted that the solution remained the one that the Chiefs of the General Staff Committee had repeated several times: accept the Federal Republic into NATO.[76]

In addition to concerns about Germany's military contribution to the EDC, France focused attention on its own contribution. In line with the recommendations made at Lisbon, France had committed itself to providing fifteen ground divisions and 2,500 combat aircraft within three years. To finance this effort, France asked the United States to grant an additional $625 million in financial aid. Yet Washington offered only $187 million, causing a political uproar in Paris. France accepted America's decision with difficulty because Prime Minister Pinay, who had promised to balance the budget without raising taxes, had premised his assumption on increased U.S. aid. Pinay dispatched Ambassador Henri Bonnet to the U.S. State Department to register France's dismay. Remarked Bonnet afterwards, "The two governments did not see the question with the same eye."[77]

Although the French government had succeeded in fashioning a fragile status quo, it did not last: beginning September 1, the Chiefs of the General Staff Committee demanded implicitly that the much talked about transition period fixed at eighteen months by the treaty be renegotiated.[78] The French military leadership became progressively dissatisfied with the EDC treaty. Although the government drafted additional protocols and clauses in an attempt to amend the treaty, the Chiefs of the General Staff remained disappointed and condemned the changes as ignoring the principal requirements. On September 5, the Combined General Staff of the Armed Forces (CGSAF) registered its complaints about the "difficulties of the treaty's application." The CGSAF charged that the document contained "inadequacies on the essential questions" dealing with national sovereignty. These inadequacies, the note continued, would give pause to the EDC's proposed members about participating in areas in which national sovereignty is the most delicate as long as there exists no supranational political authority.[79]

France was not alone in its concerns over German power; the United States also worried about Germany overshadowing France. From September 24 to 26, America's top European diplomats met in London to discuss the future of Germany. The diplomats reached the same conclusion as French officials: continuing German prosperity would end any hope of maintaining equilibrium with France and would jeopardize the further integration of Europe. A more powerful Germany would gain in confidence, perhaps seeking to unite with East Germany and expand. Although America would stand firm on rearming the Federal Republic, U.S. State Department officials continued to worry about the proper way to manage this issue. German power had to be devoted entirely to Western Europe, yet without this Europe becoming a rival power bloc. The primary goal for the United States was to maximize German power but without intimidating France.[80]

The Two Edouards Unite

The publication of a note on September 27 revealing the existence of a supposed "secret treaty" that would have granted Germany a military advantage over France threw France's political circles in an uproar. This tempest signaled the true beginning of the anti-EDC campaign and overturned the French government's waiting strategy.[81] The secret note took the center stage of debate at the 46th Radical Congress in Bordeaux on October 17. The meeting marked a new highpoint in the anti-EDC crusade, most notably the spectacular reconciliation of the "two Edouards," erstwhile rivals Daladier and Herriot. Daladier, a former prime minister, minister of war, and disciple of Herriot, had succeeded him as chairman of the Radical-Socialist Party in 1927. Over the years, however, the two became rivals. Now Daladier, a deputy in the French legislature, hurled criticisms at the European army similar to Herriot. Herriot, the eighty-year-old president of the National Assembly and leader of the Radical Socialist Party, railed against the proposed European army: "Does this treaty conform to our Constitution? I say no. . . . All the provisions of this treaty work to put France in a position of inferiority."

Herriot pointed to what he determined were three flaws in the treaty. First, although all EDC members would have the right to withdraw their troops to quell domestic disturbances, France would have to ask permission to use its troops to restore order in the French Empire. Second, Germany would have the right to form militias similar to the ones that were at the core of Hitler's army. Third, Britain was not a signatory. "I say to my American friends," Herriot remarked, "that it is impossible for us to accept a document containing so many menaces. It is impossible that our American friends would condemn France to death."

Given his great prestige, Herriot's opposition hurt chances for the EDC treaty's passage. In light of the controversial nature of the project, his party's seventy-five votes would be crucial. Pleven and Reynaud, however, supported the treaty, saying that it was designed to prevent the rebirth of the *Wehrmacht*.[82]

In addition to concerns about German prosperity, France fretted about its own. After summer recess, the National Assembly reconvened in October. Perhaps the most pressing order of business was to fix the out-of-balance budget, which was over $570,000 in the red. The combination of his no-new-taxes pledge and America's refusal to approve additional aid afforded Prime Minister Pinay little freedom of action in this area. A run of bad luck—the spread of disease among French livestock, a hot and dry summer, and higher unemployment caused by a slowdown in rearmament—boxed Pinay in further.[83]

More bad news soon followed. On October 3, Acheson sent Pinay a letter through Ambassador James C. Dunn explaining that the United States would not be able to provide its promised $650 million in aid for the French calendar year budget of 1953. France would instead get $525 million. In addition to the letter, the Department of State gave Dunn a set of verbal instructions that he might use during the course of conversation. The instructions not only said that the United States expected France to spend $4 billion on defense as mandated at Lisbon, but in light of the MSA annual review, $4.3 billion should not be out of the question. Unfortunately for Dunn, he accidentally handed over these private instructions to French under secretary of state Félix Gaillard, who then passed them on to Pinay. The Prime Minister found the message "offensive in tone." He later summoned Dunn to his office and gave him a verbal dressing down, accusing Washington of interfering in France's internal affairs: "The French Government cannot accept the use of credits voted by Parliament be submitted to the unilateral decision of a foreign government."

Notwithstanding his anger at the note, Pinay did not refuse the $525 million. At week's end, he issued a statement: "France considers its friendship for the great Republic of the United States as one of the certainties of its history and one of the constants in its national sentiment. But France is a great power which must fulfill its destiny and preserve its rank." Making his defiance of the Americans public, the prime minister basked in popular approval. Remarked a U.S. State Department official: "If this helps Pinay a lot, it is all right with us."[84]

Although Pinay met with Dunn to mend fences after the October 3 incident, France still needed financial support. He persuaded Dunn to recommend to Washington that the $650 million be restored. Normally above politics, even the French head of state waded into the fray. At an October 27 ceremony dedicating a dam built with the help of American money, President Auriol tried to counter recent U.S. criticism of his country. Many Americans not only believed that France was less than grateful for the millions of dollars of aid given to it, but that it was also overreacting to the rearmament of Germany. An emotional Auriol responded to America's decision to cut its aid to France for 1953 by 20 percent: "Without doubt the Marshall Plan helped us, and we have often cited the benefits with gratitude, but unfortunately defense of freedom in Indo-China has already cost us just about double what we have received."

Auriol also remarked on America's perceived deaf ear toward France's objections to remilitarizing Germany: "Although we have no hatred for those who made us suffer so much, and we desire to forget their cruelties if they agree not to forget them, certain apologies for their discipline and their will to power, in comparison with an alleged carelessness on the French side, hurt us profoundly. It is as if the aggressor merited more encouragement than the victim." Coming on the heels of Edouard Herriot's declared opposition toward the EDC and Pinay's implicit approval of his position, Auriol's words threatened to bring the whole European army project crashing down. Foreign Minister Schuman, however, one of the driving forces behind the European integration movement, issued a threat. If the government did not give immediate consideration to the EDC, Schuman's party, the MRP, would walk out. Realizing that he needed the MRP's one hundred votes, Pinay promised to debate the treaty's ratification in November.[85]

On October 25, Defense Minister Pleven queried Juin as to the views of the CGSC. Juin responded that according to a memorandum by the CGSC, it appeared impossible for the French military establishment to reconcile to the two tasks assigned to it: the defense of the homeland and the prosecution of the seven-year-old war in Indochina. It was now a recognized fact, Juin wrote, that as long as France continued the war in Indochina at its current level, it could not fulfill its obligations in the Atlantic Community, and that France must renounce any claims to figure in the majority in the EDC—"our Allies could very well, in light of our, wish, with a measure of reason, that the Germans one day free themselves from the malthusianism that we intend to impose upon them."

Juin continued, asking whether the decline of France's prestige in Europe and North Africa and its inability to defend its territory with its own means was considered worth the risks of paying enormous sacrifices in Indochina for the common interests and with its success even more doubtful. France must now choose. It was not a question of immediate retreat, but the search for a solution that would allow for a quick alleviation of France's effort in Indochina.

Juin also wrote that France's lack of means ruled out a military solution to the Indochina War. Instead, the solution would be found in the political arena both at home and abroad. The Chiefs of the General Staff Committee recommended the opening of talks with the Americans in view of obtaining increased aid.[86]

Taking Stock

From December 15 to 18, the tenth session of the NAC took place in Paris. At the conference, where NATO's foreign, defense, and finance ministers met, the Alliance had the opportunity to measure the results of the promises made in Lisbon ten months earlier. The Alliance also had to decide on a level of spending for 1953. In meetings held to prepare for the conference, statistics revealed a gap between the goals set in Lisbon and results achieved since then. Lisbon had set targets of fifty divisions and 4,000 aircraft by the end of 1952; seventy divisions by 1953; and ninety-eight divisions and 10,000 aircraft by 1954. London admitted that its contribution would fall short of Lisbon goals by 40 percent in men and 50 percent for aircraft. Economic woes forced Britain's forces to remain at 1952 levels. To earn needed foreign exchange, much of its weapons program would go for export.

France also admitted that it would be unable to provide the three new divisions it had promised for 1953. It cited two principal reasons why it could not meet its quota: a diminished pool of conscription-age young men resulting from low birthrates during the 1930s and a reduced level of arms shipments from the United States, France's primary supplier. There was much truth to France's complaints. Although all NATO divisions (except Britain's) received 70 percent of their tanks, trucks, and artillery from the United States and 50 percent of their communications equipment, the Korean War forced America to cut back elsewhere. Accordingly, Washington had only given one-third of the military equipment apportioned to Europe since 1950. France said, however, that without $125 million more in U.S. military aid, it might have to cut its 1953 defense budget.[87]

As 1952 drew to a close, German rearmament remained as controversial as ever. Although the Allied nations had committed to enlisting German power to augment their security, they continued to harbor apprehensions about future German behavior. They worried that a rearmed and economically growing Federal Republic might upset the balance of power within the European army. This worry fueled anxieties among the Allies, making it more difficult to obtain ratification of the EDC Treaty.

Such concerns would fail to dampen American enthusiasm for the project. Although new leadership would appear in the United States in 1953, the entering Eisenhower administration would expend even more effort to consummate the EDC. Ironically, it would achieve no more success in reaching this goal than did its predecessor.

CHAPTER FIVE

New Faces, Similar Policies

As anticipated, the Republican administration of Dwight Eisenhower took office in January 1953. Its Cold War policy highlighted three related themes: fiscal austerity, massive retaliation, and the liberation of Eastern Europe from the grip of Soviet Communism. Eisenhower believed that America needed to maintain a vibrant economy for its democratic values to flourish. He also believed that the high cost of stationing massive conventional forces in Europe harmed the U.S. economy. These beliefs led his administration to shift from conventional deterrence to a greater reliance on nuclear forces in order to cut costs. This increased reliance on nuclear forces ushered in the strategy of "massive retaliation."[1] Finally, the Eisenhower administration derided as passive the Truman administration's policy of containment. The Eisenhower White House would instead "roll back" Soviet power in Eastern Europe.[2]

Yet despite condemning Truman's foreign policy, the new administration encountered its own difficulties in obtaining approval of the EDC: French resistance continued to collide with American commitment to the plan. No French government would submit the EDC Treaty to its legislature until, among other reasons, France received guarantees that America and Britain would maintain a predetermined level of their combat troops on the continent for an extended period.[3] Although the Eisenhower administration applied pressure to end French resistance to the treaty, it took care not to alienate France.

The Eisenhower administration supported the EDC more strongly than the previous administration for two main reasons.[4] Washington officials considered France as important as Germany to a reconstructed and reinvigorated Europe. American officials held Franco-German enmity primarily responsible for many past European conflicts. Knitting strong ties between the two former enemies would therefore improve the chances for obtaining lasting peace and stability in Europe, a priority for American officials. The logic of the U.S. strategy also indicated that France would double as a security buffer against both Soviet expansionism and German revanchism. Conversely, the administration thought that an alienated France would not be a strong and reliable Alliance partner. A weakened France would, in turn, hinder European unity and thereby threaten America's plans to remove its troops from the continent. Although America used both rewards and punishments in dealing with France, the threats it issued were not always credible or effective.[5] American officials ultimately determined that weakening France through coercive diplomacy or diplomatic isolation would surely boomerang.

Eisenhower advised against the United States continuing forever its current pace of defense spending. It would do long-term damage to the U.S. economy and wash at the foundation of America's democratic liberties, thus defeating the nation's ultimate purpose. Accordingly, Eisenhower sought to shift some of the expense of defending Europe onto the backs of the Europeans. Yet they faced economic and political difficulties of their own, a reality that left the administration with little alternative but to walk away from Europe, leaving it to provide its own defense, or to stand with Europe, whatever the cost to the United States.

France faced difficult economic problems, too. Governments of the Fourth Republic had to endure the concurrent costs of the Indochina War and Alliance commitments as well as chronic economic ills. Attempts to repair the economy, however, clashed with legislative mechanisms found in the 1946 French Constitution.[6] For instance, France had long been plagued by the instability of its currency, which drove down both domestic and international confidence. Politically handcuffed, successive governments could do little to restore confidence in the franc, which resulted in much capital either fleeing the country or taking refuge in the underground economy.

Critics have argued that one of the primary faults of the 1946 Constitution lay with Article 13, which granted the National Assembly, as a whole, the indivisible right to legislate. This nondelegation clause prevented prime ministers from taking prompt and decisive action on important issues, leaving them unable to legislate even small portions of their economic programs that enjoyed widespread support.[7] In addition, although Article 17 of the Constitution limited deputies from proposing expenditures during budget debates,[8] they soon learned how to circumvent this stricture.[9] As such, a government's budget could be delayed indefinitely on point-by-point debate over purely technical matters,[10] rendering budget debates long, drawn-out affairs that produced much bickering and many fallen governments, but precious little progress.[11]

The 1946 Constitution also handcuffed strong leadership. For example, because the prime minister could not dissolve parliament, he could neither demand that the deputies accept his legislative program in its entirety nor would he have recourse if defeated on any crucial question. In consequence, parliament could alter the government's program beyond recognition and it could, as was often the case, avoid important issues altogether.[12] Taken as one, these elements produced chronic legislative gridlock.[13]

NATO'S Nuclear Strategy

Budget woes had far-reaching effects, as they would ultimately and decisively influence the Atlantic Alliance's nuclear policy. Burden sharing was a perennial concern to the Alliance; deciding who would pay what had never been truly settled. From the outset of the EDC affair, the United States had agreed to assist the Europeans both economically and militarily—but only if they took on increasing responsibilities. Eisenhower wanted to prevent defense spending from getting out of hand and doing permanent damage to American society. At the same time, he wanted to avoid having the Europeans become too dependent on the United States, thus sapping them of the will to do for themselves.

In response, his administration looked for ways to reduce substantially America's costs in fighting the Cold War. Washington initially believed that a European defense force would solve the problem by lessening the need for U.S. troops to be stationed in Europe. Impending U.S.-Soviet nuclear parity, however, led Eisenhower to place greater emphasis on tactical nuclear weapons' presumed ability to reduce defense costs significantly while still providing a powerful deterrent to Soviet aggression.

In the area of nuclear weapons, Eisenhower chose to—and often had to—work within the general framework that he had inherited.[14] This inheritance is highlighted in one of the final acts taken by the Truman administration: the January 19, 1953, report to the National Security Council, NSC-141.[15] An outgrowth of the "Ridgway Study," NSC-141 reexamined basic national security policy in light of the anticipated addition of tactical nuclear weapons to NATO's arsenal. Instead of downplaying the need for ground forces, NSC-141 called for increasing their number. Yet the NSC draft determined that for economic and political reasons, the Europeans were unable or unwilling to spend substantially more on defense, and attempts to pressure them to do so might be counterproductive.[16]

Although the Eisenhower administration accepted and even promoted the inclusion of nuclear arms in NATO strategy, it rejected NSC-141's codicil of expanding the Alliance's conventional forces. The document forecast that tactical nuclear weapons would actually add to the number of ground troops needed, a clear conflict with Alliance political realities as well as Eisenhower's fiscal desire to reduce U.S. aid to Europe and his strategic desire to keep American troops at home. In consequence, he indicated that he would accept a "leveling off" of NATO's defense buildup provided the Alliance took steps to integrate nuclear weapons into its arsenal.[17]

Given the need to augment defense and promote fiscal restraint, Allied planners had to devise a strategy that would bridge the gap. Their efforts would eventually yield a new nuclear posture for the Alliance: MC-48, NATO's "New Look." Although relying heavily on nuclear weapons to deter a Soviet attack, MC-48 also recommended that conventional rearmament go forward and that Germany contribute twelve ground divisions to Western defense.[18]

Domestic Political Turmoil

France entered 1953 in the grip of its third ministerial crisis in a year. Prime Minister Antoine Pinay had resigned two days before Christmas and no suitable candidate had yet come forth to form a government. This impasse occurred at a critical moment, for the new parliamentary majority that had unseated the Socialists governed by a thin margin and was itself torn over such major issues facing the country as budgetary and financial difficulties, the French Union, and European affairs.[19]

Finally, René Mayer, a Radical Socialist, emerged as a credible candidate for prime minister. He turned first to the Socialists for support, but they refused his appeals, citing profound differences with the majority and the proposed government program. Mayer had no choice but to seek support from the rightist RPF. Although the two sides agreed on budgetary matters, forging a common policy on the EDC presented a major obstacle because the RPF opposed the European army while Mayer strongly supported it.

To ensure his candidacy—and keep the European army project alive— Mayer made a number of compromises to appease the RPF, which feared that the treaty as it stood would destroy the French Army. These compromises concerned the status of the Saar, British ties to the EDC, and protocols concerning the EDC Treaty.[20] Mayer promised the RPF that the French Army would remain intact and that he would not pose a vote of confidence while the National Assembly debated the EDC Treaty.[21] Invested by 389 votes to 205, Mayer attempted to reform the treaty by adding protocols, a condition of the RPF's endorsement of his candidacy.

Despite the government's support, the EDC's chances plummeted for four reasons. First, because Mayer held office by the grace of the RPF, a committed foe of the European army now in the majority, he had to agree to conditions guaranteed to anger France's allies. Second, the National Assembly's Foreign Affairs and Defense committees named two anti-EDC legislators—Jules Moch and General Marie-Pierre Koenig—as their *rapporteurs,* which increased the likelihood that the project would either be defeated or bottled up in committee. A third reason is that Bidault replaced Schuman as foreign minister. Schuman's retreat from the Quai was auspicious, for he was perhaps France's only direct link to Adenauer. Schuman was also a staunch Europeanist who ensured France's foreign policy remained "pro-European." Without his presence, movement toward European union would be set back measurably, thereby endangering the ECSC, the EDC, and other organizations designed to promote European unity, secure French political leadership, advance French economic concerns, and attenuate the "German problem." Fourth, and finally, the influence of Jean Monnet, who was then installed in Luxembourg, declined even further, as a number of his allies no longer held key positions in government.[22]

Although France had not as of mid-January worked out the exact nature or wording of the protocols, Alphand provided the U.S. embassy a tentative outline. According to the draft, France requested:

1. The right to withdraw French troops for use in the French Union.
2. Alteration of the voting procedure in the EDC to ensure Franco-German equality.

3. Maintenance of the integrity of French forces.
4. A two-year interim period whereby French forces stationed in the Federal Republic would enjoy special status.
5. Financial support for French troops in Germany six months after the EDC treaty and contractual agreements had entered into force.
6. Agreements regarding United Kingdom troop deployments on the Continent.
7. An understanding of U.S. financial assistance to France.[23]

Although potentially divisive, American officials decided to adopt a nuanced attitude toward the proposed protocols, with the Department of State suggesting:

> keeping an open mind regarding minor changes to the treaty provided they did not cause considerable delay, reopen the treaty or the Contractuals to amendment, work against six-power integration, prejudice a German contribution, or poison U.S. public opinion; neither encouraging the protocols, nor opposing them if they were necessary for approving ratification; not interfering, for it was a European project. America should only concern itself with the articles that affected it: Article 13, the already-ratified Contractuals, and the EDC-NATO protocol.[24]

Notwithstanding the American administration's seemingly hands-off approach, it made clear that European unity remained its priority and that failure to reach this objective would entail costs. In January, Dulles cautioned that "if in particular France, Germany and England should go their separate ways, then certainly it would be necessary to give a little re-thinking to America's own foreign policy in relation to Western Europe."[25] For Dulles, pressure held a prime place in his diplomatic repertoire, useful for nudging countries unwilling to follow U.S. policy. In this instance, he decided that America's allies needed to know the price of inaction. To be fair, Dulles was also just voicing political realities, as the U.S. administration found itself under considerable pressure. In strategic terms, the leadership of the U.S. military doubted the West's current ability to hold a defensive line in Western Europe—NATO was still under strength.[26] In political terms, Congress certainly would deny aid to allies who seemingly refused to help themselves. American boys and treasure would not be sacrificed in vain.

French plans to alter the treaty angered official London. On the day Mayer took power, Eden told Churchill that he did not "feel like being blackmailed by the new French government into any more concessions."[27] It was clear, however, that unless British policy moved in France's direction, the French parliament would reject the EDC. On January 19, Mayer met with Sir Oliver Harvey of the Foreign Office. Mayer insisted that Britain could help to advance efforts to integrate Europe and organize the common defense by committing to the Continent militarily. Despite some differences, the two men agreed that granting "reserved rights" to the signatories of the Contractuals was a powerful and accurate way to monitor the maintenance of German democracy, a concern that transcended Franco-Anglo political differences.[28]

In Germany, reactions to the proposed protocols contained greater complexity, as its leadership appeared to move from warm acceptance to cold rejection. Soon after Mayer announced them, Adenauer said publicly that they were to be welcomed. According to James Dunn, then U.S. ambassador to France,[29] Adenauer agreed to discuss the protocols before ratification simply in an effort to help France.[30] According to Dunn, Blank and other advisors persuaded him to do nothing to encourage additional protocols.[31] Less than a week later, the chancellor told the German press club that the protocols must deal only with issues of secondary importance and avoid setting back adoption of the treaty. Yet later, his skepticism grew into outright hostility the more he learned about them.[32]

Aware that international political winds could easily blow its plans off course, the new French government had to decide, among other matters, how to handle its allies. On January 16, an ambassadors' conference took place in Paris. Along with the men who acted as France's eyes and ears abroad were Mayer, Bidault, Queuille, and Maurice Schumann,[33] who met to discuss the difficulties surrounding the EDC and the additional protocols, Britain's relations with the organization, recent discussions in Strasbourg, and the Saar question.

François-Poncet, who had met recently with Adenauer, said that the chancellor received Mayer's remarks with greater calm than the German parliament or public opinion, and indeed wished to learn more about France's plans. For constitutional reasons, however, Adenauer wanted to avoid making the protocols public before the German parliament had approved ratification, as then the whole procedure would have to begin anew. Although he preferred a simple exchange of letters following approval, Adenauer needed to know the details of the French propositions in order to direct the debate in the German legislature.

Bidault, who considered Adenauer without doubt France's best interlocutor, asked what would be the best way to reopen talks with the chancellor. He noted that several obstacles remained, such as the Saar. In addition, France needed to know the position of other interested countries, especially Britain and the United States. René Massigli, France's ambassador to London, remarked that British ties with the EDC were essential, for without an agreement with London, it would be difficult to set up a meeting with Adenauer.

Some officials also suggested that the Saar question would have to be visited in its entirety. Mayer said that France would not know what to do as long as it had not adopted a position on two questions: the future state of the Saar and the new Franco-Saarois conventions to be concluded. François-Poncet thought the question of a date was secondary; the essential point was to inform Adenauer where the French government stood, as this would aid him in dealing with his parliament.[34]

In view of the compromises Mayer had to make to secure investiture, the other EDC nations began to question France's commitment to the project. Although Bidault attempted to reassure France's partners of its pro-European sentiments, he also had to deal with domestic opponents of the EDC. On January 29, a group of high-placed French officials sent him a note attacking the project. According to the note, the EDC Treaty would both re-create the *Wehrmacht* and destroy the French Union:

> Trapped in a supranational network, France has no other choice but to bypass it entirely . . . [W]e could then enter in the six and remain at the sides of the two superpowers. . . . The essential idea that appears to emerge from a comprehensive examination of the problem is that, in matters of defense, it is in the Atlantic, not the European, framework that we must build in order to keep our place in the Alliance and our positions in the world.[35]

France faced other domestic enemies of the EDC: the PCF, the RPF, certain foreign ministry officials, and the military leadership. Moreover, progress on the European army had languished throughout the Continent over the past several months, as the Europeans wanted to see who would be the new U.S. president. They had also awaited the results of U.S. studies to determine how tactical nuclear weapons would affect NATO's conventional force requirements.[36]

Eisenhower Assesses the EDC

With the U.S. election over and the studies completed, Eisenhower wanted to assess the EDC's chances, so he dispatched Dulles and Mutual Security Director Harold Stassen to Europe on a fact-finding mission.[37] Before he departed, Dulles canvassed selected U.S. officials about the EDC and received mixed views. William Draper, the U.S. representative on the NAC, referred to it as "the most pressing current problem in Europe for the security of the United States." Unfortunately, he remarked, progress over the past nine months had been disappointing, primarily due to Franco-German disagreement. Nonetheless, he believed that if these two could iron out their differences, the other four EDC countries would surely acquiesce. Draper opined that there were but two alternatives to the EDC: the NATO option or a bilateral security pact between Bonn and Washington. Seeing both as "unacceptable or unworkable," principally due to France's expected objection, Draper concluded that the European army was the only instrument available to advance U.S. policy.[38]

Near the end of the month, Dulles convened a high-level meeting at the Pentagon, at which he wanted to discuss alternatives to the EDC. According to General Omar Bradley, the chairman of the JCS, "From the military standpoint, EDC presents a solution to the problem of German participation and it is thus desired by the military."[39] Yet Bradley also suggested that Eisenhower's enthusiasm was responsible for the American military leadership's support of the European army even though it would have preferred NATO. "The real problem," he noted, "is that of getting German participation. Anything which does not accomplish that doesn't mean very much." When Dulles expressed surprise that Bradley preferred NATO to the EDC, the general pointed out that France could limit German production under EDC rules, but not under NATO rules. Bradley's point was obvious: free of French-imposed limits, the West could make more effective use of any German military contribution.

Given these views, Paris would arguably be the most important stop on Dulles's trip. On February 2, France and the United States held two plenary sessions as well as a private meeting between Dulles, Bidault, Mayer, and Pleven. At the first session, Bidault told the U.S. delegation that:

1. Strengthening NATO to tackle world Communism was a basic element of French foreign policy.
2. France would pursue European unity and the EDC.
3. There were factors that concerned the French public and parliament.[40]
4. France could not meet its European responsibilities if nationalism were encouraged in North Africa.

5. France welcomed "belated" recognition of efforts in Asia.
6. Atlantic cooperation was needed to ensure that France no longer continued its present armament program in the same way, that is, "annual improvisation."

Dulles responded to all of France's concerns. Specifically, he said that the United States recognized the global nature of the threat and would forswear isolation. He also noted that America's main objective was to bring together France and Germany. Although the United States would not intrude, Congress might need information regarding a ratification date and the proposed protocols before it would appropriate funds. Finally, in referring to North Africa, he contended that while the United States wished to avoid dismantling the French Union, it expected France to promote self-government.[41]

In the private meeting, the prime minister stated that he needed to resolve four issues in order to push the EDC through the French legislature: protocols interpreting the treaty—but not changing it—the way France wanted; U.K. association, without which France would not budge; settling the economic future of the Saar; and burden sharing in Indochina so that Germany would not dominate the Continent in France's absence.[42]

Bonn marked the second most important stop on the tour. There Dulles met with Adenauer as well as opposition figures.[43] Although the SPD leaders made the case that the West needed to call a four-power conference to reduce Cold War tensions, and that if it were to fail the West should drop the EDC in favor of national forces, Dulles would have none of it. He argued that such a meeting would be pointless in light of past Soviet actions. The West had to instead proceed from a policy of strength. Dulles also asserted that for political and military reasons, a national German army could not take the place of the EDC.[44]

According to Dulles, the chancellor appeared confident that approval of ratification would not be long delayed in spite of the SPD's legal challenge. Regarding the French protocols, Adenauer said that although he was unfamiliar with their details, they could potentially force new negotiations or another round of ratification, pushing the project back even further. Looking down the road, he said that once the entire process was complete, Germany would be ready to proceed, as it had done all the preparations it could possibly do at that point. Along these lines, Adenauer envisioned a 50,000- to 100,000-member volunteer force that would form the core of the future army. Commenting on the Saar, he noted that although Bonn and Paris had reached political agreement, economic concerns remained unresolved. Nonetheless, he expressed readiness to resume negotiations on the matter.

Dulles endorsed the timetable Adenauer had outlined, as the other states needed to approve the treaty as quickly as possible to put pressure on France and convince a skeptical U.S. Congress that the Europeans were making progress. Dulles also assured him that the French protocols would not alter the treaty. In addition, he encouraged the chancellor to do what was necessary to end the Saar dispute, concerned that France would not approve the treaty until the issue was settled.[45]

Confident that the trip had breathed life into the project, Dulles returned from Europe encouraged about the EDC's chances, putting them at "60–40." Although France remained the biggest question mark, he did not see French concerns as insoluble. Ambassador Dillon suggested to Dulles that he try to get more precise information from Bidault when he visited Washington in late March.[46]

France Demands British Help

Throughout this affair, an essential French demand was to obtain an unambiguous British commitment to the EDC, for Britain's military presence would help to offset any potential military advantage either sought by or accorded to the Federal Republic. French efforts to enlist British support continued. From February 12–13, Anglo-French meetings took place for the purpose of discussing the projected protocols. The French proposed to establish between Britain and the European army "a relationship of organic co-operation going further than mere association." France indicated that British troops in Europe could remain at present levels and, in exchange, Britain could take part in EDC institutions. Although France suggested that Britain could use its forces elsewhere after obtaining approval from the SACEUR, Paris demanded the same right but without the need to consult the SACEUR, obviously a suggestion that London would reject.[47]

In addition to strategic concerns, financial matters also gave London pause. The high costs of stationing four British divisions in Germany had led Britain's Joint Planning Staff to recommend dropping one division for the sake of economy. Eden relented, informing the British cabinet on the twenty-fourth that if Britain agreed to consult the EDC about its troop strength on the Continent, France might approve the EDC Treaty.[48]

The French military leadership also saw British cooperation as crucial. On February 18, the French Chiefs of the General Staff Committee (CGSC) drafted a note regarding the guarantees and assurances needed from Britain. The CGSC had found Britain's protocol insufficient, believing that it should be only the basis for further discussion. According to the note, France needed British cooperation in several areas. Britain had to commit itself to maintaining a certain number of ground troops in Europe. British help was also needed "in order to block the renaissance of militarism in West Germany and a policy of revanche that could lead the Federal Republic to war." London could also support Paris on such international matters as NATO and the French Union.[49]

On March 2, London presented a memorandum to Paris that it subsequently submitted to the other EDC governments. The document laid out terms for Britain to cooperate politically with the EDC and to negotiate the question of British armed forces on the Continent. Britain also suggested altering the NATO Treaty so that it would co-terminate with the EDC Treaty. Although assuring Bidault that Britain had no intention of withdrawing its troops and would never do so without consultation with NATO, Oliver Harvey told him categorically that Britain would not commit to maintain a definite number of troops on the Continent. The French government replied ten days later saying, among other things, that there should be some link between military cooperation and British "participation" in the EDC, that Britain should make its existing commitments to NATO more explicit, and that London should set out its proposals for associating with the EDC with a protocol rather than a unilateral declaration. Although British officials concluded that the gap between the two sides had narrowed, it was not until April 1954—after lengthy negotiations—that Britain finally agreed to offer a formal agreement concerning its ties to the EDC.[50]

Paris in Twenty-Three Days

In addition to troubles with its Alliance partners, France also faced other problems: the rift between civilian and military leaders over the proposed European army opened further at the beginning of the year and would grow tremendously. Some high-ranking French officers approached members of parliament to lobby against the EDC, while others sought to influence public opinion. Juin hardened his stance, too. His promotion to marshal, the summit of France's military hierarchy, led him to shed his reserve and appeal to a higher calling—the interest of the state—when challenging civilian officials. By the end of 1952, Juin had clearly moved into the opposition.[51]

On January 4, 1953, in a speech to French reserve officers, Juin publicly criticized the EDC. He indicted the state of Western defense, charging that without a large-scale German military contribution, the Soviet bear could easily claw its way into the very heart of Western Europe:

> The enemy has installed himself in Saxony and in the salient, 150 kilometers from the Rhine. This salient is, in the heart of Germany and toward the heart of France, a . . . loaded pistol.
>
> If one transplants to the Rhine region that offensive maneuver developed by the Russians in White Russia against the Germans in 1944, and grants them [the Russians] the same concentration of forces and rhythm of advance, such an attack . . . would be capable of reaching Paris in 23 days.[52]

The French government took seriously such apocalyptic statements from the country's top military official. Yet although many civilian officials agreed with Juin, there remained a sticking point: how to obtain an acceptable balance between French and German forces. If German forces outnumbered French forces, they would pose a potential military threat to France and embolden the Federal Republic to demand greater political authority within the EDC—both unacceptable outcomes for France. Yet Paris could not supply more troops than Bonn because of the financial and manpower droughts brought on by the Indochina War. This conflict forced France to cut back its efforts to rearm, causing it to fall short of the force goals set at Lisbon in February 1952. To avoid being outnumbered in the EDC, the French government attempted simply to reduce Germany's contribution so as to achieve the desired equilibrium. This policy, however, incensed the military leadership: "In military terms, it is not possible to reduce the German contribution without compromising Western defense. The necessary balance between French and German contingents must be sought by maintaining French objectives and not by reducing German forces."[53]

A Matter of Protocol

With the EDC Treaty under attack from several quarters, the French government knew it had to attach protocols to the agreement to satisfy domestic critics who feared that the EDC would prevent France from using its armed forces to deal with extra-European crises.[54] On February

11, 1953, the French government submitted protocols to the EDC Inter-mediary Committee. These protocols included one mandating the right to interchange forces devoted to the EDC and national forces and one giving France the right to withdraw forces from the EDC to deal with crises in its overseas territories.[55] These protocols, however, sparked in-ternational criticism that they were simply a ploy to delay or prevent German rearmament, to which the French government replied that they changed neither the spirit nor the letter of the EDC Treaty. Instead, ex-plained French officials, they were simply designed to make the agree-ment more precise and facilitate ratification by the French parliament.[56]

In addition to trying to obtain British support on the Continent, France also had to win acceptance for its proposed protocols. On February 11, after having already discussed with its allies their tentative substance, Paris submitted the protocols to the heads of the EDC Interim Commit-tee.[57] Hervé Alphand presented the proposed protocols as necessary because of France's defense commitments in Indochina and other non-European territories. He insisted they would violate neither the spirit nor the letter of the EDC Treaty. He refused, however, to guarantee that no additional protocols would be offered, a point that could potentially cause difficulty in negotiations.[58]

All sides had the opportunity to air their opinions on February 24 at the EDC foreign ministers conference in Rome. There France's propos-als encountered stiff opposition. Adenauer was particularly vexed, charging that they jeopardized Western security arrangements. He claimed that the Soviet Union was stepping up military actions in East-ern Europe, and that Western Europe needed to respond or the United States might adopt a peripheral strategy. Furthermore, he charged that the protocols not only contradicted France's original project but would also hamper defense and cause ratification problems. The treaty, there-fore, had to be considered in its present unmodified state.[59]

In response, Bidault argued that the protocols were indeed consistent with the document. Moreover, he continued, if the situation were as dire as Adenauer claimed, they should be accepted so that the ratifica-tion process could proceed. The other foreign ministers then stepped in to mediate. The next day, Bidault adopted a conciliatory tone, stressing France's commitment to a European policy and its willingness to work for approval of ratification even if the protocols were rejected. Although the other foreign ministers pledged to help France, they nonetheless sided with Bonn and blamed Paris for causing ratification difficulties. In any event, the French protocols were considered merely as "interpretive texts" and set aside until later. The foreign ministers then returned the draft protocols to the Interim Committee to be studied further until the next meeting in Strasbourg.[60]

Adenauer had good reason for concern. On February 9, the Soviet Council of Ministers called for a drastic expansion of Soviet military might. This expansion included the creation of 74 bomber divisions, 10,300 planes, and 290,000 personnel for the air force. The council also planned to grace the Soviet Navy with heavy and medium-size cruisers.[61] The Soviet Union seemed destined to become a more formidable adversary. According to Matthew Evangelista, 1953 was the "high point of Soviet troop strength," when its authorized forces numbered 5.4 million. That same year, the United States had 427,000 military personnel in Europe.[62]

The Protocols

Aware that the EDC's unpopularity could ultimately sink it, Mayer tried to drum up domestic support. Speaking in Sétif at the beginning of March, Mayer defended the project by focusing attention on the protocols.[63] He warned that Germany must contribute to its own defense and not be allowed to develop its richness in times of peace "while the Western partners, including France, exhaust themselves in training and equipping armed forces." An amended treaty, however, would be the final opportunity to demand of Germany "guarantees against the rebirth of militarism, which is necessary both in her own interests and those of France." Mayer contended that once in place, the protocols would prevent Germany from reconstructing its general staff, supporting paramilitary forces, raising more troops than France, receiving direct U.S. military aid, maintaining military forces, having a ministry of defense, or reorganizing its arms industries for its own benefit. Conversely, France would retain special powers in Germany, receive the chance to reopen four-power talks, and enjoy formal defense agreements with London and Washington.[64]

Despite Mayer's advocacy, the French military leadership continued to find the treaty unacceptable. Some military officials even suggested bypassing the EDC altogether. On March 12, retired General Maxime Weygand, the former Chief of the General Staff of the French Army, met with President Auriol to voice his concerns. He told the president that German rearmament must take place within NATO, not the EDC.[65]

On March 23, the EDC Interim Committee[66] agreed to five of the French protocols. Disagreement on number six,[67] which concerned France's demand for the right to withdraw its troops from the EDC for use elsewhere, threatened to scuttle the other five. None of the other members would tolerate preferential treatment for France.[68] The next day, Prime Minister Mayer proposed a compromise. He suggested that the EDC Commissariat act immediately on any request to redeploy troops after it had been made to the Commissariat and SACEUR.[69] The Interim Committee then accepted the protocols and sent them to the six foreign ministers. In the main, this compromise agreement improved the EDC's chances in the five other nations.[70]

This was not the case in France. Although France's government had tried to attach protocols to the EDC Treaty that would ease the French military leadership's concerns, its retreat in the face of Allied opposition instead provoked the military chiefs' ire. On April 4, General Clement Blanc issued a note that underscored this very point. He wrote that because the other EDC countries had coldly received the French protocols, they had to be modified. Now, according to Blanc, it was a question of "imprecise agreements from which the repercussions could be considerable."[71]

Juin shared Blanc's concerns. He thought that the government's compromises would impair French security. In March 26 testimony to the National Assembly's National Defense Committee, Juin recommended extending the eighteen-month transition period until a European political authority was established—a year and a half was simply not long enough to resolve the EDC's political and technical difficulties. He warned that the French Army would be disorganized while German forces were not yet ready, making the transition dangerous. Juin also reaffirmed the need to rearm Germany, while noting that the EDC provided guarantees limiting German arms. He admitted that he would have considered the treaty inapplicable without the recently accepted protocols; yet he expressed misgivings about the functioning of the organization of the defense community defined in the treaty. Finally, Juin reiterated what several Allied military officials had begun to say out loud: NATO did not have the military wherewithal to defend at the Elbe.[72]

Juin again took his concerns public, this time taking an even bolder stand. In an April 4 address to the Congress of the National Union of Reserve Officers at Constantine, in North Africa, Juin warned that the NATO countries lagged far behind their projected contributions to defense, a deficit that would risk "a battle inevitably lost, invasion of the homeland and the adoption of the peripheral strategy." Although the atomic bomb would be of some help, it could not prevent an invasion. What was needed, he insisted, was German support. Nonetheless, Juin harbored reservations about the EDC, contending that it needed a supranational political authority to bolster it. He also noted that while the guarantees in the treaty should be retained, one should also guard against carrying out the treaty too strictly in all its particulars.[73]

Juin continued his campaign to modify the treaty. When on April 15 the French cabinet approved the protocols adopted by the EDC Interim Committee, Juin protested vigorously. The next day he complained to the government that the protocols it had submitted made the text less clear and failed to respond to essential goals in two areas: maintaining the unity of the French Army and the preparation and carrying out of mobilization plans.[74]

Juin soon had an opportunity to raise his concerns about the protocols face-to-face, as the National Defense Community met on April 21, two days before France would seek accord at the upcoming NAC meeting. Foreign Minister Bidault began the meeting by announcing that the new version of the protocols was not only closer to French aims but responded to the essential objections the marshal had raised in his recent letter. Juin dissented, however, insisting that the updated draft was more obscure than the first. Bidault quickly disagreed, contending that the new text had received the approval of all the countries concerned and that no ambiguity existed on its meaning. Defense Minister Pleven seconded Bidault, arguing that while the text was not perfect, as is the case with most texts subject to long negotiations, it had received, in its essentials, the support of all the signatory nations of the principles that France had initially advanced.

The Seventh Protocol

Undeterred, Juin proposed a seventh protocol. In his view, putting the treaty into force too rapidly would risk upsetting the organization and morale of French forces. Indeed, he continued, Germany would experience fewer difficulties entering the EDC because it was "bargaining from zero." France, on the contrary, would have to contend with all that already existed in the military arena, where overturning its methods could destroy or compromise the potential of French forces at a critical moment for the defense of Europe, in which France played an essential part.

Juin said the transformation produced by implementing the EDC must occur without problems. It is for this reason, he stated, that the CGSC had from the beginning recommended adopting an eighteen-month transition—yet even this period would appear too short to guarantee the progressivity and the flexibility indispensable to the treaty's application. It is necessary, he stressed, to prolong it. The marshal then proposed adding a seventh protocol to the treaty that would require that ratification be contingent on the political integration of its signatories. If adopted, however, this seventh protocol would have resulted in additional negotiations, effectively halting progress on the EDC. The meeting then turned ugly, as Pleven and Bidault faced off against Juin. Although other participants proposed compromises, Juin held his ground.[75]

Later in the day, Juin wrote to Prime Minister Mayer regarding that morning's stormy National Defense Committee session. He confessed surprise at the manner in which the decision regarding the seventh protocol had been avoided. In fact, he thought those present were not speaking the same language, and that the discussion had quickly turned into a "dialogue of the deaf."[76] He also wrote that while concerned to see the EDC quickly realized, he was also "firmly convinced" of the risks involved were France unable to find a means to prolong the intermediary period to more than eighteen months. Although the project still faced vigorous opposition from the French Army, the public, and the National Assembly, he maintained his position, which, he believed, offered a solution. Nonetheless, he warned that, "one must not count on me to aid the ratification as long as the precaution I suggest and deem indispensable is not adopted. If it turns out that I am followed neither by the government nor the parliament, the government will have to provide a replacement for my present responsibilities."

Mayer responded the next day, expressing surprise that Juin considered the discussion of the seventh protocol to have been "avoided." Mayer told him that he had given him the "opportunity to present . . . the reasons that appear to you to militate in favor of its text." He continued. "You had the floor in order to defend your thesis. You know as well as me that" it had not been adopted because it consisted of "a veritable modification of the treaty."[77]

The government's refusal to accommodate Juin only widened the distance between it and the military leadership, with several military officials later writing and distributing pamphlets and tracts denouncing the treaty. As for Juin, he would soon find himself in deep political trouble for publicly opposing the European army. A year later, France would relieve him of his national military responsibilities.

American Financial Concerns

France would receive substantial help in assembling an effective defense. Yet despite its great relative strength and prosperity, U.S. officials—most notably, Dwight Eisenhower—had qualms about the consequences of committing massive resources to the East-West conflict. In addition to strictly geopolitical matters, Eisenhower also worried about the financial cost of fighting the Cold War.[78] In his eyes, America had to defend not just material assets, but also a particular way of life: a democratic polity supported by a free-market economy. Reckless defense spending would place all this at risk. As he told Bernard Baruch, the head of the U.S. delegation to the U.N. Atomic Energy Commission, "To accustom our population to living indefinitely under such controls will gradually bring a new conception of the relation of the individual to the state—a conception that would change in revolutionary fashion the kind of government under which we live."[79]

Eisenhower's concerns about the economy were no secret; he publicly expressed hope that government spending would be cut to move toward a balanced budget, which was then $8 billion in the red. Eisenhower wanted to keep his campaign pledge to erase the deficit, and he believed that deficit spending "has a very bad effect on our whole economy." Nonetheless, he stated that in terms of current combat strength, he would not recommend any "major" cut.[80]

At a special NSC meeting near the end of March, Secretary of the Treasury George Humphrey, a fiscal conservative, called for cutting back U.S. foreign aid—it was simply too costly. Humphrey recommended instead that the United States premise its plans to defend the Continent with European conventional forces supported by America's atomic shield.[81]

Dulles and Mutual Security Director Harold Stassen rejected this recommendation, contending that increased defense spending would bankrupt Europe's economies. Reducing aid might signal to the Allies that the Communist threat had receded and they could thereby justifiably slow their efforts to rearm. Cutting aid would "take the heart out of NATO," as Europe might believe that America had returned to its isolationist ways, leaving the Old World to look out for itself.[82]

The Europeans had justification for such concerns. The United States has historically avoided tight military and political links to Europe, a condition that had endured during the twentieth century even after America attained superpower rank and two world wars engulfed Europe. This record remained etched in the minds of most Europeans. Secretary of Defense Charles Wilson stoked such fears in early May when he told a House subcommittee that the Department of Defense would reduce spending for fiscal year 1954. Economic concerns clearly influenced a range of policy options.[83]

Franco-American Talks

A team of French officials would travel to Washington in April to raise a number of important issues with their American counterparts. One issue concerned U.S. plans for the Federal Republic. Although the United States had continuously denied that it would pursue the NATO option, French fears remained strong. An internal French document noted that during his recent visit to Bonn, Dulles had proclaimed that Germany would not enter NATO. It pointed out, however, that in certain U.S. circles, most notably the Pentagon, attitudes on the subject were not as cut and dried. As such, France needed to make the following case.

To accept the Federal Republic into NATO would alter the treaty's character. "It would bring about a profound modification of the EDC system conceived precisely in function of the nonparticipation of the Federal Republic." Moreover, "If Germany, soon after ratification, asked to enter the Pact, French opinion would have the impression that the European Defense Community was just a temporary expedient for the Germans." In addition, it "would risk bringing about a complete revision of the contractual system and the abandonment of reserved rights, which would have dangerous consequences concerning East-West relations." Finally, the National Assembly would veto any attempt to admit Germany into NATO. "Given the political repercussions that this veto would trigger, it is essential to avoid such a question being raised."[84]

As for the United States, it was chiefly concerned with getting the EDC Treaty approved. At the March 25 meeting of the NSC, Dulles proclaimed that René Mayer sincerely supported the treaty and that he was America's last best hope. Were he to fall, the EDC would tumble with him. Furthermore, Adenauer would probably lose his bid for reelection, forcing London and Washington to take unilateral measures certain to meet French objections.

Dulles also pointed out the connection between the EDC and Indochina: France was simply unable to meet both commitments simultaneously. To convince Congress that France deserved continued U.S. assistance for the war, the two sides would have to find a way to end the conflict within twelve to nineteen months. As an inducement for France to approve the treaty, Eisenhower suggested naming Marshal Alphonse Juin as commander-in-chief, Allied forces Central Europe. The president hoped that this move would mitigate French fears that the EDC would diminish France's role in Europe by ensuring that it had a voice at the highest levels.[85]

That same day, David Bruce, the recently appointed U.S. observer to the EDC Interim Committee and representative to the ECSC, met with

Mayer. Bruce told him that elements within France's foreign ministry opposed the treaty. Mayer replied that he had already taken drastic measures to rectify the situation. Mayer further contended that the best way to settle the Saar dispute would be to hold direct talks with Adenauer, whom he expected to be difficult regarding France's economic and financial ties to the region. France, however, had a huge financial stake in the Saar, having poured in large sums of money. Although Mayer conceded that he could accept a European status for the Saar, he remained adamant regarding its economic and monetary status. Mayer also said that he expected to ask Washington for more money to continue the Indochina War.[86]

From March 26 to 27, France and the United States held talks in Washington. Eisenhower warned Mayer that unless France made progress toward approving the treaty, U.S. public opinion would refuse to provide financial support. Dulles told Bidault that U.S. aid depended on the treaty's progress. Despite these threats, France made no discernible progress on the treaty. Switching gears, Washington provided Paris with over $1 billion on April 26. The United States hoped that it would be money well spent.[87]

Yet as events will show, money was only part of the problem. The talks eventually snagged on the Saar. Mayer told the Americans that settling the Saar was a precondition for approving ratification of the EDC. Without an agreement on this point, it would be unclear whether EDC troops could be stationed in the Saar, or whether Saarlanders could serve in the European army. Dulles supported France on this issue, and would in turn press Adenauer, who planned to come to Washington after Mayer.[88]

German–American Talks

On March 15, Herbert Blankenhorn, Adenauer's chief aide, arrived in New York to meet with McCloy to discuss the ambitious agenda for the chancellor's upcoming visit. Blankenhorn, who traveled secretly, relayed Adenauer's concern about Germany's security. Citing the delay before the EDC became a reality and drawing attention to the Soviet Union's alleged military buildup in its satellites, the chancellor proposed that Germany begin training 100,000 men for military service just as soon as its parliament had approved ratification of the treaty. He also suggested that Washington inform both London and Paris that it wished to sever the link between the EDC Treaty and the Contractuals so that Bonn could regain its sovereignty immediately.[89]

After a short recess, the talks continued. Due to expected French re-sistance, the Eisenhower administration agreed only to the most innocu-ous German demands. This point was reiterated in a March 30 conversation Blankenhorn had with James Riddleberger, the director of the State Department's Bureau of German Affairs, who told him that if the United States were even to consider Adenauer's major proposals, it would be a tacit admission that the EDC Treaty might be defeated. Such action could adversely influence the ratification process in France, a risk the United States was unwilling to take.[90]

From April 6 to 18, Adenauer embarked on his first trip to the United States. Contrary to his initial hopes, the chancellor scaled back his high expectations. Adenauer's chief foreign policy objective was to end all in-ternational discrimination toward the Federal Republic and secure its place among the sovereign nations of the world. Although he deemed the creation of the EDC the shortest route to this goal, French opposi-tion presented the main obstacle, as Paris insisted on resolving the Saar question before it would even consider approving the EDC treaty. In addition, Adenauer also felt sharp domestic pressure from those Ger-mans who considered the Saar to be exclusively German territory. Given the high priority it accorded to the EDC, the United States ostensibly sided with France in this case, telling the chancellor to do his best to end the dispute so that the ratification process could proceed.[91]

Despite his failure to achieve his initial goals, the trip was a success for both Adenauer and the Federal Republic. President Eisenhower, in a spirit of openness, invited Adenauer to lay a wreath on the grave of the American Unknown Soldier. Following the ritualistic twenty-one-gun salute, the chancellor approached the grave and laid the wreath. In this solemn moment, the military band struck up *Deutschland über Alles,* moving the seventy-five-year-old Adenauer to tears. He later recalled it as the "greatest moment of my life."[92]

Significantly, the visit polished the chancellor's image as a great states-man and accorded Germany greater prestige in the international arena. Yet, irrespective of these important achievements, domestic electoral politics in France would alter international political calculations and make solving the German question as elusive as ever.

CHAPTER SIX

The Death of Stalin

The United States intended the EDC to enable the Europeans to defend themselves against Communism rather than relying on U.S. support. Yet the death of Josef Stalin on March 5, 1953 cast a shadow over these plans. Ailing for several years, the seventy-three-year old Stalin's demise delivered fresh hope to opponents of the EDC, who believed that perhaps the West could cut a deal with Moscow now that the increasingly erratic and paranoid Stalin was dead.[1] The Soviet Union soon gave credibility to such views by launching a "peace offensive." In a mid-March speech to the Supreme Soviet, Georgii Malenkov, the new chairman of the Council of Ministers and Stalin's likely successor, proclaimed that no international issue existed that could not be resolved through negotiation. He then singled out the United States.[2]

Moscow's unexpected conciliatory gesture forced the Eisenhower administration into an awkward position. Eisenhower wanted to respond positively, but Dulles argued that a very favorable reply would delay the EDC and German rearmament because the Soviets would use these talks as a pretext to delay. Dulles believed that the Soviet Union was in a position of weakness and that the United States should attempt to capitalize on it. Taking into account Dulles's counsel, Eisenhower on April 16 responded conciliatorily to Malenkov's peace feeler but called for acts—such as signing an Austrian peace treaty or releasing World War II POWs—not words.[3]

The Soviet Union did take positive steps, however. On March 19, the Soviet Council of Ministers resolved to pursue a policy of "concluding the war in Korea as soon as possible." The warring parties signed an armistice on July 27, ending a conflict that could have led to a direct clash between the Soviet Union and the United States. The Council of Ministers also decided on June 2 to try to improve the political situation in an increasingly unstable East Germany. The Soviet leadership also encouraged a general liberation among its East European clients. In fact, the Presidium of the Soviet Council of Ministers produced on June 2 a document drafted and signed by the head of the newly created Ministry of Internal Affairs, Lavrenti P. Beria. According to the document, "Measure to Improve the Political Situation in the GDR," the East German leadership should "abandon the policy of forced construction of socialism and work for the creation of a united, democratic, peace-loving and independent Germany."[4]

Of course Eisenhower had no way of knowing about decisions made inside the Kremlin. But while Dulles acted as a firm brake on any White House temptation to parlay with the Kremlin, there existed other reasons the president declined the Soviet offer. He had been in office fewer than three months; his predecessors had failed to develop plans to deal with a post-Stalin Soviet Union; and the United States had no ambassador in Moscow since George F. Kennan, whom the Kremlin declared persona non grata in 1952 for comparing the Soviet Union to Nazi Germany.[5]

Churchill's Summit Proposal

While Eisenhower seemed unprepared to grasp Moscow's extended olive branch, Churchill eagerly welcomed it. Less than a week after Stalin's death, the British prime minister sounded out Eisenhower about an informal four-power summit. Although Eisenhower opposed such a meeting, Churchill persisted.[6] In a May 11 address to the House of Commons, Churchill proposed that the West seek high-level talks with Moscow.[7] He also suggested creating an international security pact with and against a reunited Germany, based on the model of the 1925 Locarno Pact.

Much to Churchill's dismay, many in his own Foreign Office, as well as among Britain's principal allies, criticized his speech. Top British and French officials doubted Soviet sincerity but wanted to put it to the test, while the Foreign Office warned that the Kremlin would exploit an open-ended summit in an attempt to block the EDC.[8] The United States also reacted skeptically to Churchill's speech. Eisenhower opposed a summit with Moscow in part to protect his flank from right-wing Republicans. The German government took no comfort in Churchill's remarks either. The new face on Soviet foreign policy displayed in the wake of Stalin's death troubled Adenauer. Blankenhorn said that the chancellor was "scared stiff" by Churchill's proposal, fearful that the West might arrive at an understanding with Moscow at Germany's expense. Certain that Moscow intended its campaign to block the creation of the EDC, Adenauer tried to ensure that the Federal Republic be rearmed and granted sovereignty regardless of the fate of the European army.[9]

Churchill's proposal did elicit positive reactions from some quarters in France. On May 13 and 14, the Foreign Affairs Committee of the National Assembly adjourned until a new study of the European army was completed. It also asked the government to try to convene a four-power conference.[10] On May 20, Prime Minister Mayer contacted Eisenhower to suggest a three-power meeting. Nonetheless, Churchill's speech presented a downside for France. Although buoyed by the suggestion of a "big four" meeting, France also saw its hopes dashed by Churchill's statement that Britain was *for* but not *with* the EDC.[11] Churchill's remarks particularly wounded Mayer. In office just over four months, he had so far failed to obtain a satisfactory British association with the EDC.[12]

The Saar Dispute

In spite of the German government's efforts to approve the treaty, France continued to hold its ground. As it had long insisted, France demanded agreement on the Saar before approving ratification of the EDC. On May 12, Franco-German talks on the Saar took place. Although each side made clear its concerns, they accomplished little of substance.[13]

Frustrated by German objections, Paris wanted to bypass Bonn and negotiate directly with the Saar; and on May 20, despite Adenauer's pleas, representatives from France and the Saarland signed the Conventions Franco-Sarrois. While awaiting the region's European status, the agreement guaranteed the Saar "complete political autonomy." This guarantee notwithstanding, France and the Saar maintained a monetary and customs union, a situation that inflamed opinion in the Federal Republic.[14] On July 2, the Bundestag approved a resolution intended to serve as a blueprint for the government's future discussions on the subject:

> According to German law and international law the territory of the Saar has been a part of Germany and within German frontiers since 31 December 1937;

The administration at present in force in the Saar territory is a constituent part of Germany's internal organization, which is the occupation powers instituted by the authority temporarily assumed by them; and

In the negotiations for a treaty concerning the Saar territory which the German Federal Republic will undertake, and in the decisions of the treaty itself, the law must be reconstituted in such a way that: (a) free and democratic conditions are created within the Saar territory; (b) the de facto separation of the Saar territory from Germany is brought to an end, and recognition is given to the fact that the Saar belongs to Germany.[15]

Germany's hard-line stance not only put the ball firmly in France's court, but also risked destroying the European army project were France to refuse to back down. Moreover, were the EDC to be discarded, America might unilaterally rearm Germany or adopt a peripheral strategy. Neither prospect held any appeal for France.

Indochina Moves to the Top of the Agenda

Events continued to spiral downward for France, for on May 21, financial difficulties felled the Mayer government. America's $1 billion aid package of April 26 seemingly did nothing to ensure Mayer's survival. His fall sparked political turmoil in France. The country was waging a costly and losing battle in Indochina, Washington was growing more impatient about the EDC, and Germany was becoming more truculent over the Saar. Whoever next assumed power in France would confront a full plate of troubling political issues.

One such hopeful was Pierre Mendès France, who for some time had been a rising political star. In a mid-May interview, Mendès France, a prominent Radical Socialist and anticolonialist, commented on Indochina: "The facts long ago led us to concede that a military victory was not possible. The only solution therefore lies in negotiation. Our negotiating position was better two years ago than it was last year; better last year than it is now; it is probably not as bad now as it will be next year."[16]

Such talk irked U.S. officials, who counted on France to end the war in Indochina with a military triumph, not a negotiated settlement. America took seriously the specter of a Mendès France–led France when on June 3, although Joseph Laniel was invested, Mendès France received 301 votes for prime minister, thus failing to secure investiture by a mere

13 votes. This number meant that with the PCF, there were at least 400 French deputies willing to jettison Indochina. From this point on, Indochina became France's top foreign policy priority, setting back even further plans to create a European army.[17]

Three months later, U.S. official Ridgeway Knight submitted a report that analyzed what would happen if Laniel were to fall.[18] Knight surmised that Mendès France saw the Indochina War as a problem for the free world, not just for France. Moreover, without greater Allied backing, he might end the conflict at the bargaining table and not on the battlefield. Knight also contended that while anti-Communist, Mendès France gave less credence to the Soviet threat than did U.S. officials. Nonetheless, Knight thought that he might approve the EDC.[19]

As the year progressed and solutions regarding Indochina and the EDC continued to stall, public dissatisfaction fueled the rise of Mendès France. At the September 17–20 Radical Socialist Party's congress, the delegates blew cold air on the EDC. Mendès France delivered the most memorable speech of the congress: "Ah yes, it must change! Because, listen to rumors that mount, we are in 1788!"[20] Talk of revolution was unwelcome in Washington and in other Allied capitals. The Alliance wanted a stable and reliable partner, not one on the brink of great change.

Yet if American policy makers held deep reservations about Mendès France, such was not the case regarding Adenauer, whom they saw as their best bet. Washington also needed Adenauer's approval if a four-power summit were to succeed.[21] Although the chancellor had opposed such a meeting because he feared that Germany's interests could be bartered away, a June 10 Bundestag resolution forced him to change his policy and call for four-power talks.[22]

No sooner had the German legislature voted to test Moscow's intentions, when on June 16 and 17 anti-Soviet strikes and riots erupted in East Berlin in protest of new governmental work decrees. The uprisings continued for a couple of days before Communist authorities suppressed them, reigniting Cold War tensions and setting back plans for a four-power summit. The Eisenhower administration thought that the uprising would deflect the Soviet Union from pursuing an East-West summit on Germany. Washington expressed deep concern; if the EDC were to stall, it could hurt Adenauer's chances for reelection. An Adenauer loss would be a major blow to U.S. policy, which counted on him to steer a pro-Western course while keeping German nationalists at bay.[23]

The Eisenhower administration debated over how to respond to the uprising. Some administration officials saw the riots as an opportunity

126 · The Death of Stalin

to carry out the president's pledge to "roll back" Communism in Eastern Europe. Eisenhower and Dulles wanted to support the protesters, but they realized that U.S. intervention could lead to war. They eventually concluded that instability in Eastern Europe threatened not only Soviet security, but American interests, too. Once again, U.S. policy and strategy crumbled when confronting the facts on the ground.[24]

Summit Plans

Despite this crisis, plans for a four-power parlay were soon back on track. On June 18, however, Eisenhower vowed that there would be no high-level summit. Nonetheless, the State Department began to see a four-power conference as unavoidable. Winston Churchill, an important U.S. ally, continued to agitate for a summit meeting. As a result, the United States should try to shape its agenda. First, the Big Three would have to meet to form a united front.[25]

France had been operating without a government since the May overthrow of Mayer. After many unsuccessful attempts to install a new prime minister, President Auriol designated Joseph Laniel of the Centre national des indépendants et paysans (CNIP) on June 24. Primarily because he carried little political baggage and parliament strongly desired to end the crisis, Laniel won investiture on June 27. Laniel pledged that he would withhold the EDC Treaty from parliament until France and Germany had resolved the Saar dispute and Britain had committed to the Continent to France's satisfaction.[26] Although Laniel supported the treaty, he, too, owed his office to the Gaullists, as he received sixty-two Union républicaine d'action sociale (URAS) votes out of eighty-one.[27] To ensure this support, Laniel had to name six Gaullists to the cabinet.[28]

Less than knowledgeable about the EDC, Laniel leaned heavily on Bidault, whom he retained as foreign minister, and Paul Reynaud, the vice-premier of the French senate, for advice. Yet while Reynaud supported the project, Bidault offered less enthusiasm despite the official backing of his party, the MRP. In addition, Finance Minister Edgar Faure also opposed the plan.

As the setting for the July 10–14, tripartite talks began in Washington,[29] the three allies differed over what policy to pursue toward the Soviet Union. Uncertainty existed over what course to take toward the Soviet Union following Laurenti Beria's unexpected arrest and expulsion from the Communist Party. The conferees also had other differences. The United States wanted to use the meetings to defuse the political bombshell that Churchill had launched on May 11. France insisted on reopening four-power discussions on Germany as a condition for approving ratification of the EDC. The Federal Republic shared this demand, with Adenauer requesting that the conference take place after the September German elections. Dulles was persuaded to acquiesce to Franco-German demands, leaving Britain's foreign minister Lord Salisbury, arguing over the risks involved, isolated. Unable to resist twisting the lion's tail, Bidault told Salisbury, "It was not the fault of the French that the idea of a four-power meeting had entered European thinking . . . if a certain country took certain action which it had so far refused, the French government would ratify EDC within a month." Dulles backed France on the timing.[30]

On July 13, the British cabinet supported the Dulles-Bidault proposal for a four-power foreign ministers' meeting after the German elections in September, with the agenda confined to Germany and Austria.[31] Two days later, French HICOG François-Poncet reported from Bonn that German officials welcomed the planned four-power conference and that the three Western foreign ministers were pursuing a policy of European integration.[32] In view of the division within the Western camp over how best to deal with Moscow, Washington worried that the EDC might collapse. Accordingly, Eisenhower ordered U.S. officials to consider alternative plans; they provided him with three: creating a national German army; neutralizing Germany; and adopting the "peripheral strategy"— in other words, leaving Western Europe to fend for itself while the United States concentrated on maintaining its atomic shield.[33]

After reviewing these alternatives, the United States chose to remain committed to the European army. Russell Fessenden of the Office of European Regional Affairs noted that the NSC and the State Department had deemed none of the alternatives acceptable. They concluded that France would object even more to the NATO option than to the EDC. Moreover, any attempt to force it on France would backfire, as "the net increase in European defense potential would be substantially reduced by the negative French reaction." They also ruled out neutralizing Germany and adopting a peripheral strategy.[34]

On August 17, the United States reaffirmed its support for the EDC in NSC-160/1. According to the document, "No satisfactory substitute for this solution has been found." However, it continued, if approval of ratification were long delayed, America should review alternatives, including taking critical steps toward creating and arming German troops, but only "if this can be done without serious repercussions on our relations with the French."[35] This was a large "if" indeed.

As winter approached, Anglo-American patience with France began to wear thin. French inaction endangered the EDC, and no politically acceptable alternative was in sight. While both London and Washington supported the project, their support remained more spiritual than concrete—neither offered to extend a Continental commitment for the benefit of France. For example, when Anthony Eden returned to the Foreign Office on October 5 after a long illness, he insisted that the EDC was still "our best bet."[36]

Washington's frustration at European inaction on the EDC shown brightly. In office nine months, the Eisenhower administration had yet to devise an acceptable way of burden sharing, as Alliance politics vastly diminished the White House's range of policy options. In a late October letter to General Alfred M. Gruenther, his successor as SACEUR, Eisenhower insisted that America could not protect Europe forever. If the United States were to bring home its forces and cut back its share of European defense, Germany would surely have to take up the slack.[37]

The Adenauer Era Begins

In the meantime, the evolution of German politics revived U.S. suspicions about Germany. The September 1953 landslide reelection of Adenauer as chancellor increased his prestige and influence as well as the volume of nationalist voices then reverberating in the Federal Republic. Rumors soon began circulating that an overly confident Adenauer was considering rearming his country independently of the EDC. Moreover, U.S. officials believed that Bonn's increasing inflexibility over the Saar posed a serious barrier to a Franco-German reconciliation.[38] These matters prompted Dulles to press Adenauer to demonstrate greater flexibility in negotiations on the Saar. Dulles also made plain the unequivocal American understanding that both France and Germany were vital to the success of the EDC. There would be no independent Germany, Dulles affirmed.[39]

Yet a Franco-German rapprochement seemed unlikely, for the two sides remained miles apart on the Saar, with no breakthrough in sight. In the Bundestag's October 28 session, foreign affairs dominated debate, and in light of impending negotiations with French foreign minister Bidault, attention focused on France and the Saar. The Free Democrats, led by Thomas Dehler, Adenauer's former minister of justice, unexpectedly rejected Europeanization of the Saar.[40]

Such political shifts posed difficulties for the United States, for without Franco-German agreement on the Saar, France would reject the

EDC. American officials faced three major problems that stood in the way of an agreement: how to assure France that the Saar would not be returned to Germany; how to deal with the Saar population once it achieved complete political freedom and pro-German parties entered the political process in the region; and how the Federal Republic could enjoy equal economic rights under a Franco-Saarois customs union. In an effort to settle the matter, Adenauer and François-Poncet scheduled a set of four preliminary talks to conclude on November 24. The two sides then hoped to reach a settlement during the November 26 meeting of the ECSC foreign ministers.[41]

Concerns about France

Reflecting American concerns about current trends in French politics, the National Intelligence Estimate (NIE) 63/1 reported that France would face difficulty achieving economic growth and fiscal stability given its relative overextension abroad (Indochina) and at home. The Estimate also suggested a crucial six-month window for obtaining French approval of the EDC. Resolving the dispute over the Saar, proving the futility of discussions with the Soviets regarding Germany's future status, and continuing persistent but cautious U.S. pressure on France would, the Estimate stated, increase the likelihood of its approving the EDC Treaty. The report also warned that some demands would backfire. If, for example, America or Britain were to formally propose a plan to rearm Germany other than the EDC, France would undoubtedly use such talks as a pretext for further delay.[42]

French Domestic Opposition

Despite its relative leverage, France's government had its hands tied, for as much as Washington urged quick action on the treaty, French domestic opponents insisted on delaying matters. Again, Marshal Juin took the lead. The government's refusal to accommodate Juin poisoned its relations with the military leadership. Several military officials resorted to writing and distributing pamphlets and tracts denouncing the treaty. In a November 17 document, Juin expressed his profound dissatisfaction with the EDC Treaty. He attributed the reason why the treaty incited so much passion to its poor craftsmanship; its vague wording could give rise to all sorts of plausible interpretations that its opponents would surely exploit. Closely reading the text could lead one to fear that the

French Army would lose its personality entirely if certain precautions designed to prevent it from being dragged in some military misadventure and also permit it to carry out its duties in the French Union were adopted. Although the government had put forward additional protocols, Juin believed them inadequate because they needed to be complemented by a seventh protocol that would lengthen the interim period. "In my eyes," Juin wrote, "it is the indispensable supplementary precaution."

According to Juin, the time for remedying the treaty was running short. He said that "the EDC is a political integration for which we in our present state are neither psychologically mature nor materially ready. It is only a truly European grouping when incorporated in a superior defense community, that of [NATO], which is already functioning and is the only decision-making authority in deployment matters. The supranational political authority envisaged in the EDC can play no role but that of administrator."[43]

In addition to the military leadership, legislative opponents of the treaty also registered their displeasure. From November 17 to 27, the National Assembly debated the issue. This controversial subject produced intensely emotional exchanges. To cite but one example, former Prime Minister Edouard Daladier railed against rearming Germany, insisting that "if Germany prefers the European Army, it is because she had the certainty of establishing her hegemony over Mittel-europa, reconstituted by our efforts. . . . The Russian soldier has never set foot on French soil since the duel which opposed Czar Alexander to the Emperor Napoleon. The German soldier has invaded it three times in 70 years."

In counterpoint, Mayer later replied: "To those who say we are going to create a German Europe, I reply: If we turn our back, Europe will still exist. It will be no more less German. . . . If we admit that [France] is not strong enough to carry on a European policy, how would she be better able to follow a policy of isolation . . . ? To overthrow a foreign policy without having any alternative to offer would not only be grave, it would be criminal."[44]

Bermuda Summit Talks

France soon had an opportunity to press its demands for safeguards. In November, the Soviet Union agreed to the West's offer in October to hold a CFM meeting to discuss Germany and Austria. In advance of this big-four meeting, Churchill, Eisenhower, and Laniel, along with their foreign ministers, met in Bermuda from December 4 to 8 to discuss a possible four-power conference with the Soviets, as well as the EDC. Laniel fell ill on arriving in Bermuda, so Foreign Minister Bidault represented him during the talks.

Bidault made four key demands: the creation of a more closely integrated NATO and strengthening EDC-NATO relations; assurances that America and Britain would not withdraw from NATO after twenty years; the maintenance of an "equilibrium" between U.S.-UK forces and NATO forces through special tripartite consultation and agreement; and assurance that France would continue in its "great power" role, specifically in the NATO Standing Group. Once again, however, the Anglo-Americans took no definite action on the French proposals. For his part, Churchill championed the NATO solution, but both France *and* the United States rejected this suggestion.[45] Dulles, presaging remarks he would make a week later, warned that the failure to ratify the EDC Treaty might lead the United States to rethink its national security policy toward Europe.[46]

In their final conversation at Bermuda, Dulles told Laniel that if France could not "face up" and immediately approve the EDC, then it would be "doubtful that she could maintain a position of leadership . . . on the European continent and in world affairs."[47] Finally, the Three sent a note to the Soviet Union proposing a January 1954 four-power conference in Berlin. Although Dulles indicated that America would adopt a peripheral strategy if the EDC were rejected, such a move appeared increasingly probable whatever the fate of the European army.

On December 10, the National Security Council discussed the upcoming NAC meeting in Paris. The members agreed that the long-term goal of the United States was to bring home its forces, but that American officials should avoid all mention of this topic to avoid undermining European defense efforts. After all, if it were to become known that U.S. combat troops were to leave the Continent once the Europeans had rearmed, they might abandon the very policies designed to bring rearmament about so as to force the Americans to stay. The primary objective, Eisenhower stressed, was to get the EDC ratified and German contingents in place.[48]

Despite America's frequent denials about redeploying U.S. troops, Churchill seemed prepared for the worst. Once back in London, he expressed his anxieties to Eden:

President Eisenhower rejects the idea that if it continues to be indefinitely delayed an arrangement can be made to include a German army in NATO. It must be EDC or some solution of a "peripheral" nature . . . The consequence would be a Russian occupation of the whole of defenseless Germany and probably an arrangement between Communist-soaked France and the Soviet Union. Benelux and Scandinavia will go down the drain.[49]

Put bluntly, Churchill believed that if American combat forces were to retreat from Europe, Moscow would dominate the Continent—and in its weakened position, Britain could do little but watch. Perhaps this view might explain why Churchill so desired a four-power conference. Convinced that America would adopt a peripheral strategy, one might suggest that he wanted to reach an understanding with the Kremlin while West still had cards worth playing.[50]

The Role of Nuclear Weapons

The resolution of the EDC affair was linked to the critical role that nuclear weapons play in international politics. These weapons became a key U.S. asset during this period, as America incorporated them increasingly into its European security policy. Soviet nuclear arms also wrought important change on American policy, as Moscow's detonation of a hydrogen bomb in August 1953 convinced Washington that aggressive U.S. risk taking would threaten the very survival of the United States. A preponderance of power offered no protection from the overwhelming might of thermonuclear weapons. Given that a stable nuclear balance was now crucial to the continued existence of the United States, the country had little choice but to renounce an aggressive anti-Soviet strategy and to maintain a survivable second-strike capability.[51]

In late 1953, the Eisenhower administration announced a policy that prominently featured nuclear weapons: the "New Look."[52] This policy responded to several administration concerns: the Europeans' inability to meet the NATO-mandated conventional force buildup; the inevitability of U.S.-Soviet nuclear parity; and the need to carry out forward defense of the NATO area. The policy was also partially intended to fulfill the administration's desire to withdraw American troops from the Continent, because a nonnuclear Europe would be no match for a nuclear-armed Soviet Union. To meet these goals, the New Look called for heavy reliance on nuclear deterrence and massive retaliation if necessary. Eisenhower deemed that placing greater emphasis on nuclear arms would axiomatically lessen the need for large standing forces and thereby reduce America's military costs.

Nonetheless, the president took care to hide his true intentions regarding a redeployment of U.S. troops, for America's military presence on the Continent signaled its tangible commitment to Europe's defense. Were this commitment in doubt, the United States feared that neutralist and defeatist sentiments would then spread among the European allies, thus unraveling carefully laid defense plans.[53]

Agonizing Reappraisal

Dulles raised these issues at the annual NAC meeting, held in Paris on December 14, 1953, where he spoke of European unity, the EDC, the deployment of U.S. troops, and atomic weapons.[54] He contended that European unity provided a powerful defense against world Communism. Yet because such unity depended on a genuine Franco-German rapprochement, institutions such as the EDC were needed. American frustration with continued delay over this issue led him to warn, however, of an "agonizing reappraisal" of U.S. foreign policy if the EDC Treaty were not approved—something no nation had yet done. On the subject of nuclear weapons, Dulles mentioned Eisenhower's decision to ask for Congressional approval to share nuclear information with U.S. allies.[55] Sharing this information was a necessary step toward adopting a preemptive nuclear doctrine, a signal of new American thinking about the utility of such a posture in responding to any anticipated Soviet aggression.[56]

This speech marked a public shift in U.S. diplomatic tactics. Although the Eisenhower administration intended to withdraw U.S. forces only after the Europeans had adequately built up their defenses, it dared not say so for fear of retarding the Western allies' efforts in this area (in other words, not ratifying the EDC Treaty or lowering defense spending). America now threatened to quit the Continent if the Europeans did *not* approve the treaty. It appeared that the Eisenhower administration had lost patience with France. Yet the motivation for this threat did not emanate from the White House. In fact, David Bruce and Jean Monnet instigated Dulles's hardened tone. The shifting political sands in France meant that Monnet's influence ebbed while opposition to the EDC grew. Monnet reasoned, as a result, that U.S. pressure on France would give him a powerful lever to advance his agenda to unite Europe.[57]

Despite French criticism, Dulles continued these themes in a December 22 speech in which he clarified his "agonizing reappraisal" remark by noting that it reflected a "self-evident truth." The United States had been saying all along that the EDC was of great importance, Dulles contended, but this idea had failed to take root. Dulles presented three reasons he believed made the proposed European army essential to the defense of Europe. First, forward defense rested on, among other things, the unacceptability of German neutrality: America could not and would not defend at the Elbe unless Germany participated. NATO predicted its defense plans on this assumption.[58] Second, the EDC would assure other countries—particularly France and the Soviet Union—of controls on the size and use of German troops.[59] Third, and most important, according to Dulles, the EDC offered arrangements that would end Franco-German enmity permanently, an outcome even more important than securing German divisions in NATO.

Few acceptable alternatives to the EDC existed, Dulles argued. The NATO solution would meet the requirements of forward defense but would not provide assurances to Moscow and Paris. The NATO option required renegotiating the Occupation Statute on Germany, a precarious process given the need for French assent—which was not at all certain—as well as assent from the other members of the Alliance.[60] French veto power would inevitably surface in the face of any such talks.[61]

Yet Dulles was simply responding to the speech that Bidault had already delivered to his Atlantic colleagues about the relationship between NATO and the EDC. He insisted that Europe needed both American and British guarantees in order to create a balance between the two organizations:

[A]s we solemnly agreed to at our earlier meeting in Ottawa, a European defense organization [i.e., the EDC] would be inconceivable outside the Atlantic Alliance; the development of the latter is a condition of the existence of the former.

Today Europe is in a dangerous situation and sacrifices, unknown to national traditions, must be made for the benefit of a new equilibrium. I declare, however, that the Continent of Europe also needs a counterweight and guarantors, at least until the reconciliation [with Germany] to which we have dedicated to our lives is firmly established.

Whereas it may fall upon certain of our Atlantic allies to provide counterweight and to be guarantors, I believe it lies upon this council to formulate suitable thoughts on the matter. Conditions of defence, economy, and progress demand broader groupings and extended solidarities in the world of today. But if on our continent this would result in substituting national sovereignty only for European isolation, I am bound to say that to persevere in this future undertaking would then become so risky that many would be tempted to seek shelter in the frameworks left to us by the past.[62]

While scholars have focused much attention on Dulles' "agonizing reappraisal" remark, they have largely overlooked Bidault's speech.[63] He suggested that Europe would renounce the EDC if certain guarantees concerning Germany were not met. Bidault wanted to strengthen NATO so that German troops would supplement, not replace, American and British forces. For France, an Anglo-American Continental commitment was imperative. Despite Bidault's threats, at the end of December, France's Superior Council of the Armed Forces, convened by Pleven, declared German rearmament necessary by a vote of 22 to 1.[64]

Although it seemed that the EDC affair had finally come to a head, almost another year would pass before France and the United States arrived at an arrangement that both sides thought met their basic security needs. How they arrived at this arrangement involved diplomacy, statecraft, and chance.

CHAPTER SEVEN

The End of the Affair

Unresolved since the fall of 1950, the drive to create the EDC gained no-
ticeable momentum in 1954, as the signatory countries began to approve the treaty, Britain and the United States took steps to help defend
Western Europe, and France invested a prime minister who vowed that
his country would no longer "equivocate" on this issue. Despite these
encouraging signs, the EDC would collapse in 1954, replaced by a more
practical plan for Allied defense cooperation. This replacement laid the
groundwork for what would become the Cold War order in Western
Europe: a rearmed Germany with its power limited and balanced by a
massive and long-term Anglo-American military presence.

France on the Defensive

Signed in May 1952, the EDC Treaty had since been delayed over political disputes. As a result, none of the signatories had yet obtained parliamentary approval of the document. By April 1954, however, four out
of the six EDC member states had approved the treaty: on January 20,
the Netherlands became the first to do so, Belgium followed suit on
March 11, the Federal Republic on March 29, and Luxembourg on
April 7. Only France and Italy remained, the latter preferring to wait
until a wavering Paris had voted on the pact.

Such actions embarrassed French officials because they exposed
France as the final obstacle to its own proposal. These moves not only
stung France's wounded pride, but they also eroded Allied confidence in
France's ability to meet its international commitments. Indeed, were

France to reject the treaty outright, its international reputation would suffer, deflating French hopes of gaining additional influence within the Atlantic Alliance.

France remained the Alliance's wild card because its legislature displayed the greatest skepticism toward the EDC. Many French lawmakers opposed the treaty because they believed that adopting it would sour relations with the Kremlin, potentially missing an opportunity to resolve European security problems by negotiating rather than arms racing. They worried that remilitarizing the Federal Republic would force Moscow into a corner, leaving it little choice but to capitulate—an uncertain prospect—or respond in kind, thereby reinforcing the division of Europe. French officials also balked because neither Britain nor the United States would make a definitive military commitment to the European Continent. Given France's relative weakness and its legitimate doubts about an Anglo-American commitment to defend Europe, French deputies preferred to avoid confronting the Soviet Union if a less provocative alternative existed to promoting peace and stability.

On the one hand, Gaullist deputies disliked the EDC because its supranational character would place French military forces under international, not national, control. France would, therefore, have to ask permission before it could use French forces designated to the EDC to deal with problems in the French empire. Communist deputies, on the other hand, loathed the European army because it entailed rearming Germany, which they viewed as a reactionary nation.

A number of French legislators (and military leaders) detested the EDC because they thought that it would increase France's military commitments when more resources were sorely needed in Indochina. To guarantee French military and political superiority in the proposed European defense force, large quantities of men, money, and materiel would have to be diverted from Indochina. For supporters of the Indochina War, this diversion meant surrendering to the Viet Minh Communists and losing a prized member of the French Union. Better to postpone the EDC, they reasoned, until the tide in Indochina shifted in favor of France. Without doubt, the prospects for winning French legislative approval of the EDC seemed exceedingly slim.

Nearing the End

Marshal Juin continued his campaign to amend the EDC Treaty into 1954. On the eve of a legislative debate on the EDC, Prime Minister Joseph Laniel, who had recently taken office, asked the marshal for his personal view of the EDC Treaty. Juin responded by saying that if the debate were not handled properly, France could find itself at an impasse, "the consequences of which could be grave." Convinced that the government wanted to convey the impression that it had consulted the nation's military leadership about the EDC Treaty and that they had accorded it their blessing, Juin unsuccessfully attempted to persuade Laniel to block the debate. In response, Juin adopted a radical course.[1]

On March 27, Juin gave a speech in Auxerre in which he denounced the EDC Treaty. He declared that although the agreement included guarantees against an uncontrolled rearming of the Federal Republic, the pact's other signatories rejected its supranational features. In addition, France would enter such an organization only if the French Army composed the majority, a wish difficult to fulfill given the disarray of France's armed forces. Although the treaty contained numerous defects, Juin grumbled that he was never consulted about it except for particular points and technical matters. To remedy these defects, the French government proposed additional protocols—yet according to Juin, they were either inadequate or unclear. The solution, he proclaimed, was to replace the treaty.[2]

By March 29, Juin's remarks were front-page news. That evening while in Lyon, Juin learned from the press that Laniel had summoned him to his office to explain his remarks. His response was immediate: "I will not go." The next morning, Juin, still furious over Laniel's public request, dashed off a letter to the prime minister saying that "I do not intend to respond to a summons introduced to the public under a rather menacing form, as if running to the sound of a trumpet." Juin added that he would only meet Laniel under more discrete conditions.[3]

Laniel responded by expressing regret over the way that Juin had chosen to address him. Nonetheless, the marshal refused to meet with him. He told Laniel that he would meet with him on another day when the press had not been informed in advance. Juin's insubordination would cost him. On March 31, the cabinet met just before midnight and decided to revoke his national duties as vice-chairman of the Superior Council of War, leaving him only his NATO command.[4] The censuring of Juin provoked outrage among his supporters, who disrupted an April 4 ceremony held at the Arc de Triomphe to honor veterans of the Indochina War. They vented their anger at Laniel and Defense Minister Pleven, jostling the two men, who had to be spirited away by automobile. Though encouraged by his supporters, however, Juin refused to attend the ceremony, which could have easily turned into a plebicite.[5]

The Berlin Conference

To ease the French legislature's concerns, high-level American, British, and French officials tried to prove that they were making a good-faith effort to negotiate with the Soviet Union, but that Moscow's intransigence left no alternative but to go forward with the EDC. When Winston Churchill proposed in May 1953 a series of four-power talks, Dulles opposed the meeting because he disbelieved Soviet professions of peace and cooperation. For him, the Soviet Union was simply engaged in a cynical "peace offensive" intended to weaken Western resolve, not promote understanding.

Although Konrad Adenauer and Georges Bidault also doubted Soviet goodwill, each contended that domestic pressure was forcing his respective government at least to test Moscow's intentions by convening a high-level summit. Otherwise, according to Bidault, the French legislature would never approve the EDC Treaty. As for Adenauer, he wished to steal his opponents' thunder before the September Bundestag elections, lest they use the issue against him. In light of these concerns, Dulles invited the Soviets to discuss the German question and a peace treaty with Austria. The Soviet Union accepted the offer in late November.

From January 25 to February 18, the foreign ministers of the four powers met in Berlin, the first such meeting since 1949. In addition to discussing the German question and an Austrian peace treaty, they also dealt with Soviet demands for a five-power conference that would include China.[6] To prepare for the upcoming East-West summit talks, the three Western powers met in December 1953 to forge a common policy.[7]

The three Western foreign ministers arrived at Berlin with a unified stand on Germany. They argued that only a freely elected all-German government could legally negotiate a peace treaty with the victors of the Second World War. In support of this argument, Britain's Anthony Eden presented a five-point plan to unite Germany and achieve a peace treaty. It stipulated (1) free elections throughout Germany; (2) the convocation of a national assembly resulting from these elections; (3) the drafting of a constitution and the preparation of peace treaty negotiations; (4) the adoption of the constitution and the formation of an all-German government responsible for the negotiation of the peace treaty; and (5) the signature and entry into force of the peace treaty.[8] Soviet foreign minister Vyacheslav M. Molotov countered that the German problem could be settled only according to wartime agreements signed at Potsdam and Yalta. In counterpoint to Eden, Molotov contended that the two German states should form a provisional government that would then negotiate a peace treaty.[9]

The Western foreign ministers rejected Molotov's proposal. Dulles argued that two aspects of the German problem demanded attention. First, a divided Germany fostered instability. To prevent this outcome, Germany had to be reunified, a task the Eden Plan would accomplish. The second aspect was "insuring that a united Germany shall be a peaceful Germany." Harsh restrictions, he proclaimed, would arouse German nationalism. To avert this scenario, Dulles asserted, Germany had to be treated as an equal, and one had to find a "worthy outlet for the great energy and vitality of the German people." A natural community of European nations working for a common purpose, such as the EDC and the ECSC, sister organizations in the drive to integrate Europe, would solve this problem. Dulles stressed that the EDC, in particular, guaranteed there would be no German general staff. For the Western powers, NATO, the EDC, and the ECSC formed the backbone of their security policy for Europe, and Germany had to be free to join all three.[10]

Undeterred, Molotov presented other projects during the conference. On February 4, he offered a draft resolution similar to the one Stalin had proposed in March 1952, which envisioned a reunited but neutral Germany. Molotov later proposed that all four powers withdraw from East and West Germany within six months. Negotiations would then take place on the future of a reunited Germany. Molotov also suggested a "Draft General European Treaty" that all the European countries—including Germany—would sign until a "democratic" Germany could take its place. Unimpressed, representatives of the Western Powers spurned all of Molotov's propositions.[11]

The Future of France

Beyond the stated agenda of the conference—the future of Germany— U.S. officials also contemplated the future of France. Although they hoped that France would assume the political and military leadership of continental Europe, their faith began to falter along with their patience. American agnosticism was rooted in France's hesitance to accept the EDC and its inability to win the Indochina War. Two days before the end of the Berlin Conference, Dulles sent a note to Eisenhower affirming that the United States supported French leadership on the Continent and a tripartite role in world affairs. "But," he stressed, "if in the next several months France rejects EDC it will be impossible for the U.S. to maintain the fiction that France is capable of the role of leadership in European and world affairs and will have demonstrated its incapacity for such leadership."[12]

American concerns about France's fitness for leadership extended beyond Europe; Washington also worried that Paris would fail to fulfill its other international commitments, particularly in Southeast Asia. Convinced that a French defeat in Indochina would ease the spread of Communism throughout Asia, U.S. officials also saw repercussions worldwide. In late March, Dulles told Admiral Arthur Radford that "France is creating a vacuum in the world wherever she is." The United States had to "fill that vacuum . . . [or] we could lose Europe, Asia, and Africa all at once." Ambassador Douglas Dillon expressed similar sentiments.[13]

For the Eisenhower administration, such apocalyptic scenarios cut to the heart of the problem. In its outlook, America should play a limited role in international security arrangements. Accordingly, Europe—especially France—would assume a greater degree of responsibility in containing Communism. Such plans, however, depended on France and the rest of Europe developing sufficient political, economic, and military strength to perform this task. Yet France's poor showing in these crucial categories jeopardized U.S. goals, forcing America to do more than it deemed necessary.

Unable to bridge differences over the German question, the Conference of Berlin ended in failure. This lack of success aided EDC supporters, who could now argue plausibly that the West had attempted to negotiate seriously with Moscow but was spurned. This rebuff proved, they contended, that the Kremlin sought not to reduce tensions, but simply to prevent the creation of a militarized pro-Western Federal Republic, to undermine NATO, and to retain indefinitely its grip on Eastern Europe. The West had no choice, according to these voices, but to consolidate its own power relative to that of the Soviet bloc by dint of German men and arms.

Adenauer, under fire from domestic critics who demanded German unification, seized this argument and used it to his advantage. At a February 20 party meeting in Camberg, Germany, he argued that the results of the Berlin Conference clearly demonstrated the correctness of his policy of *Westbindung* and provided a sound reason for continuing on this path. Five days later, he announced to the Bundestag that the talks had exposed Soviet designs to dominate Europe, contending that Moscow would be dissuaded only by actions, not words.[14]

In Britain, the Berlin Conference's failure galvanized the House of Commons, which then shed its political divisions in favor of a bipartisan approach. The British government also made public in February a draft treaty that would link London to the EDC. If implemented, the treaty would lend considerable support to pro-EDC French officials, for unless Britain agreed to commit its forces to the Continent for an extended period, France's parliament would never assent to the European army.[15]

Yet the positive momentum created by the British announcement did not mitigate all French concerns. According to Bidault, France first required a satisfactory resolution of the Saar issue. It also needed U.S. aid to continue fighting the Indochina War, a need that grew stronger as France's position on the battlefield grew weaker. Although French representatives assured U.S. officials that an American bombing campaign would turn the tide in its favor, Eisenhower refused to commit U.S. power and prestige to the cause without congressional consent and British participation, neither of which appeared forthcoming.[16]

French military setbacks in the Indochina War, however, would catapult that conflict to center stage. Although geographically half a world apart, the EDC and the Indochina War were linked on several levels. Economically, the heavy financial burden of the Indochina War was preventing France from contributing as much money to the EDC as Germany. This imbalance would create a dilemma in Europe. If Germany were to provide more money to the European army's budget than France, Bonn would surely ask the organization for expanded authority and responsibilities. If these demands were accepted, the Federal Republic would eventually dominate the force. If German demands were rejected, however, Bonn might quit the organization, sapping the European army of the very strength that affirmed its existence. In either case, French security needs would remain unmet.

Militarily, waging war in Indochina exacted the efforts of France's best fighting forces, thus making them unavailable to serve in Europe, virtually ensuring that German forces in the EDC would supersede French ones, both in number and quality. France would then be militarily weaker than the Federal Republic, an outcome of grave concern.

Politically, France agonized over the wisdom of continuing the Indochina War. Given the conflict's divisiveness due to its great cost in blood and treasure, it seemed politically impossible to debate and vote on the EDC before the Geneva Conference. Precariously situated, the government of Joseph Laniel hesitated to forward the EDC Treaty to parliament because there was simply too little support to pass it, and a "no" vote could have severe consequences.

Diplomatically, French vulnerabilities led the nation's allies—particularly Germany and the United States—to suspect that Paris would try to bargain unilaterally with Moscow. On the surface at least, the interests of France and the Soviet Union ran parallel in that both expressed reservations about remilitarizing the Federal Republic and both wished to limit American influence in Europe. Moreover, the two sides had historic ties to each other, as evidenced by the Franco-Soviet Treaty of 1944. These factors led some U.S. and German officials to wonder whether Moscow and Paris might arrive at an understanding: France would veto the EDC in return for Soviet help in Indochina.

At the end of 1953 and the beginning of 1954, Washington applied pressure that further complicated the EDC question. The United States had threatened to pursue a peripheral strategy if the allies rejected the EDC, a warning that many European officials took seriously. Churchill particularly worried about the ensuing repercussions should it carry out this threat. If America chose to abstain from Continental security arrangements, it seemed doubtful that Britain would countenance close ties to the EDC. If London refused to associate closely with the proposed defense organization, the French parliament would surely reject the project, ending plans for the European army, German remilitarization, and a conventional military balance on the European mainland.

In addition to U.S. pressure, America made certain policy moves that nourished doubts about its continued political and military commitment to Europe. For example, U.S. secretary of defense Charles Wilson announced that the United States would reduce its armed forces by 400,000 men. According to André François-Poncet, France's high commissioner to Germany, this announcement caused considerable worry in Bonn that America intended to adopt a peripheral strategy.[17] Such concerns highlighted an inherent tension in America's European strategy. Ostensibly, Washington intended to raise the stakes of European inaction or rejection of the treaty—in other words, no EDC, no U.S. support. Ironically, it had another effect. By sowing doubt in Allied capitals over a continuing American resolve to defend Europe, the Europeans could easily surmise that their best course might be to delay action on the EDC and force U.S. troops to remain in Europe.

The New Look

Allied inaction on the EDC Treaty dismayed U.S. officials. Losing patience with Allied indecision, American policy makers took diplomatic steps to further the country's strategic plans. As the United States' diplomatic offensive unfolded, so did NATO's new nuclear policy, MC-48. This policy would decisively influence American nuclear strategy and play a large role in resolving the European army affair.

Approved by NATO in December 1953, MC-48 assumed that war with the Soviet Union would require the use of nuclear weapons. NATO's "New Look" incorporated tactical nuclear weapons in carrying out the Alliance's policy of forward defense. These weapons would annihilate Soviet ground formations before they became large enough to punch through Allied ground defenses. Although it appeared that these arms would reduce the need for large conventional forces, MC-48 recommended that NATO continue to build up its conventional force. The document also suggested the need for twelve German divisions, reasoning that NATO needed to establish a formidable ground defense to stop the advance of Soviet ground forces until a NATO strategic bombing campaign paralyzed Moscow's capacity to wage war.[18]

The administration began laying the groundwork for a policy shift early in the year. In his State of the Union address, Eisenhower spoke about the nation's defense planning. He indicated that "while determined to use atomic power to serve the usages of peace we take into full account our great and growing number of nuclear weapons and the most effective means of using them against an aggressor if they are needed to preserve our freedom." He also contended that America's defense would be stronger "if, under appropriate security safeguards, we share with our allies certain knowledge of the tactical use of our nuclear weapons." He then urged Congress to provide him that authority. Eisenhower also stated that nuclear weapons created "new relationships between man and materials" that would "permit economies in the use of men" as America built its military forces.[19]

In sum, Eisenhower wanted to reduce the need for manpower by substituting atomic firepower. He also sought to give the European allies control of these weapons. Adopting this policy would cost America less money and transfer to the Europeans greater responsibility for their own defense. This policy would also allow Eisenhower to pull U.S. forces out of Europe, knowing that a conventionally armed Europe could not deter a nuclear-armed Soviet Union.

Worried that the EDC might implode, the United States stepped up the pressure on its European allies to approve the treaty. Without the European army, administration plans to build a Europe powerful enough to contain Moscow with limited American help would come to naught. To encourage the allies to ratify the treaty, the Eisenhower administration threatened what it would and would not do if the EDC were to fail. Along with Eisenhower, Dulles began preparing the groundwork for a change in U.S. policy in a series of speeches in late 1953; he continued this public campaign in the new year.

In a January 12, 1954 speech devoted to U.S. security policy and the need for long-range plans, Dulles again spoke about nuclear weapons and once more linked the fate of the EDC to that of NATO. America's actions in the Cold War had so far been reactive, the secretary argued, responding primarily to Soviet initiatives. Such emergency measures would not serve enduring U.S. interests. Moreover, he noted, NATO's immense military buildup of the past three years could not be sustained indefinitely without ruinous economic consequences. America needed allies and collective security, the secretary stated; the goal of the United States was simply to make them "more efficient [and] less costly." America could accomplish this goal, he said, by "placing more reliance on deterrent power and less dependence on local defensive power." He contended that massive retaliation was designed as a long-term deterrent commensurate with American need for cost-efficient collective security arrangements. This policy would allow the West to respond instantly "at places and means of its own choosing."

The long-range view implicit in the new doctrine would permit time for spreading defense costs over a wider fiscal horizon and for encouraging a Franco-German rapprochement under the sturdy umbrella of an Allied nuclear deterrent. It also implied that America would reduce its conventional military commitment to Europe. Finally, according to Dulles, the EDC was crucial to NATO's survival. NATO would only endure if founded on a unified Europe in which the Germans were at peace with the French, and both contributed fully in its defense. Such cooperation would not occur without the EDC.[20]

Notwithstanding the great importance that Eisenhower and Dulles attached to the EDC, its fate rested in the hands of the French parliament. Moreover, strategic considerations sharply limited American leverage over France. For example, Prime Minister Joseph Laniel told U.S. officials in late 1953 that he required assurances before he would submit the EDC Treaty to the French legislature. Central among them were close UK-EDC ties; an Anglo-American commitment not to withdraw their forces from NATO after twenty years;[21] a favorable settlement of the Saar question; and the maintenance of French power in European affairs. Without these guarantees, Laniel argued, the EDC Treaty would fail.[22]

Although David Bruce, the U.S. representative to the Interim Committee, argued that Laniel and Foreign Minister Bidault continued to avoid a parliamentary debate and that it was time to press them, Eisenhower rejected this advice.[23] Recognizing that he had little room in which to maneuver, Eisenhower, at a National Security Council meeting, directed the administration to provide assurances to France that the United States would retain forces in Europe and continue to participate in NATO. Although at one point asking, "Must we go on for ever coddling the French?" Eisenhower nevertheless decided to extend the assurances.[24] Beyond these assurances the administration could do little because Bonn and London held the key to France's other demands.

Like Washington, London also recognized French demands. As a result, in the spring of 1954, both London and Washington tilted their policies toward French demands. American and British officials realized that their nations had to act quickly if they were to have any hope of influencing the French legislature, which was set to begin debating the EDC Treaty in early April. Both America and Britain had an abiding interest in creating a European army that would help to deter both Soviet and German aggression.

In early March, Eden presented proposals to the British cabinet that exceeded previous efforts linking Britain to the EDC. The first one, a declaration, stated that Britain had "no intention of withdrawing [its troops] from the continent." The second proposal declared that Britain would include British Army formations within European army formations if requested by the SACEUR. A third proposal would have Britain assign an armored division to the EDC. The cabinet adopted the proposals and then presented them to the EDC and subsequently to the British parliament.[25]

Marking further progress, Britain and the EDC signed a formal agreement on April 13 defining the terms of their association. The agreement contained three major points. First, a U.K. minister would attend the EDC's Council of Ministers meetings. Second, Britain would continue to station on the Continent "such armed forces as may be necessary and appropriate to contribute a fair share of the forces needed for the joint defense of the North Atlantic area." London also proclaimed that it did not intend to withdraw "from the continent of Europe so long as the threat exists to the security of Western Europe and of the E.D.C." Third, Britain committed itself to be on the mainland before aggression began, not after. Once established, Britain would place an armored division into a European army corps. In addition, the Royal Air Force would participate with European units. The proposal received wide support in the House of Commons, which realized that the French parliament would never assent to the project unless Britain agreed to involve itself in Continental security arrangements.[26]

The United States made a similar gesture two days later, when Eisenhower sent a text to the EDC countries outlining U.S. assurances to the European army once the treaty entered into force. It stated that America would continue to maintain in Europe forces "necessary and appropriate" for the joint defense of the NATO area; consult with the members of NATO and the EDC regarding force levels under the command of SACEUR; "encourage the closest possible integration" between EDC, NATO, and U.S. forces in terms of command, training, tactical support, and logistical organization developed by NATO; seek to share a greater degree of information about the military use of new weapons and techniques; regard a threat to the EDC as a threat to the security of the United States; and issue a stronger guarantee of continued U.S. membership in NATO once the EDC was established.[27]

These declarations nonetheless failed to pacify French opponents of the EDC, who noted that the British announcement spoke only of "cooperation" with the EDC, which suggested that London would most certainly remain apart from the European army. Gaullists in the French parliament particularly disliked the agreement because they believed that Britain's involvement with the EDC would be considerably less than that of France. Furthermore, they saw the U.S. proposal as containing nothing new, merely reaffirming old, less than satisfactory guarantees. Finally, they viewed it as strictly a personal pledge by Eisenhower, committing his successors to nothing.[28] Thus, while a step in France's direction, the Anglo-American proposals failed to overcome French parliamentary resistance to the EDC, adding considerably to Washington's frustration.

In addition to offering carrots, the United States used sticks to prod France. Many European officials took seriously the threat that the United States might refuse to commit its military forces to Europe and embrace instead a peripheral strategy. It anguished Churchill considerably. He feared that an American peripheral strategy would dissuade the House of Commons from offering a true Continental commitment. British inaction would, in turn, lead the French parliament to reject the EDC. Germany would remain demilitarized and the Soviet Union would enjoy conventional military superiority on the European mainland.[29]

The French government also expected Bonn to play its part in lessening French legislative fears. Scheduled to vote on the treaty near the end of March, the Bundestag would, by adopting the French protocols, signal its willingness to cede to France's demands. Given the high priority it accorded this issue, Paris made certain that Bonn understood the French position. In a March 22 interview with Herbert Blankenhorn, Adenauer's chief foreign policy aide, French HICOG François-Poncet underscored the importance France ascribed to the signing of the additional protocols.[30] Then on March 23, Bidault reported that he had received successively both the American and the British ambassadors and reminded them that it was essential that the Federal Republic sign the additional protocols.[31] Unfortunately for the French, the protocols were viewed negatively by the other prospective members of the EDC, not just Germany.

Disaster in Indochina

The course of the Indochina War also affected the EDC affair, as France's fading fortunes in that conflict altered both its domestic and foreign policies. The war also influenced the policies of the other states involved, for if France could not end the fighting on honorable terms, its international reputation could suffer. France had good reason to worry about its international standing. In February, the Viet Minh encircled Dien Bien Phu, a French outpost in Indochina. On February 22, Bidault told Dulles that the situation there was hopeless. More ominously, Prime Minister Laniel told a U.S. State Department official that if the garrison fell, French legislators would reject the EDC.[32]

On March 13, the Viet Minh attacked the French position at Dien Bien Phu, pounding the 13,000 defenders relentlessly. Soon after the assault began, France asked the United States to help save the beleaguered outpost in the hope of avoiding a military disaster and strengthening France's diplomatic hand at the soon-to-open Geneva Conference. The stakes were high for France, so French chief of the General Staff for National Defense Paul Ely traveled to Washington, D.C., on March 20 in hopes of eliciting U.S. military support, including transport aircraft to deliver supplies and bombers to pummel the Viet Minh. The Eisenhower administration considered a French victory crucial to its Cold War strategy, and American officials soon devised a plan. Code-named "Operation: VULTURE" and supported by members of the Joint Chiefs of Staff, the plan to aid the French outpost consisted of sending five dozen American bombers, tactical nuclear weapons, and U.S. ground forces on a mission against Viet Minh positions. Eisenhower gave the issue considerable thought, but without congressional approval and British participation, as well as the risk of war with China, he eventually said no. The U.S. administration thus resigned itself to a French defeat at Dien Bien Phu, though not Indochina as a whole.[33] The Eisenhower administration wanted to prevent a French military defeat Indochina War as well as block a French negotiated settlement. Dulles lamented the situation at the besieged French encampment, but he also remarked on April 23 that "there is, of course, no military or logical reason why [the] loss of Dien Bien Phu whould lead to a collapse of [the] French."[34]

For some U.S. officials, however, the fall of Dien Bien Phu loomed larger than the loss of a single battle. American ambassador to France Douglas Dillon predicted that if the French were to lose in Indochina, it would lead to a "neutralist government in France that could recreate the wartime Franco-USSR alliance in order to prevent German rearmament." The Congress would "pull our troops from Europe," leaving the United States in "isolation."[35] Indeed, the outcome was critical for both sides.

The attack at Dien Bien Phu prefaced the Geneva Conference, which opened on April 26. By that time the situation at the French camp had degraded. The goal of the talks was to settle the Indochina conflict, and all the major parties attended: Cambodia, China, Laos, France, the Soviet Union, the United Kingdom, the United States, the Viet Minh, and Vietnam.

The talks began inauspiciously, for the two combatants—France and the Viet Minh—possessed fundamentally incompatible objectives. France, represented by Bidault, rejected partitioning Vietnam and simply wanted to engineer a cease-fire, not a political settlement. In contrast, the Viet Minh wanted to capitalize on its commanding position on the battlefield to obtain a political settlement. In addition, the Viet Minh also called for French forces to withdraw from Vietnam, leaving the Vietnamese to settle their own disputes. Given its dominant position in the country, the Viet Minh would doubtless triumph. When one added the general mistrust on the part of all the participants, it is little surprise that the talks sputtered to a halt.[36]

Mendès France Takes Power

The fate of the EDC reached a critical juncture on May 7 when Dien Bien Phu fell, throwing France's Indochina policy into further chaos. The sixty-five-year old Laniel, shrouded in mourning black, ascended the podium of the National Assembly. His voice breaking, the chamber fell silent as he delivered the news. The hall was soon engulfed in a collective sense that France had reached its nadir.[37] Yet from the ruins of this debacle emerged a figure who would alter the political landscape profoundly: Pierre Mendès France, a leading parliamentary critic of the Indochina War. In a June 9 speech to parliament, Mendès France indicted the Indochina policy of the Laniel government and of the Fourth Republic.[38] The National Assembly toppled the hapless Laniel on June 13. President René Coty then made an appeal to Mendès France to present himself as a candidate for prime minister.[39]

Heeding Coty's wishes, on June 17, a confident Mendès France presented himself to the National Assembly. The specter that haunted American officials was on the brink of assuming power. He vowed to either settle the war in Indochina by July 20 or resign. He also pledged to resolve the long-simmering dispute over the EDC once peace was obtained in Indochina.[40] Mendès France made clear that he would be his own man. He would determine the composition of his government, choose his own ministers, and change them when he wished. He would negotiate neither his program nor the composition of his cabinet. Mendès France also said that he would forgo the votes of the Communist Party because he feared that accepting them might harm his ability to negotiate with the Viet Minh Communists. Invested the following day, Mendès France kept his word, refusing to consider the 99 Communist Party votes as contributing to his 419–47-vote victory.[41]

Although the arrival of such a dynamic figure to power augured well for France, its allies expressed doubts. Mendès France generated great distrust and hostility in Washington, for in addition to wanting to negotiate an end to the Indochina War, Americans suspected him of opposing the EDC. The United States was now forced to work with a French government seemingly prepared to undermine American policies in Europe and in Asia.[42]

Adenauer placed little confidence in Mendès France, whom he suspected of opposing the EDC. After the chancellor's party received a million fewer votes in provincial elections in North Rhine-Westphalia than it had during the September general election, Adenauer summoned French HICOG André François-Poncet and gave him a message for Mendès France: "French delays have cost me a million votes. In a few months I may lose another million. I am the only German Chancellor in history who has preferred the unity of Europe to the unity of the Reich." The chancellor also told Dulles that Mendès France "was not a Communist . . . but would be led to play the Communist game."[43]

Yet the character of the new French government offered greater diversity than Adenauer and some U.S. officials assumed. Mendès France counted among his advisors those who favored good relations with the Soviet Union, and who therefore opposed rearming Germany. Others, however, feared that if the EDC were to fail and the Allies created nothing to take its place, Germany might try to bargain with Moscow, raising the specter of a second Rapallo.[44]

Fearful that Mendès France might sabotage the EDC, the United States considered alternate plans. On June 25, the JCS endorsed two alternatives for the Federal Republic: first, full membership in NATO and, second, its independent rearming with American and British support. The JCS recommended adopting "positive measures" to encourage France to either approve the EDC or agree to the NATO option. If not, London and Washington should inform Paris that they would proceed with the second option by October 1. If neither policy were carried out, the United States should "reappraise its basic policy toward Western Europe and its NATO commitments."[45]

Despite the JCS recommendation, Eisenhower and Dulles rejected alternatives to the EDC, including NATO. They wanted instead to create a European "third force" that would enable the United States to withdraw its military forces from Europe, knowing that a robust conventional deterrent remained in their wake. They therefore invested considerable energy and political capital in support of the project. Yet this same enthusiasm also blinded them to the fact that the EDC enjoyed relatively faint support in France and that the French parliament would probably reject it.

Nonetheless, U.S. plans would remain on hold until Washington exhausted its diplomatic options, for political considerations precluded doing otherwise. To illustrate, at an Anglo-American summit in late June, the two sides publicly pledged to support the EDC; but in private they agreed to study alternative ways to rearm Germany should France reject the treaty.[46] From July 5 to 12, a joint Anglo-American study group met to consider the issues covered in the June Eisenhower-Churchill statement and to examine all the options available if France remained indecisive or rejected the treaty. The group, which met openly and informed the French beforehand, tried to devise a method that would restore German sovereignty immediately while the Alliance continued to hammer out the issue of rearmament.

Yet this move would mean separating the May 1952 Bonn Conventions, which related to the restoration of German sovereignty, from the EDC Treaty. If only the former agreement took effect, it would restore German sovereignty and thus open the door to the creation of a German general staff and a national army without limits. The practical nature of this move was questionable, for it would require French consent, an unlikely prospect under the circumstances. In the end, the joint Anglo-American statement declared that if the French parliament did not ratify the EDC Treaty, "the two governments would have to reveal to the French Government their intention to proceed by themselves if necessary. This move could not be done in any detail until the two Governments had first consulted the Federal Chancellor and made sure that he approved."[47]

The French, however, made no moves to ratify the EDC Treaty. As Mendès France stated in his investiture, resolving the Indochina affair topped his agenda. Despite his decision to put the EDC on the back burner, the Americans and the British still refused to act unilaterally. Although the Canadians expressed concerns of a possible rift between the Anglo-Americans on the one hand and the French on the other, Frank Roberts, the undersecretary of state in the German Section of the British Foreign Office, assured the Canadian High Commissioner, "We were neither thinking of rearming the Germans unilaterally nor of imposing political liberty upon Germany in disagreement with the French. The time for awkward decisions of this kind would only come very much later if and when the French remained recalcitrant."[48]

Although affording it a degree of leverage, France's stance also entailed costs, because by refusing to submit the treaty to its legislature, the French government found itself increasingly isolated. Pressure to act came not just from Bonn, London, and Washington, but from other quarters as well. Some of the EDC's smaller powers grew impatient with French procrastination. On June 30, Mendès France met with Belgian prime minister and foreign minister Paul-Henri Spaak to explain to him the parliamentary situation in France.

Mendès France explained that as far as could be determined, a majority of the deputies in the National Assembly opposed the EDC. Nonetheless, the legislature could be summoned the first two weeks of August to decide the issue. Although sympathetic to the timetable and procedure adopted by France, Spaak inquired as to the likely outcome of the vote. Mendès France told him that it would be impossible to predict the decision. Spaak reacted sharply, contending that the vote would present the other countries that had an interest in the outcome with a fait accompli. Mendès France responded that he faced two contradictory critiques. The first (for example, by the United States) was to refuse to begin new negotiations after which the French parliament could once again refuse to go along. According to Mendès France, every request along these lines was judged to be purely a delaying tactic. As a result, the French had to define their position almost unilaterally. Yet he claimed when he adopted this procedure, he was criticized for placing before the others a fait accompli.

Although Spaak understood Mendès France's position, he expressed concern over the reactions it would produce in the other countries, contending that Germany would almost certainly refuse any formula that required new parliamentary debates at home.

Spaak emphasized that Belgium would never accept "an EDC that would not be an EDC"—in other words, any agreement other than that agreed to by the six coalition partners. If, however, France rejected the EDC, Belgium would seek other options. For example, Germany in NATO (a solution he still hated); or "Belgium would resume its traditional policy of leaning on England and France" (a phrase he repeated several times). Belgium wanted to avoid an alliance between the Benelux countries, England, and the United States; an alliance between the Benelux and Germany; and a six-power military coalition.

Very pessimistic concerning the likely outcome of the French attempt to ratify the treaty, Spaak cautioned Mendès France, "You will unavoidably end up with something that will be unacceptable for the Belgians and the Germans." He feared most of all that the French parliament, in adopting a text, would force the other five countries to reject it, putting the onus for killing the project on their shoulders. Spaak insisted that the true responsibility lay with past French governments. Mendès France assured Spaak that he would not place the other countries in an embarrassing and unfair situation. Spaak said that if the EDC were to fail, he would prefer that the French make a straightforward decision to reject the project; it would be more clear and loyal, and Franco-Belgian relations would not suffer as a result. Mendès France refused to envisage a pure and simple negative French response, pledging to work hard to avoid a crisis for the Western Alliance. He understood Spaak's impatience. He said that he considered it his duty to do everything to bring to at least partial conclusion some of the attempts at coordinated or integrated Western rearmament that prefigured the future constitution of Europe. The pure and simple refusal of France would have grave consequences.[49]

In addition to placating the Belgium government, Mendès France also took care in dealing with the Federal Republic. If public opinion viewed his policy toward Bonn as too lenient, his government could fall. Yet adopting an overly hard-line policy would anger the NATO allies, further isolating France and perhaps opening the door to uncontrolled German rearmament. Mendès France's stance toward Germany, in turn, affected Adenauer's policy, because the chancellor also faced the same concerns—he could not be perceived as a French punching bag. Despite the prime minister's efforts to strike a balance, the combination of Adenauer's personal distrust of Mendès France and his need to defend himself against political attacks at home led the chancellor to go on the offensive. In early July, Adenauer took verbal shots at Mendès France during an interview with German journalist Saul Friedländer, one of the chancellor's favorite commentators, and in a speech on Radio Hamburg.[50]

According to an aide, Adenauer's statements preoccupied Mendès France. The prime minister considered that if the chancellor's remarks were taken to the letter, the planned trip to Bonn by the French diplomat Jean-Michel Guérin de Beaumont could be put in question. Although the prime minister wanted to talk on the telephone to hear the views of French HICOG François-Poncet, he suspected that the line might have been tapped. As a result, he wished to convey the impression to Bonn that he "was not willing to make the first contact between his government and Chancellor Adenauer under a seeming imperative raised yesterday night by Mr. Adenauer."[51]

Perhaps in an effort to mend fences, Adenauer turned to a domestic ally. In mid-July, H. A. Kluthe, a confidant of Adenauer, wrote to Mendès France at the urging of the chancellor. Adenauer wanted Kluthe to meet with Mendès France to clarify French policy. Kluthe said he had done his best to contradict the falsehoods about Mendès France now circling about in Bonn. He said that mistrust only helped the Communists and admitted that Adenauer's interview was "very clumsy."[52]

Mendès France responded that he was not surprised by the rumors bandied about in Bonn, only that the German government had placed credence in them. He warned that if a government based its policy on gossip, it could lead only to serious international misunderstandings. Mendès France claimed to be equally surprised that Bonn had not taken French tokens of sympathy and cooperation seriously. In response, France had received only angry rebuffs that would have provoked strong responses from any other government, but which Paris suffered in silence. Mendès France asked only that Bonn take his words seriously. He also assumed that Spaak had been in contact with Bonn. He said that it would not be his fault if France's National Assembly rejected the treaties and that Adenauer was mistaken to believe that there was a majority in favor of ratification.[53]

Kluthe replied that he had shown his letter to Adenauer, who was favorably impressed with its positive tone. Kluthe then suggested that the two leaders meet.[54] Mendès France responded that he would be pleased to meet the chancellor, perhaps even before the Brussels Conference where the EDC members would meet in late August to resolve the impasse over the European army.[55]

Beat the Clock

In the meantime, Mendès France had to meet his self-imposed deadline, so he focused attention on Indochina. Soon after investiture, Mendès France traveled to Geneva to jump-start the stalled talks there. Another personage also stepped forward who would figure prominently at the Geneva Conference: China's foreign minister, Zhou Enlai. Recently having taken charge of the Communist delegates at Geneva, Zhou began to meet secretly with Mendès France. Zhou made it clear to Mendès France that he would be willing to compromise even if it came at the expense of the Viet Minh. Although a Francophile, Zhou had hardheaded reasons for accommodating France. Instead of demanding, as the Viet Minh wanted, a unified Vietnam and recognition of the Pathet Lao and the Free Khmer, Zhou said he would accept partition of the country, no recognition of the Laotian and Cambodian Communist groups, and some degree of French influence in Vietnam. China would benefit by keeping divided a traditional enemy, keeping Cambodia and Laos free of Viet Minh influence, and denying the United States a pretext for intervention. It is also possible that China feared an American nuclear strike.[56]

Mendès France also intended to meet the Soviet representative while he was in Geneva. Some Western governments feared that France's vulnerabilities would lead Mendès France to try to fashion a deal with Moscow. Although speculation abounded as to what was said between France and the Soviet Union, it appears that there was no agreement to kill the EDC in exchange for Soviet help in Indochina. On July 10, Mendès France and Molotov met to discuss Asian affairs. According to Mendès France, at the end of their conversation, Molotov broached the issue of European affairs. Mendès France demurred, saying that while he would be most interested in hearing Molotov's views on other subjects, he preferred to discuss only the issues related to the Geneva Conference.[57]

Distrusting Mendès France, Dulles flew to Paris on July 13 to ensure that the EDC and Indochina were not mixed together at Geneva. Dulles also warned him that time was on the Soviets' side, and France therefore had to act quickly. If Germany were not rearmed, the U.S. Congress would certainly withdraw financial support, thereby forcing America to adopt a peripheral strategy. Mendès France expressed his own concerns, contending that past French governments had presented a false picture of the EDC's chances of passage. He then suggested that it would be better to wait for the right moment rather than send the treaty to certain defeat.[58]

On July 20, Mendès France faced his self-imposed one-month deadline for ending the Indochina conflict. Failure to achieve an agreement meant that he had to step aside or lose his reputation as a man who could be trusted. Molotov then took charge of the situation. He called for Mendès France, Eden, Pham Van Dong, and Zhou Enlai to meet to settle matters. At Molotov's not too subtle urging, a cease-fire was agreed to for Vietnam, Laos, and Cambodia. According to the Geneva agreement, signed on July 21, Vietnam was temporarily partitioned at the seventeenth parallel pending national elections to be held in two years as a step toward reunification. Meanwhile, French troops would evacuate territory north of the parallel, and Viet Minh troops would leave territory south of the demarcation line. The war had cost France 92,000 dead and 114,000 wounded.[59]

On July 21, Mendès France and Molotov met again; this time they discussed Europe. According to his recollections, he told Molotov that he hoped to resolve European affairs soon, but that he could not predict what would occur. He then told Molotov that it was time for the Soviet Union to show its cards, reminding him that Moscow had up until now made no concessions. Molotov reacted negatively, however, emblematic of the Soviet attitude for the remainder of the EDC affair.[60]

Showdown in Brussels

With a cease-fire agreement in place, Mendès France could concentrate on the European army. He faced a difficult challenge, for he had to submit the EDC Treaty to a French legislature largely hostile to the project. Despite this obstacle, France's allies pressured it to proceed. From August 19 to 22, the prospective members of the EDC gathered in Brussels, Belgium, in a final attempt to end the deadlock over the plan. Mendès France, in an effort to make the EDC Treaty acceptable to his legislature, proposed an additional protocol.[61] The protocol contained clauses that would have delayed the supranational character of the treaty for eight years; allowed France alone to retain national military forces; required that the EDC and NATO be coterminus; and mandated that if NATO dissolved, or if Germany reunited, the EDC would cease to exist.[62]

In spite of French claims otherwise, critics contended the protocol would so modify the treaty as to require reconsideration by national parliaments that had already approved the pact. The other conferees rejected this demand. To them it appeared solely designed to postpone German rearmament indefinitely. Mendès France felt humiliated.[63]

Returning to Paris empty-handed would have provided his opponents with ample political ammunition, so Mendès France consulted the Americans, the British, and the Germans. Meeting with Winston Churchill and Anthony Eden, he told the British leadership that the EDC would not pass, and that he would not put the issue to a vote of confidence. He would, however, be ready to restore German sovereignty in case the French parliament did reject the treaty. He then offered an alternative: a coalition of the six EDC nations plus Britain. He characterized this alternative as "constructing a little box inside the big NATO box." Mendès France said he was sure that the National Assembly would pass this substitute.[64]

The next day, Mendès France explained to Douglas Dillon, the U.S. ambassador to France, why, in his view, the Brussels Conference had failed. He contended that with the memories of past French governments' stalling tactics fresh in their minds, the other five governments had mistrusted France from the outset. Everyone assumed that it was just a bargaining position. Consequently, no one believed that his opening statement accurately appraised the situation in France. The prime minister then told Dillon that the vote on the treaty would probably come on the thirtieth and that he expected it to fail. In such case, he would move to restore German sovereignty and work closely with Britain and the United States to secure a German military contribution. He next suggested creating an organization comprising the six EDC nations and Britain. This organization would have no supranational features, thus pleasing London, and no anti-German features, thus satisfying Bonn. The resulting creation would then form a "little box in the big NATO frame."[65] The day before the vote, Mendès France made it clear to Adenauer that in case France rejected the EDC, he would be ready to immediately grant West German sovereignty, contrary to the terms of the 1952 treaty that stipulated that the EDC treaty must be ratified first.[66]

The Crime of August 30

Determined to settle the issue, Mendès France submitted the treaty, without amendments, to a French legislature generally opposed to the agreement. No other French government had gone this far.[67] He told the National Assembly that the Federal Republic must be tied to the West. Despite his pleas, on August 30 the National Assembly struck down the EDC treaty, 319 votes to 264. Opponents of the EDC—Communists and Gaullists alike—locked arms and serenaded the chamber with the *Marseillaise*. Political shock waves ensued.

By rejecting the EDC Treaty, the National Assembly undermined American plans to reduce the U.S. financial and military commitment to Western Europe. In response, U.S. officials appeared finally ready to abandon efforts to wait on France. The following day, Dillon offered the State Department several suggestions on post-EDC U.S. policy toward France. He advised that primary concern must be given to strengthening the Federal Republic's ties with the West and supporting Adenauer. As French consent would aid the success of this policy, he counseled, the United States should not isolate France. However, Dillon continued, "If, as we expect, [the] French prove unreasonable in negotiations re[garding] Germany, particularly in regard to rearmament, and should [the] US be forced to act in concert with [the] UK over French objections, our attitude towards France should be one of firmness and regret that France herself is not prepared to take the steps necessary to increasing Western strength."[68]

Eisenhower also seemed ready to proceed without France. On September 3, he provided Acting Secretary of State Walter Bedell Smith with a list of possible EDC substitutes: "(a) . . . a revision of the EDC idea by the nations concerned. (b) . . . a meeting of the entire NATO group, with a view of including Germany as an equal partner therein. (c) . . . unilateral agreements with Germany—to which agreements we would, of course, have to get the concurrence of a sizable number of Western and Atlantic nations."[69]

A week later, Dulles made the president aware of two plans under study by the State Department: "1) Bring Germany directly into NATO, entrusting the control of the size, composition and disposition of German forces to a NATO agreement with the German government voluntarily agreeing to limit its arms, and 2) if the French should object to this scheme, to take steps along with Britain, Germany, and possibly others, to go ahead with German rearmament under a defense agreement with-

out the cooperation of the French. The second measure, though a last resort, might convince the French of the seriousness of our resolve."[70]
Time seemed to be running out on U.S. patience with France.

Churchill was fatalistic about the potential fallout from the vote, sur-
mising in a memo, "There is one even more horrible and deadly alternative . . . that America might go it alone. She is quite strong enough to do
so. All that would happen is that we would have no influence on her
policy and no protection, and that at present and for some years, the
dangerous years, no means of defense . . . only a revised NATO to include Germany under safeguards can secure our freedom and the freedom of the world."[71]

The reaction in Germany was predictable: fury at the French vote. Adenauer and many members of his party had supported the EDC, despite its
flaws, because they saw it as the best—even the only—chance to achieve
security in Western Europe and sovereignty for West Germany. Other
members of the party supported the EDC because the latter signaled closer
ties to Europe rather than to America or Britain. The chancellor, who considered resigning, called it "a black day for Europe." Emerging from his
Black Forest retreat, an enraged Adenauer granted an interview to the
Times of London. In it he attacked Mendès France and the French parliament: "I regret to say that M. Mendès-France wanted to destry the
E.D.C." Adenauer also warned that the French vote would fuel the rise of
nationalism in Germany, which would then look toward the Soviet
Union. He insisted, however, that German policy toward France would
remain unchanged: "There is no question of isolating France. For France
has isolated herself from Europe and the United States." In addition to
setting back Alliance plans to create a European army, Adenauer was
also angry because the vote had weakened the chancellor and his supporters, for they lost important elections in Schleswig-Holstein.[72]

Negative reactions also surfaced in France. One source of domestic
opposition to the EDC Treaty centered on the clauses pertaining to nuclear weapons. In November 1953, the CGSC had registered its opposition to the EDC Treaty's restrictions on acquiring nuclear weapons. This
concern resurfaced after the defeat of the treaty. On August 31, the
CGSC told the civilian leadership that with the demise of the EDC, the
question of German rearmament remained unanswered. The chiefs then
advanced an argument for rearming Germany premised on recent tech-
nological advances in the field of atomic weaponry.[73]

French military officials argued that the United States had made such
progress in the development of tactical nuclear weapons in 1953, it was

likely that these devices would be ready for deployment in 1957. Accordingly, generals Clement Blanc and Pierre Fäy, along with Admiral Henri Nomy, sent a note to the National Defense Committee on September 6 concerning Washington's recently announced nuclear strategy, the "New Look."[74] They contended that the covering zone could not transformed "except with the complete agreement and, in consequence, the active participation of the country [involved]." France should therefore insist that Germany be the designated zone and play a major role in European defense. "In short," the note continued, "in the new concept, the contribution of Germany is necessary from the geographic as well as the military point of view. It ensures placing the atomic battlefield as far east as possible and therefore contributes to distancing French territory from the area subject to the risks of the greatest destruction."[75]

On September 1, the Permanent Secretary General of National Defense issued a note to the NDC as well: "The adoption of the forward defense strategy, an essential element of the defense concept, renders German participation a necessity flowing from geography. Failing this participation, it would be necessary to increase the covering forces of the members of NATO in proportions judged incompatible with French economic possibilities." The French chiefs of staff therefore believed it necessary that measures be "quickly adopted that would permit the putting in place of the first German contingents." They then urged the government to seek a "political solution to the German question in the context of the Atlantic defense." The NDC adopted these conclusions on September 10. At that meeting, General George Catroux declared, "There is a risk of seeing the possessors of the atomic weapon keep their atomic power in priority for their own interests. There will be states that have the atomic bomb (and will not use it among themselves). There will be states without the bomb, which will be the battlefields. We need our atomic weapons."[76]

With the EDC experiment over, the time appeared ripe for introducing a more practical, less divisive solution to the question of German rearmament. Eden suggested reviving the dormant 1948 Brussels Treaty. The day after, the British cabinet agreed to modify the Brussels Treaty with the NATO solution put into effect at the same time.[77] The French were also thinking along parallel lines about a possible replacement for the EDC. On September 8, André Gros, a legal counselor at the Foreign Affairs Ministry, forwarded a note to *Direction Politique* giving his observations on accepting Germany into a revamped Brussels Treaty Organization (BTO), later renamed the Western European Union (WEU). The French plan was ready on September 9: Germany would enter an enlarged Brussels Treaty Organization, then later enter NATO. Eden was given the details the following day.[78]

Eden traveled to the Continent to confer with the Allied foreign ministers, who welcomed his proposal. Eden told Dulles on September 13 that the plans were going well: "I think we have the foundation for a practical plan which our experts in NATO could work out quickly with German participation." Dulles responded on September 14 criticizing the Brussels proposal. This response upset Eden, who feared that Dulles might endanger his plan.[79] On September 15 and 16, Eden met with Mendès France and he accepted the agreement.[80]

Dulles expressed his displeasure with France by skipping Paris and traveling to Bonn on September 16 to discuss with Adenauer the restoration of German sovereignty. The next day, Dulles met with Eden in London. The secretary of state doubted the Brussels Pact's chances, warning that the United States would provide it less support than it had given to the EDC. Nevertheless, unable to provide a credible alternative, Dulles was forced to acquiesce.[81]

On September 18, François-Poncet disclosed the French proposal to Adenauer. It contained a number of conditions: (1) Germany would not raise forces outside the European army; (2) German forces would serve only in mixed units; (3) Germany would renounce the use of force in trying to regain its lost territories; (4) Britain would maintain a sufficient level of troop strength on the Continent and guarantee that its forces stationed in the Federal Republic would not fall below a certain minimum level, and the United States would be expected to make similar commitments; and (5) the powers of the Supreme Commander would be reinforced.[82] Adenauer accepted the French plan with the understanding that the Federal Republic would also enter NATO. France made a large concession: Germany would enter the WEU and NATO simultaneously, a gesture to which Bonn reacted favorably. However, Adenauer also told U.S. HICOG James B. Conant that if France rejected it, Germany would seek a separate security pact with Britain and the United States as long as the Federal Republic regained its sovereignty.[83]

Held from September 28 to October 3, the London Conference settled problems whose solutions had remained elusive for years, as several key French demands were satisfied. With Eden chairing the conference, new arrangements on German sovereignty and rearmament were sketched out as the conference transformed the complexities of the EDC into a much simpler association (the WEU was less structured than anticipated) of the Federal Republic with the West through NATO and the WEU, the latter subservient to the former. In addition, on October 1, Germany renounced unilaterally the manufacture of atomic, biological, and chemical (ABC) weapons on its soil, for Adenauer realized that without this gesture France would have refused to go any further. In return, France accepted Germany into NATO, and the anti-German clauses in the Brussels Pact were deleted.[84]

On the second day of the conference, another cardinal French requirement was met. Dulles promised that the United States would renew the assurances it had offered to the EDC to the WEU. Eden declared Britain's intention of maintaining in Europe its existing level of armed forces—SACEUR, four divisions, and the Second Air Force of around 780 aircraft—which would not be withdrawn against the wishes of a majority of the Brussels powers or short of an emergency. France had sought such a British pledge since 1952. Ironically, the Anglophobic Adenauer found himself in debt to Britain for helping to rescue his European policy.[85]

From October 20 to 23, the Paris Conference made final adjustments to the agreements made at the London Conference.[86] The conferees decided that the West German contribution would be no fewer than twelve divisions and 1,300 aircraft. Adenauer renounced the manufacture of ABC weapons and the production of long-range missiles, guided missiles, and warships of more than 3,000 tons without approval. In addition, the attendees also signed accords granting Germany and Italy entry into the WEU and Germany into NATO. France and Germany also reached agreement on the Saar, which would receive European status and the appointment of a neutral Saar Commission. In addition, a plebiscite would take place in which Saarlanders could express their preference for or against Europeanization. They would be forbidden, however, from choosing to unite with Germany. Finally, the French would lift their ban on German parties in the Saar. It looked as though the German rearmament question had finally come to an end.

Unexpectedly, the National Assembly, in an initial vote on December 24, 1954, rejected a key section of the Paris Accords. When informed of the vote, Eisenhower erupted: "Those damn French! What do they think they're trying to do? This could really upset the apple cart in Europe." Later, receiving a call from Dulles, Eisenhower quipped: "Well, Foster, they surely have gotten things in an awful mess, haven't they?" After the call, the president analyzed the situation:

You know, here this plan like EDC was designed to protect all of Europe, the French included. They are really endangering the whole safety of Europe by such votes, but you see, I honestly believe that what they are trying to do is this: They know we are going to have to keep bases and troops on the continent of Europe for a long time. They know we must somehow or other get a strong alliance of free nations of Europe. Now, what the French would like would be to act in that concert of nations in Europe very much like we do. We are not a member of the European union and neither are the British. The French would like to be part of it without having the responsibility of being in it. It's the old French game of diplomatic doodling to see how much they can get out for themselves and never mind the rest of the world.

Later in the day, Dillon met privately with Mendès France. Although the French prime minister thought that a strong joint statement by London and Washington would do more harm than good, he did want some pressure put on the French over the weekend. Adenauer, in contrast, while furious at the French vote, nonetheless wanted to stand pat for the time being, fearing the fall of Mendès France. He feared that if France voted no, public opinion in Germany would swing in a neutralist direction, perhaps seeking negotiations with the Soviets.[87]

Following the vote, Dillon suggested that the administration join the British in issuing a strongly worded statement to the French. Among other points, it should warn France that if the National Assembly were to reject the treaty when it was considered in its entirety, Britain and the United States would rearm Germany unilaterally. Both Eisenhower and Dulles rebuffed this suggestion, however, despite pressure from London. The president said that he preferred to leave the door open to Mendès France in hopes that he might secure enough deputies to win the upcoming vote.[88]

Intervening before the next scheduled French parliamentary vote on the London and Paris treaties was an important NATO council meeting. At that meeting, held December 17 and 18 in Paris, the Council adopted a policy that committed the Alliance to a "forward defense" strategy. This new strategy actually placed greater burdens on the alliance. It called for continued rearmament, including twelve German divisions.[89] Shortly thereafter, an important meeting took place in Mendès France's office on December 26 concerning France's future nuclear effort.

According to Bertrand Goldschmidt, a French scientist who attended the meeting, "Mendès France's conclusion was clear: he had become very aware of the gap on the international scene, even in disarmament negotiations, between the powers with the weapons and the rest, as well as the advantage that France had over Germany because of the latter's renunciation. He was therefore favorable to consideration of a secret research program to manufacture nuclear weapons and atomic submarines."[90]

Eisenhower's decision to avoid pressuring France soon worked. On December 30, the French parliament ratified the London-Paris Accords 287 votes to 260, clearing the way for an amended Brussels Treaty. Dulles congratulated Mendès France as the long crisis had come to a close. By May 1955, the interested parties had ratified the treaty, ended the occupation regime in Germany, and accepted Bonn into NATO and the WEU. All that remained was the ratification by the other countries involved.[91] May 5 marked the end of the ratification process, the end of the occupation regime in West Germany, and the establishment of the revamped WEU. And on May 9, Germany entered NATO, prompting Adenauer to boast: "West Germany is now a member of the strongest alliance in history. It will bring us to unification."[92]

Conclusion:
Passions and Interests

The French nation has for centuries played an important, and at times dominant, role in the international arena. Louis XIV's France eagerly bid for dominance in Europe while Napoleonic France bestrode the Continent like a colossus. Yet the latter part of the nineteenth century saw French power and influence in Europe eclipsed by a relentlessly ascendant Germany. On the road to German unification, Bismarck's army destroyed the Second Empire along with Napoleon III's vain pretensions, while two generations later, Kaiser Wilhelm II's soldiers battered France's self-confidence even further. Worse was yet to come. In that terrible summer of 1940, Hilter's *Wehrmacht* pummeled the French Army and robbed France of its self-esteem, replacing it with unanswerable questions and unending recriminations. Although the Fourth Republic sought to restore France's pride and self-image, the nation's international reputation continued to plummet, a fall intensified by colonial setbacks in Indochina, Algeria, and elsewhere. France had seemingly lost its way as it lurched from crisis to crisis. Given its outwardly dismal record, few mourned the Fourth Republic's passing in 1958.

This unflattering portrait has undergone significant upward revision. Recent scholarship has gone a long way toward polishing the Fourth Republic's soiled image. The present study continues the trend but takes it a step further. It argues that Fourth Republic France played a crucial international role after 1945 and to a significant degree shaped the Cold War system in Western Europe. The main elements of this system were the economic and military transformation of the Federal Republic of

Germany into a bulwark again Soviet Communism, as well as the long-term presence of Anglo-American military forces on European soil to monitor German behavior and to tie the fate of America and Britain to the defense of non-Communist Europe.

This last element illustrates a critical way in which France molded the system. By rejecting key Anglo-American demands, France forced both Britain and the United States to guarantee, against their wishes, to station massive numbers of their armed forces on the European continent for an extended period. Anglo-American ground troops ensured that neither Germany nor the Soviet Union would dominate Europe, while at the same time relieving France of a costly burden. This accomplishment suggests that contrary to the views of certain scholars of international relations, such as Kenneth Waltz, "second-rank" powers can indeed force significant change on the strategies of more powerful allies, including one of superpower status.[1] In this instance, France obtained the system that it preferred while the Eisenhower administration fumed about the situation, unable to institute an alternative plan that the French would find acceptable. In similar fashion, Germany, which was even weaker than France, nonetheless skillfully forced the great powers to compromise time and time again.

This case should also give pause to international relations scholars who emphasize the "inevitability" of the Cold War order in Western Europe. The preceding account demonstrates that the system that emerged was far from inevitable. Instead, it resulted from much debate and compromise both among and within the countries involved in the EDC affair. The system, therefore, resulted from a degree of contingency even in the face of powerful structural pressures.

France fashioned the pace and conditions of Germany's rearmament, an achievement even more noteworthy given the wretched condition in which France found itself following the Second World War. Although prominent French officials favored rearming Germany, they resisted the pace and timing demanded by the United States. Aware that defying America outright posed a risk, these French officials employed other means to achieve their objectives. These alternate means succeeded, for France regulated this affair in a manner consistent with its own concerns.

Remarkably, France accomplished these objectives in the face of great internal division. Much of the French public along with the military leadership and leading political parties loathed the EDC, the framework in which France would rearm Germany. The fact that the Fourth Republic accomplished its objectives despite these enduring obstacles offers profound theoretical implications. For example, many international relations scholars dispute the neorealist claim that the international system shapes political outcomes. Some of these scholars argue that the source of grand strategy lay at the domestic level.[2] Yet the ability of French policy makers to overcome tremendous domestic opposition implies that that international security concerns exert a much greater influence on policy formulation than they believe.

This book also revises the view of U.S. foreign policy at the height of the Cold War. Although America made establishing the EDC a top priority, its overwhelming power failed to force the European allies to go faster and farther than they deemed prudent. In fact, France and Germany often determined the pace and scope of European security policy. Overwhelming power, therefore, did not guarantee specific outcomes. Equally surprising is the United States' willingness to accommodate the security concerns of the European allies and the Soviets. American officials such as John Foster Dulles recognized the anxieties that a rearmed Germany would produce in the Soviet Union and sought to reassure Moscow. This point suggests that Cold War politics were not always black-and-white.

America's recognition of French and Soviet sensibilities contrasts to its heavy-handedness in other areas. Although recent scholarship lavishly praises Eisenhower's handling of foreign policy,[3] his administration stumbled on a number of occasions. The Americans knew that their plans to create a Europe powerful enough to deter Soviet aggression— and hence allow American forces to withdraw from the Continent— would be impractical given nonnuclear West European states. Absent the American nuclear umbrella, a nonnuclear Europe could never deter a thermonuclear-armed Soviet Union. Eisenhower, therefore, decided to grant the Europeans a measure of control over U.S. nuclear weapons. Contrary to his expectations, NATO's new nuclear doctrine had the effect of shackling American forces to the Continent rather than freeing them.

Ironically, Eisenhower's policy was inferior to the policy France forced on him. Yet despite his disappointment, the long-term positioning of American troops on the European mainland produced extremely beneficial effects. The presence of a large U.S. conventional military force helped to redress the East-West military imbalance. It also enabled the Alliance to avoid a host of problems concerning NATO's new nuclear regime. Deciding which nation would control the nuclear trigger, and the possibility of a new German army, the *Bundeswehr*, gaining access to nuclear arms were problems that would have been rendered intractable had American ground forces been absent.

The favorable reassessment of the Fourth Republic presented here does not imply that omniscient wise men unfailingly guided the nation's progress with jeweler-like precision. France's belated resolution of its colonial and financial difficulties surely gives lie to that proposition. Moreover, luck also played a role in France's ultimate success in this affair. Yet as Branch Ricky once observed, "Luck is the residue of design." By fits and starts and over time, leading French policy makers steered France in a direction that enabled it to reach most of its important strategic goals.

Far from having a marginal part, France played a pivotal role in post-1945 international politics. Consistently, when they lacked French cooperation, Allied strategic plans skidded to a halt. Both Britain and the United States depended on France to contribute in a meaningful way to European security arrangements. They expected it to take the lead in containing both the Soviet Union and a remilitarized Federal Republic. Although France acknowledged and accepted the hard logic of rearming Germany, it refused to consent to this policy unless its own concerns were satisfied.

At the heart of French concerns lay the fear that remilitarizing the Federal Republic might provoke Soviet retaliation or overturn the balance of power between France and Germany. According to French planners, the best safeguard against these dangers would be the massive and permanent presence of Anglo-American military forces on the European mainland. While both London and Washington intended to remain off the Continent and shift the burden onto France, their plans could not proceed without French consent. France was able to delay Anglo-American plans by refusing to vote on the EDC Treaty until the Western European nations put their own house in order, and Britain and the United States committed themselves to defending the Continent. Important French policy makers helped to forge a system that both protected and advanced important French interests. Thus, in contrast to the caricature of France as inveterately emotional, these officials ensured that French national security policy was governed less by the passions and more by the interests.

Notes
Sources
Index

Notes

Introduction

1. In addition to France and Germany, the EDC was slated to include Belgium, Italy, Luxembourg, and the Netherlands. Primary works on the EDC include Edward M. Fursdon, *The European Defense Community: A History* (New York: St. Martin's, 1980); Fursdon, "The Role of the European Defense Community," in *NATO: The Founding of the Atlantic Alliance and the Integration of Europe,* ed. John R. Gillingham and Francis H. Heller (New York: St. Martin's, 1992), 213–240; Daniel Lerner and Raymond Aron, eds., *France Defeats EDC* (New York: Praeger, 1957); Pierre Guillen, "Les chefs militaires français, le réarmement de l'Allemagne et la CED (1950–1954)," *Revue d'histoire de la deuxième guerre mondiale et des conflits contemporains* 33 (January 1983): 3–33; Raymond Poidvein, "La France devant le problème de la C.E.D.: incidences nationales et internationales été 1951 à été 1953," *Revue d'histoire de la deuxième guerre mondiale et des conflits contemporains* 33 (January 1983): 35–57; Michel Dumoulin, ed., *La Communauté Européenne de Défense, leçons pour demain? The European Defense Community: Lessons for the Future?* (Brussels: P.I.E.-Peter Lang, 2000); Jasime Aimaq, *For Europe or Empire?: French Colonial Ambitions and the European Army Plan* (Lund: Lund University Press, 1996); Kevin Ruane, *The Rise and Fall of the European Defense Community: Anglo-American Relations and the Crisis of European Defense, 1950–55* (New York: St. Martin's, 2000); Rolf Steininger, "John Foster Dulles, the European Defense Community, and the German Question," in *John Foster Dulles and the Diplomacy of the Cold War,* ed. Richard H. Immerman (Princeton, NJ: Princeton University Press, 1990), 57–75; Ronald W. Pruessen, "Cold War Threats and America's Commitment to the European Defense Community: One Corner of a Triangle," *Journal of European Integration History* 2

(1996): 51–69; David Clay Large, "Grand Illusions: The United States, the Federal Republic of Germany, and the European Defense Community," in *American Policy and the Reconstruction of West Germany, 1945–1955*, ed. Jeffrey Diefendorf, Axel Frohn, and Hermann-Josef Rupieper (New York: Cambridge University Press, 1993), 375–394; and James McAllister, *No Exit: America and the German Problem, 1943–1954* (Ithaca, NY: Cornell University Press, 2002).

2. See Gregory Mitrovich, *Undermining the Kremlin: America's Strategy to Subvert the Soviet Bloc, 1947–1956* (Ithaca, NY: Cornell University Press, 2000).

3. In this study, "Germany" and "Germans" refer to the Federal Republic of Germany (West Germany) and its citizens unless stated otherwise. Likewise, "Allies" refers collectively to the founding members of the Atlantic Alliance: Belgium, Canada, Denmark, France, Great Britain, Iceland, Luxembourg, the Netherlands, Norway, Portugal, and the United States, as well as Germany and Italy.

4. This international force would also guarantee Germany's security, though British officials thought that article 4 of the March 1948 Brussels Treaty and article 5 of the North Atlantic Treaty already appeared to provide for German defense. They believed that if the Soviet bloc attacked the Federal Republic, the Western occupying powers—Britain, France, and the United States—would certainly regard this move as an attack on themselves. See "Brief for the Secretary of State in New York. Germany: Defence Questions," September 6, 1950, FO 371/124933, British National Archives [hereafter BNA], Kew, Richmond, Surrey.

5. The Council of the Republic, the French Senate, would approve the Paris Accords in April 1955. Yet like Britain's House of Lords, it is a withered arm of government that can hinder but not block legislation.

6. It must be noted that the United States initially employed diplomatic pressure to obtain French acquiescence. Secretary of State Dean Acheson spearheaded this strategy, yet it proved short-lived and ineffective while in operation.

7. Frank Costigliola, *France and the United States: The Cold War Alliance since World War II* (New York: Twayne Publishers, 1992), 45–47.

8. Walter LaFeber, *America, Russia, and the Cold War, 1945–1996* (New York: McGraw-Hill, 1997), 167.

9. Frank A. Ninkovich, *Germany and the United States: The Transformation of the German Question since 1945*, updated ed. (New York: Twayne Publishers, 1995), 105; and Thomas A. Schwartz, *America's Germany: John J. McCloy and the Federal Republic of Germany* (Cambridge, MA: Harvard University Press, 1991), 293.

10. Costigliola, *France and the United States*, 91; Mark S. Sheetz, "France and the German Question: Avant-garde or Rear-guard? Comment on Creswell and Trachtenberg," *Journal of Cold War Studies* 5 (2003): 37–45; Pierre Mélandri, *Les États-Unis face à l'unification de l'Europe, 1945–1954* (Paris: A. Pedone, 1980); and Jean-Baptiste Duroselle, *France and the United States:*

From the Beginnings to the Present, trans. Derek Coltman (Chicago: University of Chicago Press, 1978), chap. 8.

11. A 1,000-square-mile coal-rich area located on the Franco-German border, the Saar has long sparked passionate emotions in both France and Germany. Although traditionally German territory, France annexed the Saar after the First World War. A 1935 plebiscite, however, forced France to return the region to Germany. Then in 1947, Britain, France, and the United States declared the region semiautonomous but economically tied to France. Germany rejected what it believed to be French designs on the region and fought hard for its return. At a press conference in early 1950, Chancellor Konrad Adenauer threatened, "If the Saar government attempts to separate from Germany, with French agreement, then there may be developments of which no one can see the consequences." Quoted in Charles Wighton, *Adenauer: A Critical Biography* (New York: Coward-McCann, 1964), 118.

12. William I. Hitchcock, *France Restored: Cold War Diplomacy and the Quest for Leadership in Europe, 1944–1954* (Chapel Hill: University of North Carolina Press, 1998), 5–8.

13. The French Army has been traditionally known as *la grande muette,* or "the silent one."

14. See Paul M. Pitman, "Interested Circles: French Industry and the Rise and Fall of the EDC," in Michel Dumoulin, ed., *La Communauté Européenne de Défense, leçons pour demain? (The European Defense Community, Lessons for the Future?)* (Bruxelles: PIE–Peter Lang, 2000).

1. From Hot War to Cold War

1. See the letter from General Jean Humbert, the acting chief of the general staff, to the prime minister, July 29, 1947. In addition, Robert Schuman outlined his views on France's strategic vulnerability in a June 14, 1948, document. Both documents are found in the George Bidault Papers, Archives nationales [hereafter AN] 457 AP 151.

2. Soviet pressure in the Mediterranean and the Middle East, the breakdown of Four-Power control in Germany, the failure of the November–December 1947 Council of Foreign Ministers meeting, and the Soviet-sponsored Prague Coup in early 1948 proved to be links in a chain of events that hardened policies on both sides of the Iron Curtain.

3. George-Henri Soutou, "Le Général de Gaulle et l'URSS, 1943–1945: idéologie ou équilibre européen," *Revue d'histoire diplomatique* 108 (1994): 303–355.

4. See John W. Young, *Britain and European Unity, 1945–1992* (New York: St. Martin's Press, 1993), 10. Britain argued that while it was committed to a policy of ultimate independence for its colonies, France was not. According to Foreign Office official William Blanch, differences in ultimate aim and method over this issue might "prove a constant source of irritation." February 7, 1947, FO 371/67671, BNA.

5. See "Record of Conversation between the Secretary of State and M. Bidault at 1 Carlton Gardens after Dinner on 29th November, 1947," Ernest Bevin Papers, FO 800/447, BNA.

6. For a reiteration of British policy toward the Ruhr, see "Record of Conversation at the Kremlin on Monday, 24th March, 1947, 10:00 P.M.–11:15 P.M.," Ernest Bevin Papers, FO 800/447, BNA.

7. "The Ambassador in France to the Secretary of State," September 27, 1945, *Foreign Relations of the United States* [hereafter *FRUS*] *1945* 3:878.

8. "The Ambassador in France to the Secretary of State," November 3, 1945, *FRUS 1945* 3: 890–891.

9. "The Ambassador in France to the Secretary of State," December 8, 1945, *FRUS 1945* 3: 916, fn 81. Bidault later told Bevin that France had done Britain a great favor by rejecting the setting up of central administrations two years earlier, otherwise the Communists would be in power in Cologne. See "Record of Discussion between the Secretary of State and M. Bidault at the Foreign Office on 17th December, 1947," Ernest Bevin Papers, FO 800/447, BNA.

10. "Conversation between the Secretary of State and M. Bidault at Dinner at the British Embassy on October 11th, 1946," Alfred Duff Cooper Papers, DUFC 4/5, Churchill Archives Centre, Churchill College, Cambridge University.

11. Michael Creswell and Marc Trachtenberg, "France and the German Question, 1944–1955," *Journal of Cold War Studies* 5, no. 3 (Summer 2003), 14. According to British records, while discussing the issue of Germany, Bidault told Bevin in late 1947 that the French government was "now prepared to go as far as possible in a study of pending questions provided this was done as between the three Governments and the French were not left alone. Subject to this one proviso they were ready to talk about anything." See "Record of Discussion between the Secretary of State and M. Bidault at the Foreign Office on 17th December, 1947," Ernest Bevin Papers, FO 800/447, BNA. France also dropped its demand that the Ruhr be detached from Germany. See letter from Ernest Bevin to Clement Attlee, April 16, 1947, Ernest Bevin Papers, FO 800/447, BNA.

12. William I. Hitchcock, "Response to 'France and the German Question, 1945–1955' by Michael Creswell and Marc Trachtenberg," *Journal of Cold War Studies* 5 (2003): 35.

13. It is likely that the French leadership did not seriously envision close relations with Moscow, but domestic political realities forced French officials to make a show of good faith. In fact, both Britain and France took a harder line at the December 1947 Council of Foreign Ministers meeting than the United States. See Marc Trachtenberg, *A Constructed Peace: The Making of the European Settlement, 1945–1963* (Princeton, NJ: Princeton University Press, 1999), 68–69. See also "Record of Conversation between the Secretary of State and M. Bidault at 1 Carlton Gardens after Dinner on 29th November, 1947," Ernest Bevin Papers, FO 800/447, BNA.

14. According to Foreign Secretary Bevin, "Any suggestion that the Treaty was not directed primarily against Germany would rouse suspicion and perhaps opposition not only in Moscow but in some other quarters, including, I would imagine, the Communist Party in France and their sympathisers in Belgium and elsewhere." Telegram, January 23, 1947, FO 371/67670, BNA.

15. Quoted in Dietmar Hüser, "Charles de Gaulle, Georges Bidault, Robert Schuman et l'Allemagne 1944–1950: Concepts—Actions—Perceptions—," *Francia* 23 (1996): 64, n. 55.

16. For more information on the Treaty of Dunkirk, see John Baylis, "Britain and the Dunkirk Treaty: the Origins of NATO," *Journal of Strategic Studies* 5 (1982): 236–247; and Sean Greenwood, "Return to Dunkirk: The Origins of the Anglo-French Treaty of March 1947," *Journal of Strategic Studies* 6 (1983): 49–65. See also Bert Zeeman, "Britain and the Cold War: An Alternative Approach. The Treaty of Dunkirk example," *European History Quarterly* 16 (1986): 343–367.

17. Trachtenberg, *A Constructed Peace*, chap. 3.

18. "Record of Conversation between the Secretary of State and M. Bidault at the Foreign Office on 25th November, 1947," and "Record of Discussion between the Secretary of State and M. Bidault at the Foreign Office on 17th December, 1947"; both documents found in Ernest Bevin Papers, FO 800/447, BNA. "Conversation between the Secretary of State and Mr. Marshall at the Foreign Office on 17th December, 1947," Ernest Bevin Papers, FO 800/447, BNA. Bevin and Bidault also agreed that that they had to move cautiously and discreetly in order not to provoke the Soviet Union.

19. Maurice Vaïsse, "L'échec d'une Europe franco-britannique: la naissance du Pacte de Bruxelles (1948)," in *Histoire des débuts de la Construction européenne (mars 1948–mai 1950)*, ed. Raymond Poidevin (Brussels: Bruylant, 1986), 374. For the text of the treaty, see *American Foreign Policy, 1950–1955 Basic Documents*, vol. 1 (Washington, DC: USGPO, 1957), 968–971 [hereafter Basic Documents].

20. For background on the Brussels Pact, see ibid.; and John Baylis, "Britain, the Brussels Pact and the Continental Commitment," *International Affairs* 60 (1984): 615–629.

21. See Marc Trachtenberg, "The German Threat as a Pretext for Defense against Russia," http://www.polisci.ucla.edu/faculty/trachtenberg/appendices/appendixII.html, Appendix Two (accessed 8/30/05). Shortly after the signing of the Brussels Treaty, French President Vincent Auriol remarked that war with the Soviet Union would be much worse than war with Germany. A Franco-Soviet war would cause a civil war in France because the French Communist Party would fight in support of the Soviets. Moreover, such a conflict could destroy the entire political leadership of France. Auriol therefore believed that the West should do nothing to provide the Soviet Union with an excuse to precipitate a crisis. See "Conversation between Secretary of State and M. Vincent-Auriol on 17th April, 1948," Ernest Bevin Papers, 800/447, BNA.

22. At the beginning of 1948, French General George Revers said that the French Army had four infantry divisions and two armoured divisions in Europe and two infantry divisions in Africa. He also indicated that while France had 900,000 men trained, 300,000 had no equipment. "Note On A Meeting Between C.I.G.S. And General Revers At The War Office On 21st January 1948," Bernard Law Montgomery papers [hereafter BLM] 183/16, Imperial War Museum. In a September 8, 1948, estimate, Field Marshal Bernard Law Montgomery, Britain's Chief of the Imperial General Staff, wrote that BTO had twenty-five divisions available, at least nine of which were of "doubtful value" (BLM 207/2). According to one source, Foreign Minister Bidault remarked in private, "If the Russians are smart, they will attack right away." Quoted in Jean-Claude Demory, Georges Bidault (Paris: Editions Julliard, 1995), 275. See also "Conversations with M. Bidault and M. Couve de Murville on 16th March, 1948," Ernest Bevin Papers, FO 800/447, BNA.

23. On the day of the signing of the Brussels Treaty, Truman declared that U.S. forces would remain in Europe. See Trachtenberg, A Constructed Peace, 85. According to French General Alphonse Juin, however, the Americans did not take the BTO seriously: "They have not the men, nor are they in a position to deliver adequate munitions in time." "Summary of Conversations with General Juin at Rabat—Jan. 7th, 8th and 9th, 1949," Sir Basil Liddell Hart papers, LH 11/HB1949/5, Liddell Hart Centre for Military Archives [hereafter LHCMA], King's College, London.

24. See "Conversation between the Ministers for Foreign Affairs of the United Kingdom, France, Belgium, Netherlands and Luxembourg on 17th March, 1948 (after the signature of the Brussels Treaty)"; and "Second Conversation between the Ministers for Foreign Affairs of the United Kingdom, France, Belgium, Netherlands and Luxembourg on 17th March, 1948," Ernest Bevin Papers, FO 800/447, BNA.

25. See Vaïsse, "L'échec d'une Europe franco-britannique," 382–384; and Melvyn P. Leffler, A Preponderance of Power: National Security, the Truman Administration, and the Cold War (Stanford, CA: Stanford University Press, 1992), 205.

26. FRUS 1948 3:54–56, 59–75. The conferees excluded France from the talks because of the fear that French communists would inform Moscow.

27. For a text of the North Atlantic Treaty, see Lawrence S. Kaplan, The United States and NATO: The Formative Years (Lexington: University Press of Kentucky, 1984), Appendix C.

28. France would become the leading recipient of U.S.-administered Mutual Defense Assistance Program (MDAP) funds. See Irwin M. Wall, The United States and the Making of Postwar France, 1945–1954 (New York: Cambridge University Press, 1990), 74, 188.

29. Drafted in 1949 by the U.S. Joint Chiefs of Staff with the concurrence of the U.S. State Department, DC-6, which won NATO approval on January 6, 1950, accorded to the United States the primary responsibility for strategic bombing in NATO defense plans, a function that would be carried out primarily by the U.S. Strategic Air Command (SAC). For the text of DC-6 and

background information, see *FRUS 1949* 4:352–356; and ibid., 4:1. See also Ernest R. May, "The American Commitment to Germany, 1949–55," *Diplomatic History* 13 (1989): 431–432. In spite of this responsibility thrust on it, SAC was not at that moment a formidable military organization. When Lieutenant General (later General) Curtis E. LeMay assumed command of SAC in 1948, he found it in sad shape. He immediately set about turning it into an awesome strike force. See Samuel R. Williamson and Steven L. Rearden, *The Origins of U.S. Nuclear Strategy, 1945–1953* (New York: St. Martin's Press, 1993), chap. 7.

30. For an extended discussion of these points, see Kaplan, *The United States and NATO*, chap. 7. See also Trachtenberg, *A Constructed Peace*, 87–90; and Mark Cioc, *Pax Atomica: The Nuclear Defense Debate in West Germany During the Adenauer Era* (New York: Columbia University Press, 1988), 4–5.

31. John S. Duffield, *Power Rules: The Evolution of NATO's Conventional Force Posture* (Stanford, CA: Stanford University Press, 1995), 30.

32. Moreover, reviving and harnessing German industry would also ease the burden on U.S. industry and American taxpayers, who were footing the bill.

33. Lawrence W. Martin, "The American Decision to Rearm Germany," in *American Civil-Military Decisions: A Book of Case Studies*, ed. Harold Stein (Birmingham: University of Alabama Press, 1963), 645; Georgette Elgey, *La République des Illusions (1945–1951) ou la vie secrète de la IVe République* (Paris: Libraire Arthème Fayard, 1993), 475; *FRUS 1948* 3:59–75; Saki Dockrill, *Britain's Policy for West German Rearmament, 1950–1955* (New York: Cambridge University Press, 1991), 16–17; and the *New York Times*, May 7, 1950. This list of pronouncements by Allied officials on the desirability of a German military contribution to Western defense is representative but by no means exhaustive. See James McAllister, *No Exit: America and the German Problem, 1943–1954* (Ithaca, NY: Cornell University Press, 2002) for further evidence.

34. "The Under Secretary of the Army to the Secretary of State," April 10, 1950, *FRUS 1950* 3:43–48; and "Memorandum Prepared in the Bureau of German Affairs, 'Germany in the European Context,'" February 11, 1950, *FRUS 1950* 4:599.

35. For revisionist interpretations of America's postwar international economic policy, see Fred L. Block, *The Origins of International Economic Disorder: A Study of United States International Monetary Policy from Second World War to the Present* (Berkeley: University of California Press, 1977); Joyce and Gabriel Kolko, *The Limits of Power: The World and United States Foreign Policy, 1945–1954* (New York: Harper & Row, 1972); and Alan S. Milward, *The Reconstruction of Western Europe* (London: Meuthen, 1984). Challenging these views in a more orthodox vein is Robert A. Pollard, *Economic Security and the Origins of the Cold War* (New York: Columbia University Press, 1985).

36. Stephen L. Rearden, *History of the Office of the Secretary of Defense: The Formative Years, 1947–1950* (Washington, DC: Office of the Secretary of

Defense, 1984); and Leffler, *A Preponderance of Power,* 271, 275–276, 304–305, 308. Johnson replaced James Forrestal as secretary of defense in March 1949.

37. David Clay Large, *Germans to the Front: West German Rearmament in the Adenauer Era* (Chapel Hill: University of North Carolina Press, 1996), 38–39; Timothy Ireland, *Creating the Entangling Alliance: The Origins of the North Atlantic Treaty Association* (Westport, CT: Greenwood, 1981), 184; and Phil Williams, *The Senate and U.S. Troops in Europe* (New York: St. Martin's Press, 1985), 23.

38. Quoted in Gordon D. Drummond, *The German Social Democrats in Opposition, 1949–1960: The Case Against Rearmament* (Norman: University of Oklahoma Press, 1982), 39.

39. In fact, Adenauer, who had become chancellor on September 21, 1949, headed a four-party coalition, the other two being the Free Democratic Party (FDP) and the Deutsche Party (DP). In December 1949, several liberal parties consolidated to form the FDP. Theodor Heuss (1884–1963), the Federal president from 1949 to 1959, was the party's leader. Because no postwar German party had ever won an absolute majority in the Bundestag (until 1957), coalition government has been the norm. As such, the FDP has played a disproportionate role in German politics, having, since 1949, been in every cabinet except two. The other party, the DP, a small group that drew its support from the north of Germany, joined Adenauer's coalition in 1949 and remained there throughout the 1950s.

40. Reacting to Adenauer's remarks in the *Plain Dealer,* André François-Poncet, the French high commissioner for Germany, said "the creation of a German army in any form was absolutely out of the question." Quoted in Thomas A. Schwartz, *America's Germany: John J. McCloy and the Federal Republic of Germany* (Cambridge, MA: Harvard University Press, 1991), 121. See also Charles Williams, *Adenauer: The Father of the New Germany* (New York: John Wiley & Sons, 2000), 356.

41. Konrad Adenauer, *Memoirs, 1945–1953* (Chicago: Henry Regnery and Company, 1966), 267–270; Margaret Carlyle, *Documents on International Affairs, 1949–1950* (London: Oxford University Press, 1953); Pierre Mélandri, "Les Etats-Unis et le Plan Pleven," *Relations internationales* 4 (1977): 202; and Drummond, *The German Social Democrats in Opposition,* 38–39.

42. See Georges-Henri Soutou, "Georges Bidault et la construction européene, 1944–1954" in *Revue d'histoire diplomatique* 105 (1991): 267–306; and John W. Young, *France, the Cold War and the Western Alliance, 1944–1949: French Foreign Policy and Postwar Europe* (New York: St. Martin's Press, 1990), 134–154.

43. Quoted in "Brief for the U.K. Delegation," April 26, 1950, *Documents on British Policy Overseas* [hereafter referred to as *DBPO*], Series II, Volume II: *The London Conferences, Anglo-American Relations and Cold War Strategy, January–June 1950* (London: HMSO, 1987), 138–41.

44. "The Ambassador in France to the Secretary of State," April 22, 1950, *FRUS 1950* 3:60–62.
45. Parliamentary Debates (Hansard), House of Commons, Fifth Series, vol. 472, Session 1950, Columns 1288–1290, 1321 (London: HMSO, 1950).
46. Ibid., vol. 473, Columns 191, 323–324.
47. Ibid., Columns 323–324.
48. "The Secretary of State to the United States High Commissioner for Germany, at Frankfurt," March 31, 1950, *FRUS 1950* 3:833–834.
49. This paper had not been cleared within the State Department. See "The Current Position in the Cold War," April 14, 1950, *FRUS 1950* 3:859, fn. 1. See also "United States Objectives and Programs," April 14, 1950, *FRUS 1950* 1:262–263.
50. Longtime French foreign minister Robert Schuman.
51. "Memorandum by Mr. John Foster Dulles, Consultant to the Secretary of State, to the Under Secretary of State," April 21, 1950, *FRUS 1950* 3:60.
52. *L'Année Politique 1950* (Paris: Editions du Grand Siècle, 1951), 112; and Pierre Gerbet, *La construction de l'Europe* (Paris: Imprimerie Nationale, 1994), 102. In fact, Clay had publicly called for a limited German military contribution to Western defense in November 1949. See Martin, "The American Decision to Rearm Germany," 647.
53. See François Duchêne, *Jean Monnet: The First Statesman of Interdependence* (New York: W. W. Norton, 1994); and Éric Roussel, *Jean Monnet, 1888–1979* (Paris: Librairie Artème Fayard, 1996).
54. See Wall, *The United States and the Making of Postwar France*, 193–199; John Gillingham, *Coal, Steel, and the Rebirth of Europe, 1945–1955: The Germans and the French from Ruhr Conflict to Economic Community* (New York: Cambridge University Press, 1991), 156–162; and Milward, *The Reconstruction of Western Europe.*
55. "The Secretary of State to the Acting Secretary of State," May 8, *FRUS 1950* 3:1007–1013; "The Secretary of State to the Acting Secretary of State," May 9, 1950, *FRUS 1950* 3:1013–1018; and *L'Année Politique 1950*, 113.
56. For the text of Schuman's declaration, see "The Chargé in France to the Acting Secretary of State," May 9, 1950, *FRUS 1950* 3:692–694. France, Germany, Italy, Luxembourg, and the Netherlands signed the Treaty of Paris, which instituted the ECSC on April 18, 1951. It began operations on August 10, 1952, in Luxembourg. For the text of the treaty, see *Basic Documents*, 1039–1078.
57. Adenauer quoted in Ronald Granieri, *The Ambivalent Alliance: Konrad Adenauer, The CDU/CSU, and the West, 1949–1966* (Providence, RI: Berghahn Books, 2003), 37.
58. "The Acting Secretary of State to the Secretary of State, at London, May 10, 1950," *FRUS 1950* 3:695–696.
59. "Statement of Hon. Paul G. Hoffman, Administrator, Economic Cooperation Administration, Accompanied by Mark H. Connell, Assistant, Economic Cooperation Administration," June 23, 1950, *Executive Sessions of the Sen-*

ate Foreign Relations Committee, vol. 2, *Eighty-First Congress, First and Second Sessions, 1949–1950* (Washington, DC: U.S. G.P.O., 1976), 546.

60. For the text of the May 5, 1949, Statute of the Council of Europe, see the Council's website <http://www.coe.int>

61. "Europe of the Six" refers to Belgium, France, Germany, Italy, Luxembourg, and the Netherlands.

62. See Walter Lipgens and Wilfred Loth, eds., *Documents on the History of European Integration*, vol. 3, *The Struggle for European Union by Political Parties and Pressure Groups in Western European Countries, 1945–1950* (Berlin/New York: Walter de Gruyter, 1988), 123–125. Britain's absence from the ECSC would later pose difficulties for the French, as they strove unsuccessfully for British cooperation in other areas. For background on Mollet, see Denis Lefebvre, *Guy Mollet: Le mal aimé* (Paris: Librairie Plon, 1992).

63. Successfully fulfilling its mission, the EPU dissolved in 1958. See Jacob J. Kaplan and Günther Schleiminger, *The European Payments Union: Financial Diplomacy in the 1950s* (Oxford: Clarendon, 1989); Graham L. Rees, *Britain and the Postwar European Payments System* (Cardiff: University of Wales, 1963); Gillingham, *Coal, Steel and the Rebirth of Europe*, 175; Leffler, *A Preponderance of Power*, 349–351; and Alan S. Milward, *The European Rescue of the Nation-State* (Berkeley: University of California Press, 1992), 348–349. For texts of the September 19, 1950, "Agreement and Protocol of Provisional Application of the Agreement," see *Basic Documents*, 1012–1039. For information concerning how the signatories implemented the complex agreements, see Louis C. Boochever, Jr., "The European Union," Department of State, *Bulletin* 26 (1952): 732–736.

64. For America's concerns about Germany's political health, see Frank M. Buscher, "The U.S. High Commission and German Nationalism, 1949–52," *Central European History* 23 (1990): 57–75.

2. A Year of Living Dangerously

1. See James McAllister, *No Exit: America and the German Problem, 1943–1954* (Ithaca, NY: Cornell University Press, 2002), chap. 2.

2. For the debate over the size of the Soviet Army during this period, see Phillip A. Karber and Jerald A. Combs, "The United States, NATO, and the Soviet Threat to Western Europe: Military Estimates and Policy Options, 1945–1963," *Diplomatic History* 22 (1998): 399–429; John S. Duffield, "Progress, Problems, and Prospects," *Diplomatic History* 22 (1998): 431–437; and Matthew A. Evangelista, "The Soviet Threat: Intentions, Capabilities, and Context," *Diplomatic History* 22 (1998): 439–449. See also Matthew A. Evangelista, "Stalin's Postwar Army Reappraised," *International Security* 7 (1982/1983): 110–138; John S. Duffield, "The Soviet Military Threat to Western Europe: US Estimates in the 1950s and 1960s," *Journal of Strategic Studies* 15 (1992): 208–227; and John S. Duffield, *Power Rules: The Evolu-*

tion of NATO's Conventional Force Posture (Stanford, CA: Stanford University Press, 1995).

3. See Gregory Mitrovich, *Undermining the Kremlin: America's Strategy to Subvert the Soviet Bloc, 1947–1956* (Ithaca, NY: Cornell University Press, 2000). Despite its ability to militarily overrun Western Europe, U.S. officials did not believe that the Soviet Union would run the risk of initiating global war. See McAllister, *No Exit*, 146–148, 173–175.

4. Mitrovich, *Undermining the Kremlin.*

5. There were, in addition, a series of smaller shocks interspersed among these three larger ones. In 1948, the Soviet Union sponsored the Berlin Blockade and a coup in Czechoslovakia; Moscow created the German Democratic Republic (GDR) on October 7, 1949; British atomic scientist Klaus Fuchs was arrested on charges of espionage on February 2, 1950; Senator Joseph M. McCarthy (Republican-Wisconsin) delivered his infamous Wheeling, West Virginia speech, in which he made accusations of massive communist infiltration in the U.S. State Department, on February 9, 1950; and Peking and Moscow signed the Sino-Soviet Treaty of Friendship on February 14, 1950. The cumulative effect of these events contributed to a growing sense of alarm among U.S. officials and the general public.

6. Although the United States planned to use strategic bombing to destroy Soviet forces had they overrun Western Europe, this strategy would have undoubtedly inflicted severe punishment on the European allies.

7. For an indication of the extent to which these ideas permeated the thinking of U.S. officials, see Mitrovich, *Undermining the Kremlin*, chap. 2. See also NSC 100, January 11, 1951, *FRUS 1951* 1:7–18. In addition, the U.S. Central Intelligence Agency (CIA) reported on April 3, 1948, that the Soviet Air Force had accorded "first priority" to developing an "interceptor fighter force based on jet aircraft." This force would concentrate on stopping strategic bombers from reaching Moscow and other areas the Soviet leadership deemed vital. In addition, the CIA report indicated that the Soviet Union was also creating its own strategic bombing force. The report proved accurate, as the Soviet Union introduced a long-range bomber, the Tu-4, in 1948 and committed MiG-15 jet fighters to the Korean War. See Mark A. O'Neill, "Air Combat on the Periphery: The Soviet Air Force in Action during the Cold War, 1945–1989," in *Russian Aviation and Air Power in the Twentieth Century*, ed. Robin D. Higham, John T. Greenwood, and Von Hardesty (London: Frank Cass Publishers, 1998), 208.

8. See Melvyn P. Leffler, *A Preponderance of Power: National Security, the Truman Administration, and the Cold War* (Stanford, CA: Stanford University Press, 1992), 302–304, 333–334, 338–340, 393.

9. For a study that views the Korean War as a turning point in the Cold War, see Robert Jervis, "The Impact of the Korean War on the Cold War," *Journal of Conflict Resolution* 24 (1980): 563–592. For a study that emphasizes the continuity of U.S. policy before and after the outbreak of the Cold War,

see Walter LaFeber, "NATO and the Korean War: A Context," *Diplomatic History* 13 (1989): 461–477.

10. U.S. officials had other worries as well. Korea's geographic location made it a tempting target for the Soviet Union. Moreover, American officials thought that abandoning Korea would harm U.S. credibility worldwide. See William Stueck, *The Korean War: An International History* (Princeton, NJ: Princeton University Press, 1995), 16, 25. Then in January 1951, Soviet leader Josef Stalin directed his military forces to prepare for war games in Budapest, Hungary, in preparation for an invasion to topple Yugoslavia, which was led by Stalin's rival, Marshal Josip Broz Tito. See O'Neill, "Air Combat on the Periphery," 218.

11. Aaron L. Friedberg, *In the Shadow of the Garrison State: America's Anti-Statism and Its Cold War Strategy* (Princeton, NJ: Princeton University Press, 2000), 98–108; and Samuel F. Wells, "Sounding the Tocsin: NSC 68 and the Soviet Threat," *International Security* 4 (1979): 116–158.

12. Contrary to conventional wisdom, NSC 68 did not fundamentally alter America's national security policy. As the historian Melvyn Leffler notes, NSC 68 "explicitly endorsed the goals that had been enumerated in NSC 20/4 of November 1948" by urging America to harness its military-industrial resources to achieve a preponderance of power over the Soviet Union. See Leffler, *A Preponderance of Power*, 356. For the text of NSC 20/4, see *FRUS 1948* 1:262–267.

13. For the text of NSC 68, see *FRUS 1950* 1:237–292. Steven J. Zaloga writes that from 1947 to 1952, the Soviet Union built 847 Tu-4s. He also notes, however, that they possessed insufficient range to reach the continental United States. In response to doubts about the survivability of the Tu-4s, exposed during the Korean War, Stalin ordered a program to develop jet-powered bombers while also ringing Moscow with an elaborate strategic air defense system. See Steven J. Zaloga, "Soviet/Russian Strategic Nuclear Forces, 1945–2000" in *The Military History of the Soviet Union*, ed. Robin Hingham and Frederick W. Kagen (New York: Palgrave, 2002), 201.

14. President's Secretary's Files [hereafter PSF]: NSC Meetings 71–79, Box 210 Folder: NSC Meeting #75, 12/14/50, Harry S. Truman Library [hereafter HSTL], Independence, Missouri. I thank Gregory Mitrovich for providing me a copy of this document.

15. NSC 68, *FRUS 1950* 1:237–292.

16. David T. Fautua, "The Long Pull Army: NSC 68, the Korean War, and the Creation of the Cold War U.S. Army," *The Journal of Military History* 61 (1997): 93–120.

17. As noted in chapter one, many diplomatic historians believe that the term "unilateralism" better describes the conduct of U.S. foreign policy than the term "isolationism."

18. NSC 82, PSF: Subject Files, Box 193 Folder: NSC Memo Approvals #359, 9/11/50, HSTL. I thank Gregory Mitrovich for providing me a copy of this document.

19. See "Report to the National Security Council by the Secretary of State," July 3, 1950, *FRUS 1950* 4:691–696.
20. Marc Trachtenberg and Christopher Gehrz, "America, Europe and German Rearmament, August–September 1950," *Journal of European Integration History* 6 (2000): 9–35; and Christopher Gehrz, "Dean Acheson, the JCS and the 'Single Package': American Policy on German Rearmament, 1950," *Diplomacy & Statecraft* 12 (2001): 135–160. Truman approved NSC 82 on September 11, 1950.
21. Gehrz, "Dean Acheson, the JCS and the 'Single Package,' " 146.
22. Trachtenberg and Gehrz, "America, Europe and German Rearmament," 16–17.
23. Gehrz, "Dean Acheson, the JCS and the 'Single Package,' " 146.
24. Irwin M. Wall, *The United States and the Making of Postwar France, 1945–1954* (New York: Cambridge University Press, 1990), 198; Frank A. Ninkovich, *Germany and the United States: The Transformation of the German Question Since 1945*, updated ed. (New York: Twayne Publishers, 1995), 79; David Clay Large, *Germans to the Front: West German Rearmament in the Adenauer Era* (Chapel Hill: University of North Carolina Press, 1996), 85; Robert Gildea, *France Since 1945* (New York: Oxford University Press, 1996), 13; and William I. Hitchcock, *France Restored: Cold War Diplomacy and the Quest for Leadership in Europe, 1944–1954* (Chapel Hill: University of North Carolina Press, 1998), 140.
25. "United States Delegation Minutes, First Meeting of the Foreign Ministers, New York, Waldorf Astoria, September 12, 1950, 3 P.M.," *FRUS 1950* 3: 1191–1197.
26. "United States Minutes, Private Meeting of the Foreign Ministers, New York, Waldorf Astoria, September 12, 1950," *FRUS 1950* 3:1198–1201.
27. "Statement Made by M. Schuman Before the North Atlantic Council on September 16, 1950," C5-VR/3, NATO Archives, Brussels, Belgium.
28. The SFIO had been primarily responsible for bringing down the two previous governments, the latter after only forty-eight hours. Parliament therefore expected the Socialists to take up the task of building a new cabinet. They finally persuaded Pleven to seek investiture, and threw their votes behind him. See Owen Taylor, *The Fourth Republic of France: Constitution and Political Parties* (New York: Royal Institute of International Affairs, 1951), 205–206.
29. *L'Année Politique* 1950 (Editions du Grand Siècle, 1951), 152, 386. For more on Jules Moch, see Eric Mechoulan, *Jules Moch: Un Socialiste Dérangeant* (Bruxelles: Bruylant, 1999), the first scholarly biography based on the private archives of the Moch family.
30. "The Secretary of State to the President," September 20, 1950, *FRUS 1950* 3:335–337.
31. Quoted in Georgette Elgey, *La République des Illusions(1945–1951) ou la vie secrète de la IVe République* (Paris: Libraire Arthème Fayard, 1993), 570.
32. September 23, 1950, Sir William Elliot papers, Elliot 1/4/1, LHCMA.

33. "Resolution on the Defence of Western Europe," C5-D/11 (FINAL), NATO Archives; and *FRUS 1950* 3:348–358. Mark Sheetz disputes this point. He argues that Schuman agreed to accept German defense contributions in principle because "for the French 'en principe' connotes a highly theoretical proposition with a low probability of realization, and because he was instructed not to accept them in practice." See Mark Sheetz, "France and the German Question," *Journal of Cold War Studies* 5 (2003): 37–45. Yet Britain's ambassador to France, Sir Oliver Harvey, reported that Roland de Margerie, the assistant political director at the Quai d'Orsay, thought that, in general, the results of the meeting in New York "had not been unsatisfactory." See Telegram, October 18, 1950, FO 371/85089, BNA. The NAC produced other decisions, including ending the state of war with Germany, declaring the Federal Republic to be the legitimate successor to the Third Reich, increasing the number of Allied forces on German soil, and committing the German unification. See Ronald Granieri, *The Ambivalent Alliance: Konrad Adenauer, the CDU/CSU, and the West, 1949–1966* (Providence, RI: Berghahn Books, 2003), 42.

34. According to a leading student of the Indochina War, the defeat at the French fort at Lang-Son was devastating. "The French had suffered their greatest colonial defeat since Montcalm had died at Quebec [in 1759]. They had lost 6,000 troops, 13 artillery pieces and 125 mortars, 450 trucks and three armored platoons, 940 machine guns, 1200 sub-machine guns and more than 8,000 rifles." See Bernard B. Fall, *Street Without Joy* (Mechanicsburg, PA: Stackpole Books, 1994), 32–33.

35. Jean Doise and Maurice Vaïsse, *Diplomatie et outil militaire (1871–1969)* (Paris: Imprimerie nationale, 1987), 402.

36. Pierre Guillen, "Les chefs militaires français, le réarmement de l'Allemagne et la CED (1950–1954)," *Revue d'histoire de la deuxième guerre mondiale et des conflits contemporains* 33 (1983): 3–33.

37. Letter of October 14, 1950 quoted in Jean Monnet, *Memoirs*, trans. Richard Mayne (New York: Doubleday & Company, 1978), 345.

38. Ibid., 406.

39. Monnet feared that French resistance to German rearmament would not only prove futile but would also do irreparable harm to the ECSC. See ibid., 345–346. See also Thomas A. Schwartz, *America's Germany: John J. McCloy and the Federal Republic of Germany* (Cambridge, MA: Harvard University Press, 1991), 186–197. See also Philippe Vial, "Jean Monnet, un père pour la CED?" in René Girault and Gérard Bossuat, *Europe brisée, Europe retrouvé: Nouvelles réflexions sur l'unité de l'Europe au XXe siècle* (Paris: Publications de la Sorbonne, 1994); and Renata Dwan, "Jean Monnet and the European Defense Community, 1950–54," *Cold War History* 1 (2000): 141–160.

40. *L'Année Politique 1950*, 222–224.

41. Quoted in Guillen, "Les chefs militaires français," 4, 6.

42. Guillen, "Les chefs militaires français," 8–9; and Elgey, *La République des contradictions*, 238.

43. "Entretien Entre Monsieur van Zeeland et Monsieur Schuman, le 26 octobre 1950," Service Public Fédéral des Affaires Etrangères et du Commerce Extérieur et Coopération au Développment [hereafter SPFAE], CED, 15.397.

44. Note, December 5, 1950, Archives du Ministère des Affaires Etrangères [hereafter AMAE], Cabinet du Ministre, Cabinet du Robert Schuman (1948–1953), vol. 148; and Note, December 14, 1950, ibid.

45. "Mr. Bevin to Sir O. Franks," October 28, 1950, *DBPO*, Series II, Volume III, German Rearmament, September–December 1950 (London: Her Majesty's Stationery Office, 1989), 230–232.

46. November 1, 1950, SPFAE, CED, 15.397.

47. "Minutes of the Fourth Meeting, First, Second, and Third Sessions Held on 28–31 October 1950," Record-DC-004, NATO Archives. See also November 1, 1950, SPFAE, CED, 15.397.

48. Quoted in Philippe Vial, "Limites et contradictions d'une méthode: Monnet et les débuts de la construction communautaire (1950–1954)," in *Cinquante ans après la declaration Schuman, histoire de la construction européenne*, ed. Laurent Catala (Nantes: Presses académiques de l'Ouest, 2001), 63. See also Vial, "Jean Monnet, un père pour la CED?" 210–220.

49. See Philippe Vial, "De la surenchère atlantiste à l'option européenne: Monnet et les problèmes du réarmement occidental durant l'été 1950," in *Jean Monnet: L'Europe et les Chemins de la Paix*, ed. Gerard Bossuat and Andreas Wilkens (Paris: Publications de la Sorbonne, 1999), 307–342. See also Vial, "Jean Monnet, un père pour la CED?"

50. "The Secretary of State to Certain Diplomatic Offices," July 22, 1950, *FRUS 1950* 3:138–141.

51. France would then be spending 10 percent of its national income for defense. It already had 695,000 men under arms, the cream of which were fighting in Indochina.

52. "Memorandum du Gouvernement Français au Governement des Etats-Unis, August 5, 1950, AMI 4/2/4; and "Memorandum du 15 août 1950," AMI 4/2/8, Fondation Jean Monnet pour l'Europe, Lausanne, Switzerland [hereafter FJME]. See also "Projet de memorandum," August 16, 1950, Service Historique de l'Armée de l'Air, E 1565, Paris, France.

53. "The Ambassador in France to the Secretary of State," August 17, 1950, *FRUS 1950* 3:220–224; "The Secretary of State to the Embassy in France," August 15, 1950, *FRUS 1950* 3:1382–1383; "The Ambassador in France to the Secretary of State," September 1, 1950, *FRUS 1950* 3:1383–1387; and Wall, *The United States and the Making of Postwar France*, 195–196.

54. Vial, "De la surenchère atlantiste à l'option européenne," 331–342.

55. See Department of State, *Bulletin* [hereafter *DOSB*] 23, no. 593 (November 13, 1950): 777; "The Secretary of State to the Embassy in France," November 3, 1950, *FRUS 1950* 3:426–431. But see also "The Secretary of State to the Embassy in France," October 27, 1950, RG 59, RPPS 1947–1953, C&A

Files, Box 28, Europe 1950, NARA; and November 7, 1950, SPFAE, CED, 15.397.

56. Leffler, *A Preponderance of Power*, 410; Mitrovich, *Undermining the Kremlin*, 208, ns. 5–6; and Trachtenberg and Gehrz, "America, Europe and German Rearmament," 11.

57. By some estimates, the Soviet Union lost twenty-seven million people in the Second World War, a butcher's bill of staggering proportions.

58. See Marc Trachtenberg, *A Constructed Peace: The Making of the European Settlement, 1945–1963* (Princeton, NJ: Princeton University Press, 1999), 96–100. See also the Central Intelligence Agency's thinking on the probable Soviet reaction to a full-scale U.S. mobilization: "Memorandum for the National Security Council," December 11, 1950, PSF: Subject File, National Security Council, Box 191, Folder: Central Intelligence, HSTL.

59. According to the Policy Planning Staff, "In light of (a) the official declaration by the Soviet Union that it will not tolerate the rearming of Western Germany and (b) of the German reluctance to rearm, we should handle with the greatest care our efforts to organize and train our Western German and military units." "Memorandum Prepared by the Policy Planning Staff," December 9, 1950, *FRUS 1950* 1:462–466.

60. There was growing nationalist sentiment in the Federal Republic even before the NATO rearmament decision, which was of great concern to the U.S. High Commission in Germany, the Central Intelligence Agency, and other American governmental agencies. These sentiments can be attributed to Germany's increased self-confidence, its aversion to Allied occupation policies, and its anticipation of NATO's rearmament proposal. See Frank M. Buscher, "The U.S. High Commission and German Nationalism, 1949–52," *Central European History* 23, no. 1 (1990): 57–75. And as Henry Byroade, the State Department's Director of the Bureau of German Political Affairs, suggested to Acheson, "Even confronted with the Soviet menace as we are, we cannot ignore from the long range point of view the vital importance of obtaining the right kind of Germany." June 13, 1950, RG 59, PPPS, C & A Files, Germany 1950–1953, Box 16, National Archives and Records Administration [hereafter NARA]. Nonetheless, on July 28, the Allied High Commission approved the establishment of a 12,000-man police force. See Dennis L. Bark and David R. Gress, *A History of West Germany*, vol. 1, *From Shadow to Substance, 1945–1963*, 2nd ed. (Cambridge, MA: Blackwell Publishers, 1993), 278–279.

61. "Memorandum by the President to the Secretary of State," June 16, 1950, *FRUS 1950* 4:688–689.

62. See John Gillingham, *Coal, Steel, and the Rebirth of Europe, 1945–1955: The Germans and the French from Ruhr Conflict to Economic Community* (New York: Cambridge University Press, 1991); and Melvyn P. Leffler, "The Struggle for Germany and the Origins of the Cold War," German Historical Institute, Occasional Paper no. 16 (1996).

63. The CIA declared that "France is of greater strategic importance than any other continental country except the USSR . . . If France is lost, Europe is lost." See "The Current Situation in France," December 31, 1947, PSF: Intelligence Files, Box 254 Folder: O.R.E. 1947, HSTL. The CIA later proclaimed that "France is a key to the economic recovery and the military defense of Western Europe." See "Opposition to ECA in Participating Countries," February 10, 1949, PSF: Intelligence Files, Box 256 Folder: O.R.E. 1948, HSTL. The State Department concurred in this assessment, contending that, "France is the key continental country of the Western European defense system. Its geographical location makes it the strategic heart of the area; its manpower must provide the bulk of the immediately available ground forces." See "France," May 19, 1950, European Program Division, ECA, Box 27, Entry 353, National Archives II, College Park, MD. Paul Nitze, the head of the Policy Planning Staff, noted, "We do not have the possibility of saying to the French that we will take another course of action if they do not cooperate." See "Substance of Discussions of State-Joint Chiefs of Staff Meeting," November 7, 1951, RG 59, RPPS 1947–1953, Box 77, NARA. Dwight Eisenhower's secretary of state, John Foster Dulles, asserted that "French soil is essential to an effective continental defense system." See "The Secretary of State to Prime Minister Churchill," August 20, 1954, *FRUS 1952–1954* 5:1051–1052. See also "Review of Current World Situation and Ability of the Forces Being Maintained to Meet United States Commitments," January 15, 1951, *FRUS 1951* 1:62–75. Field-Marshall Lord Montgomery drew similar conclusions about France's strategic value. As he advised in 1948, "The main defensive effort in the West has got to be borne by the continental Nations of Western Union. . . . If we lost in the West, and the U.K. goes, we lose everything . . . France must be the hard core, militarily, of the Western Union." See "Memorandum by C.I.G.S." August 18, 1948, Ernest Bevin Papers, FO 800/453, BNA.

64. Ronald McGlothlen, *Controlling the Waves: Dean Acheson and U.S. Foreign Policy in Asia* (New York: W. W. Norton, 1993), 179–201; and Lloyd C. Gardner, *Approaching Vietnam: From Dienbienphu through Vietnam, 1941–1954* (New York: W. W. Norton, 1988), chap. 3. Truman also attempted to answer Republican critics who charged that his administration was soft on Communism in Asia. See Stueck, *The Korean War,* 41–42, 366. The CIA stressed the importance of French North Africa to U.S. strategic interests. See "The Current Situation in French North Africa," December 18, 1947, PSF: Intelligence Files, Box 254 Folder: O.R.E. 1947, HSTL.

65. Paul Porter, the U.S. special representative for economic affairs in Europe at Paris, wrote to William Draper, the U.S. permanent representative on the NAC and special representative in Europe at Paris, about the "need to create stable center governments in the six countries expected to comprise the European Defense Community." Memorandum, March 5, 1952, RG 59, RPPS, 1947–1953, C & A files, Box 29, NARA. When asked by President Truman what might happen if de Gaulle came to power, General Eisenhower re-

sponded that "he has so blatantly attacked NATO and American policy and position that, from the standpoint of effective cooperation, I don't know what would be the results of such a development." Letter, March 11, 1952," PSF: General File, 1945–1953, Box 113, Folder: North Atlantic Treaty [1 of 2], HSTL. The United States' displeasure with de Gaulle and his so-called "anti-Americanism" was a long-standing feature of Franco-American relations. America's disapproval of the French Communists goes without saying. See Deborah Kisatsky, "The United States, the French Right, and American Power in Europe," *The Historian* 65 (2003): 615–642.

66. Robert McGeehan, *The German Rearmament Question: American Diplomacy and European Defense After World War II* (Urbana: University of Illinois Press, 1971), 247–248; and Telegram, July 12, 1954, AMAE, Secrétariat Général, CED III, vol. 72. Renata Dwan argues that Monnet wanted the United States to pressure France. She also writes that in 1952, "US officials noted how the EDC was increasingly identified as a US, rather than a French, initiative and Washington feared that further pressure on Europe might actually backfire and damage the EDC's ratification chances." See Dwan, "Jean Monnet and the European Defense Community," 149, 153. It should also be remembered that article 10 of the NATO Treaty requires unanimous agreement.

67. During the early years of the Cold War, both Bidault and Schuman served several times as foreign minister. More importantly, they powerfully influenced the conduct of French foreign policy. See Jean-Claude Demory, *Georges Bidault, 1899–1983* (Paris: Editions Julliard, 1993); Jacques Dalloz, *Georges Bidault: Biographie Politique* (Paris: Editions l'Harmattan, 1992); and Raymond Poidevin, *Robert Schuman, homme d'état: 1886–1963* (Paris: Imprimerie Nationale, 1986).

68. The U.S. Congress would not have looked favorably on a French refusal of the American plan.

69. See Hans-Peter Schwarz, *Konrad Adenauer: A German Politician and Statesman in a Period of War, Revolution and Reconstruction*, vol. 1, *From the German Empire to the Federal Republic, 1876–1952*, trans. Louise Willmot (Providence, RI: Berghahn Books, 1995), 527. Britain would support Adenauer's request to raise a federal force by suggesting that he obtain the approval of the Federal Parliament to raise a force of up to 100,000 volunteers. See "Brief for the Secretary of State in New York. Germany: Defence Questions," September 6, 1950, FO 371/124933, BNA.

70. McAllister, *No Exit*, 178–181; and Large, *Germans to the Front*, 90.

71. Telegram, [mid-] October 1950, AMAE, Europe 1949–1955, Allemagne, vol. 70. Structural reasons concentrated great power in Adenauer's hands in the realm of foreign policy because the Allied High Commission (AHC) refused to allow the Federal Republic to establish a foreign ministry until March 1951. Adenauer then folded the foreign ministry into the chancellorship, giving himself the portfolio of foreign minister in addition to that of chancellor. Not stopping there, Adenauer made the nascent German defense

ministry a department in the chancellor's office. When added to his position as special envoy to the AHC, Adenauer thus held unprecedented power for a leader of a democracy. See William Glenn Gray, *Germany's Cold War Campaign to Isolate East Germany, 1949–1969* (Chapel Hill: University of North Carolina Press, 2003), 16; and Charles Wighton, *Adenauer: A Critical Biography* (New York: Coward-McCann, 1964), 140–141. According to the most detailed biography of Adenauer, "In most of the fundamental issues of foreign policy," Adenauer relied "predominantly on Blankenhorn," so his remarks most likely represented the chancellor's views. See Schwarz, *Konrad Adenauer,* 470.

72. Telegram, 15 October 1950, AMAE, Europe 1949–1955, Allemagne, vol. 70.

73. Gordon Drummond, *The German Social Democrats in Opposition, 1949–1960: The Case Against Rearmament* (Norman: University of Oklahoma Press, 1982), 49–50, 54; Schwarz, *Konrad Adenauer,* 555–556; Large, *Germans to the Front,* 103; and Granieri, *The Ambivalent Alliance,* 42–43.

74. Trachtenberg, *A Constructed Peace,* 110–111. The British also began to drag their feet. See Spencer Mawby, *Containing Germany: Britain and the Arming of the Federal Republic* (New York: St. Martin's, 1999).

75. Adenauer quoted in Granieri, *The Ambivalent Alliance,* 9.

76. Ibid.

77. Ibid., 6–7.

78. Ibid., 20.

79. This proposal had been preceded by East bloc demands, the so-called Prague Communiqué, on October 21, which was in response to the New York communiqué of September. For the text of the November 3 Soviet note, see "The Ambassador in the Soviet Union to the Secretary of State," November 4, 1950, *FRUS 1950* 4:902–903.

80. "Memorandum for the Record of State-Joint Chiefs of Staff Meeting," March 15, 1951, RG 59, RPPS 1947–1953, Box 77, NARA.

81. Ely and Stehlin quoted in Guillen, "Les chefs militaires français."

82. "Note," November 4, 1950, AMAE, Cabinet du Ministre, Cabinet du Robert Schuman (1948–1953), 148–149.

83. Procés-Verbal de la séance du Comité de Défense Nationale, December 16, 1950, Vincent Auriol Papers, Archives nationales 552 AP 44, 4AU 5/Dr 1.

84. Schwartz, *America's Germany,* 150.

85. *FRUS 1950* 3:582–609; and *L'Année Politique 1950,* 272–273.

86. *FRUS 1950* 3:566-subseq. For the text of MC 30, see "Report by the North Atlantic Military Committee," December 12, 1950, *FRUS 1950* 3:538–547. See also *DBPO*, Ser. 2, Vol. II, Nos. 106, 115–116, 130, 136; and Jacques Bariety, "La décision de réarmer l'Allemagne, l'échec de la Communauté Européenne de Défense et les accords de Paris du 23 octobre 1954 vus du côté français," *Revue belge de Philologie et d'Histoire* 71 (1993): 358.

3. Washington Pulls, London Follows, Paris Accepts, Bonn Hesitates

1. Moreover, many Germans opposed rearming their country. Even people in Adenauer's own party rejected this idea. One German deputy, Maria Dietz, declared that as a mother, she would "rather resign my seat in the Bundestag than move my little finger to help rearmament and burden my conscience." See Ronald Granieri, *The Ambivalent Alliance: Konrad Adenauer, The CDU/ CSU, and the West, 1949–1966* (Providence, RI: Berghahn Books, 2003), 39.

2. See "Annual Message to the Congress on the State of the Union," January 8, 1951, *Public Papers of the Presidents of the United States: Harry S. Truman 1951* [hereafter *PPPUS: HST 1951*] (Washington, DC: U.S. G.P.O., 1952), 6–13.

3. See Marc Trachtenberg, "A 'Wasting Asset,'" in *History and Strategy*, Marc Trachtenberg (Princeton, NJ: Princeton University Press), chap. 3.

4. "Review of Current World Situation and Ability of the Forces Being Maintained to Meet United States Commitments," January 15, 1951, *FRUS 1951* 1:62–75. Britain's military leadership reached similar conclusions years earlier. According to the Chiefs of the Imperial General Staff, "Without the military re-birth of France we cannot hold Western Europe. France must be the keystone. At present she is quite ineffective and torn by political dissension; she would collapse like a pack of cards if war broke out. We must instil a fighting spirit into her and give her the wherewithal to fight." See "Staff Conference to Be Held on 9th September, 1948. Oral Statement by C.I.G.S.," September 8, 1948, BLM 207/3.

5. Moch quoted in Charles S. Maier, "Finance and Defense: Implications of Military Integration 1950–1952," in *NATO: The Founding of the Atlantic Alliance and the Integration of Europe*, Francis H. Heller and John R. Gillingham, eds. (New York: St. Martin's, 1992), 343.

6. *L'Année Politique 1951*, 2, 4, 9; and Maier, "Finance and Defense" in Heller and Gillingham, *NATO*, 343. At a January 10 Anglo-American press association luncheon, Moch declared: "I have committed myself to have before the end of 1951 five divisions on ready alert in Germany and ready to be mobilized in three days." Quoted in *L'Année Politique 1951*, 4.

7. See Yoram Gorlizki and Oleg Khlevniuk, *Cold Peace: Stalin and the Soviet Ruling Circle, 1945–1953* (New York: Oxford University Press, 2004), 100–101.

8. For the text of the Soviet notes, see *DOSB* 24 (1951): 12; and ibid., 90–92.

9. Note, "Les Etats-Unis et le rétablissement de la souveraineté allemande," January 4, 1951, AMAE, Europe 1944–1960, Allemagne, 399. The next day, the French sent a note to the Soviet Union in reply to a Soviet note of December 15. See Royal Institute of International Affairs, *Chronology of International Events and Documents* 7 (18 December 1950 to 18 December 1951): 56–57.

10. Telegram, January 5, 1951, AMAE, Europe 1944–1960, CED, 67.

11. *L'Année Politique 1951*, 22; and AMAE, Europe 1944–1960, CED, 67.

12. "The United States High Commissioner in Germany to the Secretary of State," January 5, 1951, *FRUS 1951* 3:1317–1321.
13. Granieri, *The Ambivalent Alliance,* 45–46.
14. Ibid., 20, 30.
15. American documentation on these talks may be found in *FRUS 1951* 3:990–1047.
16. "The United States Deputy High Commissioner for Germany to the Secretary of State," January 10, 1951, *FRUS 1951* 3:990–991. Konrad Adenauer had expressed his concern over this very issue when he and Marshal Lord Montgomery had met on January 4. According to Montgomery, Adenauer had said that "there was a strong feeling in France . . . that it should be the aim of [that country], in conjunction with Russia, to keep Germany down. . . . As long as this attitude persisted it was difficult for Germans to understand that they must be prepared to fight alongside the Western Allies." Furthermore, Adenauer claimed that he had no idea "what was required of Germany, militarily, nor the present plans for the defense of the West. It was difficult for Germany to consider what contribution she should make until she had been told what was required, and what conditions on Germany rearmament were to be imposed." Quoted in *Monty: The Final Years of the Field Marshal, 1944–1976,* Nigel Hamilton (New York: McGraw-Hill, 1986), 772.
17. This refers to the Conference for the Organization of a European Defense Community, which would open in Paris on February 14.
18. "The United States Deputy High Commissioner for Germany to the Secretary of State," January 17, 1951, *FRUS 1951* 3:992–993.
19. Adenauer already outlined these conditions on January 14. See *FRUS 1951* 3:994, fn. 3.
20. "The United States Deputy High Commissioner for Germany to the Secretary of State," January 17, 1951, *FRUS 1951* 3:993–996.
21. "The United States Deputy High Commissioner for Germany to the Secretary of State," January 27, 1951, *FRUS 1951* 3:996–1001; and "The Secretary of State to the Office of the United States Deputy High Commissioner for Germany, at Frankfurt," February 1, 1951, *FRUS 1951* 3:1002–1003.
22. "The United States Deputy High Commissioner for Germany to the Secretary of State," February 2, 1951, *FRUS 1951* 3:1003–1005; and "The United States Deputy High Commissioner for Germany to the Secretary of State," February 3, 1951, *FRUS 1951* 3:1005–1008.
23. The NATO Council and Defense Committee met at Brussels on December 18, 1950, and the foreign ministers of France, the United Kingdom, and the United States met on December 19, 1950. For U.S. documentation on these meetings, see *FRUS 1950* 3:582–606.
24. "The United States High Commissioner for Germany to the Secretary of State," February 10, 1951, *FRUS 1951* 3:1013–1014.
25. "The United States Deputy High Commissioner for Germany to the Secretary of State," February 17, 1951, *FRUS 1951* 3:1016–1020.

26. Philippe Vial, "Les militaires français face aux constructions européennes de défense (été 1951–automne 1954)," mémoire de maîtrise, Université de Paris I, 1988, 11–19.

27. "Procés Verbal du séance du Comité de Défense Nationale," January 19, 1951, Vincent Auriol Papers, AN 552 AP 45, 4AU/Dr.2.

28. "The Ambassador in France to the Secretary of State," January 23, 1951, *FRUS 1951* 4:297–298.

29. *FRUS 1951* 4:304–348. Following Pleven's return from the United States, debate opened in the National Assembly on February 7. See *L'Année Politique 1951*, 50–51.

30. Quoted in Pierre Guillen, "Les chefs militaires français, le réarmement d'Allemange et la CED (1950–1954)," *Revue d'histoire de la duexième guerre mondiale et les conflits contemporains* 33 (1983): 10–11.

31. Ibid.

32. See Philippe Vial, "Limites et contradictions d'une méthode: Monnet et les débuts de la construction européenne," in *Cinquante ans après la declaration Schuman, histoire de la construction européenne*, ed. Michel Catala (Nantes: Ouest Editions, 2001), 27–28.

33. Ministère des Affaires Economiques et Financières [hereafter referred to as AMAEF]/B 48883. See also "The Ambassador in France to the Secretary of State," February 15, 1951, *FRUS 1951* 3:767–777.

34. Edward M. Fursdon, "The Role of the European Defense Community," in *NATO: The Founding of the Atlantic Alliance and the Integration of Europe*, ed. John R. Gillingham and Francis H. Heller (New York: St. Martin's, 1992), 225; and *L'Année Politique 1951*, 56–57.

35. See *FRUS 1951* 3:765ff; Fursdon, "The Role of the European Defense Community," 226; and Elgey, *La République des Contradictions*, 243–244. For the text of the official French summary of the memo, see *L'Année Politique 1951*, 625–626.

36. "Procés Verbal du séance du Comité de Défense Nationale," February 20, 1951, Vincent Auriol Papers, AN 552 AP 45, 4AU/Dr.3.

37. Ibid., March 17, 1951.

38. "Report by the Joint Intelligence Committee on Estimate of the Scale and Nature of the Immediate Communist Threat to Security of the United States. The Current Situation," JCS 1924/49, *Records of the Joint Chiefs of Staff 1946–1953, Strategic Issues* (Bethesda, MD: University Publications of America, 1980), part 2, reel 6.

39. "Supplementary Study on the January 15, 1951, Review of the Current World Situation and Ability of the Forces Being Maintained to Meet United States Commitments," April 13, 1951, *FRUS 1951* 1:76–82.

40. Jean Monnet, *Mémoires*, trans. Richard Mayne (Garden City, NY: Doubleday, 1978), 352–358; and Vial, "Limites et contradictions d'une méthode."

41. Irwin M. Wall, *The United States and the Making of Postwar France, 1945–1954* (New York: Cambridge University Press, 1990), 208.

42. For documentation on these meetings, see *FRUS 1950* 3:1396 ff.

43. "The Ambassador in France to the Secretary of State," April 18, 1951, *FRUS 1951* 4:383–387.
44. "The Secretary of State to the Embassy in France," April 30, 1951, *FRUS 1951* 4:387–388.
45. "Special Message to the Congress on the Mutual Security Program," May 24, 1951, *PPPUS: HST 1951,* 302–312.
46. See "Exposé de la délégation française sur la division européenne et le groupement de combat," March 8, 1951, Jean Monnet Papers, AMI 7/1/2 ter, FJME.
47. "Compte-Rendu de la Quatrième Séance Plénière tenue le 8 mars 1951, à 16 heures," Jean Monnet Papers, AMI 7/1/2, FJME; and "Exposé de la Délégation Allemande," Jean Monnet Papers, AMI 7/1/2 bis, FJME. See also "The Ambassador in France to the Secretary of State," March 9, 1951, *FRUS 1951* 3:774–778.
48. "The Allied High Commissioners for Germany to the Governments of the United States, the United Kingdom, and France," June 8, 1951, *FRUS 1951* 3:1044–1046. *Jean Monnet, Robert Schuman Correspondance, 1947–1953* (Lausanne: Foundation Jean Monnet Pour l'Europe, 1986), 112–114.
49. Raymond Poidevin, "La France devant le problème de la C.E.D.: incidences nationales et internationales été 1951 à été 1953," *Revue d'histoire de la deuxième guerre mondiale et des conflits contemporains* 33 (1983): 35–36; and *L'Année Politique 1951,* 171–172. On June 27, the French cabinet reacted forcefully to McCloy's statement; ibid., 35.
50. Jean Lacouture, *De Gaulle,* vol. 2, *The Ruler, 1946–1970* (New York: W. W. Norton, 1989), 148–149.
51. *L'Année Politique 1951,* 151–158, 200; Wall, *The United States and the Making of Postwar France,* 210–212; Jean Fauvet, "Birth and Death of a Treaty," in *France Defeats EDC,* ed. Daniel Lerner and Raymond Aron (New York: Praeger, 1957); Jacques Bariety, "La décision de réarmer l'Allemagne, l'échec de la Communauté Européenne de Défense et les accords de Paris du 23 octobre vus du côté français," *Revue belge de Philologie et d'Histoire* 71, no. 2 (1993): 358–359; Dorothy Pickles, *French Politics: The First Years of the Fourth Republic* (New York: Royal Institute of International Affairs, 1953), chap. 9; Philip M. Williams, *Crisis and Compromise: Politics in the Fourth Republic* (London: Longman, 1954); and Frank Giles, *The Locust Years: The Story of the Fourth French Republic, 1946–1958* (London: Secker and Warburg, 1991). For David Bruce's assessment of the elections, see "The Ambassador in France to the Secretary of State, June 18, 1951," *FRUS 1951* 4:393–397; and "The French Communist Party and the National Elections of June 17," State Department, Correspondence, 1951–1952, Box 42, folder 2, HSTL.
52. Vial, "Limites et contradictions d'une méthode," 27; and Pitman, "The Rise and Fall of the Europeanist Coalition, 1947–1952."
53. "Notes on a Meeting at the White House," January 31, 1951, *FRUS 1951* 3:449–458; and Edward M. Fursdon, *The European Defense Community: A History* (New York: St. Martin's, 1980), 117–118.

54. According to public opinion polls, Eisenhower was one of the most admired men in the United States. See Ernest May, "The American Commitment, 1945–1955," *Diplomatic History* 13 (1989): 452.

55. Louis Galambos, ed., *The Papers of Dwight David Eisenhower*, vol. 12: *NATO and the Campaign of 1952* (Baltimore and London: Johns Hopkins University Press, 1989), 460, fn. 4; Monnet, *Memoirs*, 358–360; May, "The American Commitment to Germany," 452; and Fursdon, *The European Defense Community*, 119. For NSC 115, see "Memorandum From the Secretary of State and the Acting Secretary of Defense to the President," *FRUS 1951* 3:849–852.

56. Charles Wighton, *Adenauer: A Critical Biograpy* (New York: Coward-Mc-Cann, 1964), 144.

57. Poidevin, "La France devant le problème de la C.E.D.," 36. At the insistence of Monnet, one spoke henceforth of a European Defense Community or EDC rather than a European army. See "Interim Report," July 24, 1951, *FRUS 1951* 3:843–846. The Spofford Plan called for national units of 5,000 to 6,000 men. "Rapport Intérimaire des Délégations aux Gouvernements participant à la Conférence," Paris, July 24, 1951 (Paris: Imprimerie nationale, 1951), 17–20. For German demands, see Wighton, *Adenauer*, 145–146.

58. "Interim Report," July 24, 1951, *FRUS 1951* 3:843–846.

59. "Rapport à Monsieur le Ministère des Affaires Étrangères sur les Négociations Relatives à l'Organisation d'une Communauté Européenne de Défense," August 14, 1951, René Mayer Papers, AN 363 AP 28.

60. Andrew J. Birtle, *Rearming the Phoenix: American Military Assistance to the Federal Republic of Germany* (New York: Garland, 1991), 93; "Memorandum of Conversation, by the United States Representative at the Four-Power Exploratory Talks," *FRUS 1951* 3:1146; "Copy of Message from Secretary Acheson to Foreign Minister Schuman, dated August 9, 1951," AMI 8/3/5, FJME; Letter from Schuman to Acheson, August 25, 1951, AMI 8/3/12, FJME; and Poidevin, "La France devant le problème de la C.E.D.," 38.

61. Birtle, *Rearming the Phoenix*, 95.

62. Secrétariat Général, August 23, 1951, AMAE, Vol. 62.

63. "Procès Verbal du Comité de la Défense Nationale," August 27, 1951, Vincent Auriol Papers, AN 552 AP 45, 4AU5/Dr.4.

64. Guillen, "Les chefs militaires français," 13.

65. Quoted in ibid.

66. Poidevin, "La France devant le problème de la C.E.D.," 44; and Weighton, *Adenauer*, 147. For the American minutes of the proceedings, see *FRUS 1951* 3:1228–1308.

67. The TCC was comprised of America's Averell Harriman, the director of the Mutual Security Agency and special assistant to the president; France's Jean Monnet; and Great Britain's Sir Edwin Plowden, chief planning officer and chairman of the British Economic Planning Board. Collectively, they were known as the "Three Wise Men."

68. "Memorandum for the Secretary of Defense," July 13, 1950, *FRUS 1950* 3:133–134.
69. Monnet, *Memoirs*, 363.
70. It is unclear to which London Conference Stehlim was referring. Perhaps he meant the Paris conference.
71. Note, "Problèmes financiers de la Conférence de Londres et de la Conférence de Paris," November 6, 1951, B 48883, Archives du Ministère des Affaires économiques et financières.
72. Poidevin, "La France devant le problème de la C.E.D.," 42.
73. Guillen, "Les chefs militaires français," 5, 11, 16–17.
74. Ibid., 5, 16.
75. "Organisation de l'Armée Européenne," November 15, 1951, Georges Bidault Papers, AP 156, AN 457.
76. Guillen, "Les chefs militaires français," 17.
77. Poidevin, "La France devant le problème de la C.E.D.," 42–43; and "Report by the Foreign Minister to the North Atlantic Council," November 27, 1951, *FRUS 1951* 3:938. See also "Verbatim Record of the Third Meeting of the Eighth Session of the North Atlantic Council Held at the Foro Italico, Rome, on Monday, 26th November 1951, at 3:30 P.M.," Eisenhower Papers, Principal Files, Box 197, North Atlantic Council Meeting, November 26, 1951, Dwight D. Eisenhower Library [hereafter DDEL].
78. *L'Année Politique 1951*, 327.
79. "Summary of the TCC Report," December 17, 1951, *FRUS 1951* 3:389–392; and Edwin Plowden, *An Industrialist in the Treasury: The Postwar Years* (London: Andre Deutch, 1989), 130–131.
80. "The Ambassador in France to the Secretary of State," December 17, 1951, *FRUS 1951* 4:455–459.
81. Georges Bidault Papers, AN 457 AP 156.
82. William C. Foster was the administrator for economic cooperation until September 1951, then the deputy secretary of defense.
83. "The Director of the Planning Staff of the Bureau of European Affairs to the Economic Cooperation Administration," December 26, 1951, *FRUS 1951* 4:474–479.
84. Gorlizki and Khlevniuk, *Cold Peace*, 99.
85. The Conservative Party returned to power in Great Britain in October 1951.
86. On December 6, Churchill spoke on the European army in the course of a debate on defense. See Parliamentary Debates (Hansard), House of Commons, Fifth Series, Columns 2594–2597; and AMAE, Europe 1944–1960, Généralités, CED, Vol. 67.
87. Roger Bullen and M. E. Pelly, eds., "Minute from Mr. Eden to Mr. Churchill," *DBPO*, Series II, Volume I: *The Schuman Plan, the Council of Europe and Western European Integration, 1950–1952* (London: HMSO, 1986), no. 417.
88. René Mayer papers, AN 363 AP 28; *FRUS 1951* 3:974–975; "Extract from a record of a meeting held in the Hotel Matignon, Paris on 17 December

1951 at 5:30 P.M.," *DBPO*, Series II, Volume 1, no. 418; and *L'Année Politique 1952*, 307–312. For evidence of legislative resistance, see Nathan Leites and Christian de la Malène, "Paris From EDC to WEU," RM-1668-RC, RAND Corporation, 1956.
89. Vial, "Les militaires français," 101.
90. Guillen, "Les chefs militaires français," 17.

4. Progress, Promises, and Problems

1. See Ronald Granieri, *The Ambivalent Alliance: Konrad Adenauer, The CDU/CSU, and the West, 1949–1966* (Providence, RI: Berghahn Books, 2003), 48–49.
2. See Marc Trachtenberg, *A Constructed Peace: The Making of the European Settlement, 1945–1963* (Princeton, NJ: Princeton University Press, 1999).
3. In an early February meeting of the CDU-CSU parliamentary bloc, Adenauer vigorously reaffirmed his government's requirements. According to a press service report, the chancellor declared in violent terms that he would not sign the General Convention or its annexes or the EDC Treaty as long as the Allies failed to consider German wishes relative to the Saar and its desire to enter NATO. See "Monsieur Muuls, Ambassadeur de Belgique à Monsieur P. van Zeeland, Ministre des Affaires Etrangères à Bruxelles," February 6, 1952, SPFAE, CED, 15.397. Among other reasons, Adenauer intended his February outburst to shore up his standing with the more nationalist members of his coalition.
4. Although France annexed the Saar after the First World War, a plebiscite forced it to return the region to Germany in 1935.
5. Signed on March 3, 1950, the Franco-Sarrois Convention granted France a fifty-year lease of the Saar mines. On May 5, the Federal Republic issued a note to the Allied High Commission protesting these conventions. For the text of the Franco-Sarrois Convention, see Denise Folliot, ed., *Documents on International Affairs* (London: Oxford University Press, 1955), 231–240. France eventually returned the Saar to Germany in 1957.
6. Charles Wighton, *Adenauer: A Critical Biography* (New York: Coward-McCann, 1964), 160.
7. Prof. Walter Hallstein, the Federal Republic's secretary of state for foreign affairs and a personal advisor to Adenauer, made similar public statements on January 2. For the text of the communiqué of the Six-Power Ministerial Conference, see *L'Année Politique 1952*, 475; or Folliot, *Documents*, 74. For U.S. documentation of the meetings, see *FRUS 1952–1954* 5:579ff. Hallstein's remarks were probably approved by the chancellor. Along with Herbert Blankenhorn, Hallstein assisted Adenauer in conducting German foreign policy. See Granieri, *The Ambivalent Alliance*, 32; and Mark Cioc, *Pax Atomica: The Nuclear Defense Debate in West Germany During the Adenauer Era* (New York: Columbia University Press, 1988), 16.
8. "Note Pour le Ministre," January 12/15, 1952, SPFAE, CED, 15.397.

9. Ibid.
10. Ibid.
11. AMAE, Europe 1944–1960, Allemagne, 370.
12. "The Ambassador in France to the Department of State," January 28, 1952, *FRUS 1952–1954* 5:595–596.
13. "Foreign Minister Schuman to the Secretary of State," January 29, 1952, *FRUS 1952–1954* 5:7–11. According to David Bruce, "Schuman's unfortunate [letter] was approved by [the] French Cabinet and thus represents an official statement." "The Ambassador in France to the Department of State," February 1, 1952, *FRUS 1952–1954* 5:12–13.
14. Quoted in Melvyn P. Leffler, *A Preponderance of Power: National Security, the Truman Administration, and the Cold War* (Stanford, CA: Stanford University Press, 1992), 455.
15. Georgette Elgey, *La République des Illusions (1945–1951) ou la vie secrète de la IVe République* (Paris: Librarie Arthème Fayard, 1965), 263; and *FRUS 1952–1954* 5:571ff.
16. Pierre Gerbet, *La construction de l'Europe* (Paris: Imprimèrie nationale, 1983), 157.
17. "Premierless Again," *Newsweek* 39 (January 21, 1952): 36. The Gaullists controlled 118 seats, the largest single voting bloc, the Communists 101, and the Socialists 106. For background on Mendès France's emergence as a critic of the Indochina War, see Jean Lacouture, *Pierre Mendès France,* trans. George Holoch (New York: Holmes & Meier Publishers, 1984), chap. 8.
18. Pierre Guillen, "Les chefs militaires français, le réarmement de l'Allemange et la CED (1950–1954)," *Revue d'histoire de la deuxieme guerre mondiale et des conflits contemporains* 33 (1983): 16–17.
19. "Interim Finance Bill Is Adopted in France," *New York Times,* January 1, 1952, 6.
20. Lansing Warren, "Military Costs Raise French Trade Deficit and Higher Prices Reduce Sales Abroad," *New York Times,* January 3, 1952, 54; Rene Dabernat, "Rearming Snarls French Recovery," *New York Times,* January 3, 1952, 57; and Jean Weiller, "Relations commerciales et financières de la France au course de la reprise des années 1952 à 1956," *Cahiers de l'Institut de Science Economique Appliquée,* Serie P9, no. 145 (January 1964): 12–13.
21. "Increased Outlay for Defense Pledged; Special Military Budget Is Established," *New York Times,* January 3, 1952, 57. Bidault quoted in the *Times* [London], January 1, 1952, 5.
22. "Another Cabinet Crisis," *Newsweek* 39 (January 14, 1952): 37; and "Premierless Again," *Newsweek* 39 (January 21, 1952): 36.
23. "Faure to the Fore," *Time* 59, no. 4 (January 28, 1952): 26.
24. "The Ambassador in France to the Department of State," January 25, 1952, *FRUS 1952–1954* 6:1140–1141.
25. Edward M. Fursdon, *The European Defense Community: A History* (New York: St. Martin's, 1980), 137–138; and Raymond Poidevin, "La France devant le problème de la C.E.D.: Incidences nationales et internationales (éte

1951 à été 1953)," *Revue d'histoire de la deuxième guerre mondiale et des conflits comtemporains* 33 (1983): 45.

26. William I. Hitchcock, *France Restored: Cold War Diplomacy and the Quest for Leadership in Europe, 1944–1954* (Chapel Hill: University of North Carolina Press, 1998), 163.

27. Guillen, "Les chefs militaires français," 18.

28. Ibid., 16–17.

29. "Proces-Verbal Du Comité de Défense Nationale du 9 Février 1952," Vincent Auriol Papers, AN 552 AP 46, 4AU6/Dr. 1, February–April 1952.

30. "In Fear and Hatred," *Time* 59 (February 25, 1952): 32.

31. *L'Année Politique 1952*, 489–90; "The Chargé in France to the Department of State," February 17, 1952, *FRUS 1952–1954* 5:615–616; Pierre Gerbet, *Le Relèvement, 1944–1949* (Paris: Imprimerie nationale, 1991), 158–159; *Journal Officiel*, Débats, February 17, 1952, 726; and Georgette Elgey, *La République des Contradictions (1951–1954)* (Paris: Fayard, 1968), 267–272.

32. For the official summary of the TCC's report to the North Atlantic Council, see Department of State, *Bulletin* 26 (March 10, 1952): 368–370.

33. Fursdon, *The European Defense Community*, 141; Leffler, *A Preponderance of Power*, 455–456; "Substantial Achievement," *Time* 59 (March 3, 1952): 23; *Executive Sessions of the Senate Foreign Relations Committee*, "Editor's Note," Vol. 4, Eighty-Second Congress, Second Session, 1952 (Washington, DC: USGPO, 1976), 141; and Poidevin, "La France devant le problème de la C.E.D.," 45. For the text of the Tripartite Communiqué, see Department of State, *Bulletin* 26, No. 663 (March 13, 1952): 325. For the text of the Quadripartite Communiqué, see Department of State, *Bulletin* 26 (March 17, 1952): 423. For the text of the TCC Report on Germany, see Department of State, *Bulletin* 26 (March 13, 1952): 325.

34. Leffler, *A Preponderance of Power*, 455–456; "Serious Joke," *Time* 59 (February 25, 1952): 29; "Background Paper Prepared in the Department of State," February 6, 1952, *FRUS 1952–1954* 5:203–206; "Report of the Secretary of State on the London and Lisbon Conference," *ESSFRC*, March 3, 1952, 163–188; and Department of State, *Bulletin* 26 (March 17, 1952): 423–426. On February 4, Germany gave reasons why it could not contribute more. See "The Ambassador in France to the Department of State," February 12, 1952, *FRUS 1952–1954* 5:32–33.

35. See *FRUS 1952–1954* 5:7–28.

36. Department of State, *Bulletin* 26 (March 10, 1952): 368–370.

37. The fourteen NATO members also agreed to let the organization review and critique their annual defense budgets, issuing a communiqué and declaration of aims on February 25. See Department of State, *Bulletin* 26 (March 10, 1952): 367–368.

38. *FRUS 1952–1954* 5:107ff.; Robert Wampler, "Conventional Goals and Nuclear Promises," in *Eisenhower: A Centenary Assessment*, ed. Stephen E. Ambrose and Gunter Bischoff (Baton Rouge: Louisiana State University

Press, 1995), 356–358, 363–367; and Irwin M. Wall, *The United States and the Making of Postwar France, 1945–1954* (New York: Cambridge University Press, 1991), 225–227. The figures for Allied defense expenditures are taken from Saki Dockrill, "Cooperation and Suspicion," *Diplomacy and Statecraft 5* (March 1994): 148. Dean Acheson, *Present at the Creation: My Years in the State Department* (New York: W. W. Norton, 1987), 615–627.

39. See Paul M. Pitman, "The Rise and Fall of the Europeanist Coalition, 1947–1952," unpublished paper delivered at the April 2002 meeting of the Society for French Historical Studies, Toronto, Canada, April 15–16, 2002.

40. In 1951, 31 percent of French governmental expenditures went to defense, one third of that earmarked for Indochina. See Dockrill, "Cooperation and Suspicion," 148. See also René Massigli, *Une comédie des erreurs: Souvenirs et réflexions sur une Étape de la construction européene, 1943–1956* (Paris: Plon, 1978), 312; Pierre Mélandri, *Les Etats-Unis face à l'unification de l'Europe* (Paris: A Pedone, 1980), 89–90; Elgey, *La République des Illusions*, 276–277; Vial, "Les chefs militaires Français," 101; *L'Année Politique 1952*, 20; and "The Fall of No. 13," *Time 59* (March 10, 1952): 36. For France's 1952 performance in the dollar zone, see Weiller, "Relations commerciales et financières de la France," 15–17.

41. "Report of the Secretary of State on the London and Lisbon Conferences," *ESSFRC*, March 3, 1952, 163–188.

42. Jacques Dumaine to Edgar Faure, February 26, 1952, AMAE, Europe 1944–1960, Généralités, 66; "Paper Prepared by the Director of the Office of European Regional Affairs," September 10, 1954, *FRUS 1952–1954* 6:1166–1179; and Acheson, *Present at the Creation*, 623–625.

43. "Report of the Secretary of State on the London and Lisbon Conferences," *ESSFRC*, March 3, 1952, 163–188.

44. AMAE, Europe 1944–1960, Généralités, 66, 41–44; and "The United States Delegation to the Department of State," February 21, 1952, *FRUS 1952–1954* 5:120–123.

45. Philippe Vial, "Les militaires français face aux constructions européenes de défense (été 1951–automne 1954)," mémoire de maîtrise, université de Paris I, 1988, 103; Guillen, "Les chefs militaires français," 19; and Georges Bidault Papers 457 AP 156.

46. "Revolt Against the General," *Time 59* (March 17, 1952), 28.

47. Elgey, *La République des Contradictions*, 278; and Jacques Dalloz, *Georges Bidault: Biographie Politique* (Paris: L'Harmattan, 1992), 240.

48. Poidevin, "La France devant le problème de la C.E.D.," 43.

49. Quoted in Ruud van Dijk, "The 1952 Stalin Note Debate: Myth or Missed Opportunity for Unification?" Cold War International History Project, Working Paper 14 (May 1996).

50. For the text of the note, see Folliot, ed., *Documents on International Affairs,* 85–89; "The Soviet Ministry for Foreign Affairs to the Embassy of the United States," March 10, 1952, *FRUS 1952–1954* 7:169–172; and Department of State, *Bulletin* 26 (April 7, 1952): 531–532.

51. For the text of the U.S. note, see Denise Folliot, ed., *Documents on International Affairs, 1952* (New York: Oxford University Press, 1955), 89–91; and Department of State, *Bulletin* 26 (April 7, 1952): 530–531.
52. For the text of the Soviet note, see Department of State, *Bulletin* 26 (April 7, 1952): 819–820.
53. Guillen, "Les chefs militaires français," 18.
54. Ibid., 17.
55. Ibid., 18.
56. Telegram, March 12, 1952, AMAE, Secrétariat Général, CED I, vol. 64.
57. Anthony Eden, *Full Circle: The Memoirs of Anthony Eden* (London: Cassell & Company Ltd., 1960), 46–49; Saki Dockrill, *Britain's Policy for West German Rearmament, 1950–1955* (New York: Cambridge University Press, 1991), 98–99; and "Memorandum by the Secretary of State for Foreign Affairs," March 28, 1952, PREM 11/373, BNA.
58. Eden, *Full Circle,* 46–49; Poidevin, "La France devant le problème de la C.E.D.," 41; "Guarantee for Europe," *Time* 59 (28 April 1952): 29; "British Pledge On European Defence," *Times* [London], 16 April 1952, 6; Massigli, *Une comédie des erreurs,* 318; and *L'Année Politique 1952,* 328.
59. General ——, "Avant qu'il ne soit trop tard," *Le Monde,* March 14, 1952.
60. Vial, "Les militaires français," 103.
61. "Proces-Verbal Du Comité de Défense Nationale du 24 Avril 1952," Vincent Auriol Papers, 552 AP 46, 4AU6/Dr. 1, February–April 1952, AN.
62. Folliot, ed., *Documents on International Affairs, 1952,* 105–116; Leffler, *A Preponderance of Power,* 458–459; Poidevin, "La France devant le problème de la C.E.D.," 43; and *L'Année Politique 1952,* 521–522. For summaries of the Contractual Agreements released to the press, see Department of State, *Bulletin,* 26, no. 676 (June 9, 1952): 888–895. For the text of the Contractual Agreements, along with the text of the treaty establishing the European Defense Community, see 82nd Congress, 2nd Session, Executive Q and R, June 2, 1952.
63. *L'Année Politique 1952,* 336–337; AN 363 AP 28; and "The Ambassador in France to the Department of State," June 20, 1952, *FRUS 1952–1954.* For the joint U.S.-U.K. statement, see Folliot, ed., *Documents on International Affairs, 1952,* 169. Although the United States was not a party to the EDC treaty, it did sign the protocol and related conventions. The protocol to the North Atlantic Treaty affirmed that member states of the North Atlantic Treaty would consider an attack on the European territory of the EDC states or their forces in certain defined areas to be an attack on the signatories of the NAT, who would then respond accordingly, within the meaning of Article 5. The Administration submitted these documents to the Senate, which approved them on June 30. *L'Année Politique 1952,* 522; and "Strength for the West," *Time* 59 (June 9, 1952): 29. For the text of the treaty, see Folliot, ed., *Documents on International Affairs 1952,* 116–162. Acheson, Eden, Schuman, and Adenauer also signed a declaration expressing concern over the integrity of the EDC.

64. "Strength for the West," *Time* 59 (June 9, 1952): 29.
65. Indeed, Kurt Schumacher remarked, "Whoever signs the General Treaty ceases to be German." Quoted in Gordon Drummond, *The Social Democrats in Opposition, 1949–1960: The Case Against Rearmament* (Norman: University of Oklahoma Press, 1982), 69.
66. "Terms of the Peace," *Time* 59 (May 26, 1952): 31–32.
67. See Pitman, "The Rise and Fall of the Europeanist Coalition, 1947–1952."
68. Guillen, "Les chefs militaries français," 18.
69. Vial, "Les Militaires Français," 113; Guillen, "Les chefs militaires française," 18–19, 27–28; Fursdon, *The European Defense Community*, 198–199; and Letter of July 26, 1952, Alphonse Juin Papers, Service Historique de l'Armée de Terre [hereafter SHAT], Château de Vincennes, Paris, France. Larmmat defended himself in a letter to the ministers of defense and foreign affairs. See AMAE, Secrétariat Général, CED I, Vol. 63.
70. Philippe Vial, "Limites et contradictions d'une méthode: Monnet et les débuts de la construction communautaire (1950–1954)," in *Cinquante ans après la declaration Schuman, histoire de la construction européene*, ed. Michel Catala (Nantes: Ouest Editions, 2001), 28–29.
71. Poidevin, "La France devant le problème de la C.E.D.," 47–48.
72. Ibid., 46.
73. Ibid., 48.
74. Vial, "Les militaires français," 113.
75. Guillen, "Les chefs militaires français," 21–22.
76. Ibid., 22.
77. "Global Squawk," *Time* 60 (August 11, 1952): 27.
78. Vial, "Les militaires français," 117.
79. Guillen, "Les chefs militaires français," 24.
80. "Summary Minutes of the Chiefs of Mission Meeting," September 24–26, 1952, *FRUS 1952–54* 6:644–662.
81. Elgey, *La République des Contradictions*, 299–300.
82. "Turning Point?" *Time* 60 (October 27, 1952): 35–36, 38; and "Herriot Opposes Europe Army Pact, Putting It in Peril," *New York Times*, October 18, 1952, 1, 3.
83. "Lesson from a Piece of Cheese," *Time* 60 (September 15, 1952): 38, 40.
84. Wall, *The United States and the Making of Postwar France*, 229–30; and "Pride & Prejudice," *Time* 60 (October 20, 1952): 34. Pinay's financial troubles did not end there. He even asked Britain's treasury secretary, Robert A. Butler, for a loan of $55 million before Christmas and $83 million afterwards. See Butler's letter to Eden, December 17, 1952, Anthony Eden Papers, FO 800/789, BNA.
85. Quoted in "Flood, Fret & Tears," *Time* 60 (November 3, 1952): 38. Auriol vented his frustration to a visiting Anthony Eden about American behavior. Auriol recoiled at remarks made by Senator Tom Connelly, a Texas Democrat, mocking France and extolling the importance of Germany. Auriol also disparaged the term American "aid," saying that properly speaking it was

America's contribution to the common defense. See "Conversation in Paris Between the Secretary of State and President Auriol," 16 December, 1952, Anthony Eden Papers, FO 800/789, BNA.

86. SHAT, Alphonse Juin Papers, Dossier 1: Politique militaire nationale, 1952–1953, Sous dossier 1: 1952.

87. "Disappointing Performance," *Time* 60 (December 8, 1952): 28–29.

5. New Faces, Similar Policies

1. See Marc Trachtenberg, *A Constructed Peace: The Making of the European Settlement, 1945–1963* (Princeton, NJ: Princeton University Press, 1999), 162, 185–188, 190. Eisenhower had other reasons for wanting to reign in military spending. He worried that maintaining a large military industry during peacetime would subvert American democracy. See his farewell address in *Public Papers of the Presidents of the United States: Dwight D. Eisenhower 1960–1961* [hereafter *PPPUS: DDE*] (Washington, DC: U.S. G.P.O., 1961), 1035–1040.

2. See Gregory Mitrovich, *Undermining the Kremlin: America's Strategy to Subvert the Soviet Bloc, 1947–1956* (Ithaca, NY: Cornell University Press, 2000); Robert R. Bowie and Richard H. Immerman, *Waging Peace: How Eisenhower Shaped an Enduring Cold War Strategy* (New York: Oxford University Press, 2000), 74–77; Aaron L. Friedberg, *In the Shadow of the Garrison State* (Princeton, NJ: Princeton University Press, 2000), 127–133; and James J. Carafano, "Mobilizing Europe's Stateless: America's Plan for a Cold War Army," *Journal of Cold War Studies* 1 (1999): 61–85.

3. See the message that James Bonebright, Jr., the deputy assistant secretary of state for European affairs, sent to U.S. secretary of state John Foster Dulles, March 4, 1953, "British Association with the EDC and the Extension of the NAT commitments," RG 59, Records of the Office of European Regional Affairs [hereafter ROERA], 1946–1953, Files of J. Graham Parsons, Box 2, National Archives and Records Administration [hereafter NARA].

4. Personal contacts also whetted America's enthusiasm for the EDC. John Foster Dulles and Jean Monnet, the architect of the EDC, were longtime friends. This friendship offered Monnet greater access to the Eisenhower administration and thus a greater opportunity to influence U.S. foreign policy. Another Monnet ally, David Bruce, was named the U.S. Observer to the EDC and Representative to the ECSC. Bruce's deputy, William Tomlinson, was also close to Monnet. See Renata Dwan, "Jean Monnet and the European Defense Community," *Cold War History* 1, no. 3 (April 2001): 150.

5. Notwithstanding its efforts, one prominent scholar argues that America's influence on post-1945 France was simultaneously pervasive yet ineffective. See Irwin M. Wall, *The United States and the Making of Postwar France, 1945–1954* (New York: Cambridge University Press, 1993). See also Dwan, "Jean Monnet and the European Defense Community," 157.

6. For the text of the 1946 Constitution, see Maurice Duverger, *The French Political System,* trans. Barbara and Robert North (Chicago: The University of Chicago Press, 1958), 200–216.

7. "Reform of the French Constitution," *The Economist* (January 3, 1953): 28; and O. R. Taylor, *The Fourth Republic of France: Constitution and Political Parties* (London and New York: Alden & Blackwell Ltd., 1951), 33.

8. Phillip M. Williams, *Politics in Post-War France: Parties and the Constitution in the Fourth Republic* (New York: Longmans, Green and Co., 1954), 426. Article 17 states: "The deputies to the National Assembly have the right to initiate expenditure. However, no proposal entailing an increase in the expenditure forecast or additional expenditures may be submitted during the discussion of the budget or of anticipated or supplementary credits."

9. Phillip M. Williams, *Crisis and Compromise: Politics in the Fourth Republic* (Hamden, CT: Archon Books, 1964), 267–269.

10. According to one scholar of the French parliamentary system, procedure gave the legislature the upper hand, as the government could not even set the timetable, a task controlled by the legislature. Moreover, "Debates can be curtailed only with the agreement of the Assembly and 'organized' only if the Assembly so decides. The President has neither the Speaker's power to select amendments, nor his discretion in calling on speakers, nor his authority in calling to order a deputy who is being irrelevant. Deliberate time-wasting is, therefore, possible." Dorothy Pickles, *France: The Fourth Republic* (New York: Barnes & Noble, Inc., 1954), 49–50.

11. Duncan MacRae, Jr., *Parliament, Parties, and Society in France, 1946–1948* (New York: St. Martin's Press, 1967), 6–9.

12. Although in theory the president has the right to dissolve the Assembly under Article 51 of the Constitution, this authority is limited, as dissolution can take place only under certain highly unlikely scenarios. See Duverger, *The French Political System,* 54–55.

13. As Phillip Williams notes, "Up to 1953 financial questions were fatal to all the six governments turned out by the Assembly." Williams, *Crisis and Compromise,* 265.

14. Moreover, Eisenhower helped to construct this framework beginning in 1949 when he was acting chairman of the Joint Chiefs of Staff. See Robert Wampler, "Conventional Goals and Nuclear Promises: The Truman Administration and the Roots of the NATO New Look," in *NATO: The Founding of the Atlantic Alliance and the Integration of Europe,* ed. Francis H. Heller and John R. Gillingham (New York: Palgrave MacMillan, 1992), 162, 165–166; and Wampler, "Eisenhower, NATO, and Nuclear Weapons," in *Eisenhower: A Centenary Assessment,* ed. Günter Bischof and Stephen E. Ambrose (Baton Rouge: Louisiana State University Press, 1996), 165–166. The Eisenhower administration also inherited a $78.6 billion budget from its predecessor that limited its options.

15. "Report to the National Security Council by the Secretaries of State and Defense and the Director for Mutual Security," January 19, 1953, *FRUS 1952–1954* 2:209–222.
16. The U.S. government argued in 1952 that nuclear weapons would not change NATO's forward defense requirement of 175 divisions. America's European allies, however, struggling to continue their rearmament programs, called into question this logic by asserting that tactical nuclear weapons might reduce conventional manpower needs, and thus save money. Pressed by Britain, the U.S. Joint Chiefs of Staff told General Matthew Ridgway to undertake a study in 1952 designed to determine how atomic weapons would affect NATO conventional force requirements for 1956. Contrary to expectations, Ridgway's report called for even more forces. These opposite pressures—Ridgway's recommendation to increase forces and NATO's European members' desire to level off if not decrease defense spending—laid the groundwork for the "New Look" strategy as embodied in MC-48. See Wampler, "Conventional Goals," 354–355, 366–368. This policy is discussed below in the text in greater depth.
17. Wampler, "Conventional Goals," 168–169.
18. Wampler, "Eisenhower, NATO, and Nuclear Weapons," 169–170.
19. *L'Année Politique 1953*, 1.
20. Ibid., 471.
21. According to Mayer, "Negotiations should be undertaken in order to prepare, to complete, to make more precise or clear by additional protocols certain clauses of these diplomatic instruments, as well as to prepare a closer association of Great Britain with the Community. . . . These protocols should permit us to maintain the unity and integrity of our army and the French Union." Quoted in Jacques Dalloz, *Georges Bidault: Biographie Politique* (Paris: Editions l'Harmattan, 1992), 311.
22. Frank Giles, *The Locust Years: The Story of the French Fourth Republic, 1946–1958* (London: Secker and Warburg, 1991), 178–179; and Philippe Vial, "Limites et contradictions d'une méthode: Monnet et les débuts de la construction communitaire (1950–1954)," in *Cinquante ans après la Declaration Schuman, Histoire de la Construction Européenne*, ed. Michel Catala (Nantes, Ouest éditions, 2001), 29–30.
23. "The Ambassador in France to the Department of State," January 15, 1953, *FRUS 1952–1954* 5:702–704.
24. "The Secretary of State to the Embassy in France," January 24, 1953, *FRUS 1952–1954* 5: 706–708. Article 13 referred to the right to withdraw forces from the European army to use for strictly national purposes.
25. Department of State, *Bulletin* 28 (February 9, 1953): 212–216.
26. On January 7, however, General Matthew Ridgway attempted to assure General Clement Blanc that SHAPE was giving no thought to adopting a peripheral strategy. "Memorandum of Conversation," 13 January 1953, Alfred M. Gruenther Papers, NATO, Box 1. Secret Correspondence, DDEL.

27. Quoted in Saki Dockrill, *Britain's Policy for West German Rearmament, 1950–1955* (New York: Cambridge University Press, 1991), 117.
28. "Conversation Avec Sir Oliver Harvey," January 19, 1953, René Mayer Papers, AN 363 AP 22.
29. Dunn served as U.S. ambassador to France until March 1953.
30. More than likely, Adenauer was also attempting to help himself. Given that he faced election in September, the chancellor had to put the best face possible on a project that he had strongly supported.
31. "The Ambassador in France to the Department of State," January 10, 1953, *FRUS 1952–1954* 5:704–705.
32. See Edward M. Fursdon, *The European Defense Community: A History* (New York: St. Martin's, 1980), 207; and *L'Année Politique 1953*, 315.
33. Schumann was the secretary of state for foreign affairs (August 1951 to June 1954) and the chairman of the National Assembly's Foreign Affairs Committee.
34. "Compte rendu," January 29, 1953, René Mayer Papers, AN 363 AP 22; and Henri Bonnet Papers, AN 363, AP 22. See also Raymond Poidevin, "La France devant le problème de la C.E.D.: Incidences nationales et internationales (été 1951 à été 1953)," *Revue d'histoire de la deuxième guerre mondiale et des conflits contemporains* 33 (January 1983): 52.
35. Quoted in Dalloz, *Georges Bidault*, 311–312. The note was signed by Guy Le Roy de La Tournelle, the Quai d'Orsay's director of political and economic affairs; André Gros, the chief of the juridical service; François Seydoux de Claussonne, the director of the office of European affairs; Pierre de Luesse, the chief of the press service; and Jean-Marc Boegner, the director of pacts.
36. These were the "New Approach" studies begun by General Alfred M. Gruenther in late 1953. See Wampler, "Eisenhower, NATO, and Nuclear Weapons," 165.
37. For documentation on their January 31 to February 8 trip, see *FRUS 1952–1954* 5:1548ff.
38. "The United States Special Representative in Europe to the Department of State," January 26, 1953, *FRUS 1952–1954* 5:708–710.
39. "Memorandum of Discussion of State-Mutual Security Agency-JCS Meeting, Held at the Pentagon Building," January 28, 1953, *FRUS 1952–1954* 5:711–717.
40. Bidault informed Dulles that France would approve ratification of the EDC treaty provided certain issues of great concern to the French Parliament and public were resolved satisfactorily: (1) preservation of France's world position; (2) the integrity of the French Union; (3) the cohesion of the French military; (4) the danger of creating a German national army; (5) a stronger British association with the EDC to help offset West Germany's influence; (6) agreement on protocols interpreting the treaty; (7) uncertainty concerning a U.S. and U.K. presence in Europe; and (8) a settlement of the Saar dispute

with Germany. "The Ambassador in France to the Department of State," February 3, 1953, *FRUS 1952–1954* 5:1557–1560.

41. "Conversations franco-américaines du 2 Février 1953," René Mayer Papers, 363 AP 22, AN Conférences internationales, 1953, Sd 2: "Entretien franco-américaines du 2 février 1953"; and "The Ambassador in France to the Department of State," February 3, 1953, *FRUS 1952–1954* 5:1557–1560.

42. "The Chargé in the United Kingdom to the Department of State," February 4, 1953, *FRUS 1952–1954* 5:1560–561. Dulles informed Eisenhower that his talks in Paris were "useful." Both he and Stassen felt that Mayer and Pleven were determined to "push this to a successful conclusion." In brief, he wrote that success was not only "possible," but "even probable." "The Secretary of State to the President," February 3, 1953, *FRUS 1952–1954* 5:1564.

43. Erich Ollenhauer was the head of the SPD, Carlo Schmid was the vice president of the Bundestag, and Herbert Wehner was an important figure in the party who became its deputy chairman in 1958.

44. Gordon D. Drummond, *The Social Democrats in Opposition, 1949–1960: The Case Against Rearmament* (Norman: University of Oklahoma Press, 1982), 101; and "The Secretary of State to the Department of State," February 6, 1953, *FRUS 1952–1954* 5:1568–1569.

45. "The Secretary of State to the Department of State," February 6, 1953, *FRUS 1952–1954* 5:1569–1571; and "The Secretary of State to the President," February 6, 1953, *FRUS 1952–1954* 5:1571–1572.

46. "Notes of the Secretary's Staff Meeting," February 10, 1953, *FRUS 1952–1954* 5:1578–1579; and "Memorandum of Discussion at the 131st Meeting of the National Security Council on Wednesday, February 11, 1953," February 12, 1953, *FRUS 1952–1954* 5:1579–1581.

47. For an English translation of the French memorandum, see PREM, 11/373, "French Memorandum Communicated by M. Bidault dated 12th February, 1953," PREM, 11/373, BNA.

48. René Mayer Papers, 363 AP22, AN. See also Dockrill, *Britain's Policy for West German Rearmament, 1950–1955*, 116–117; *FRUS 1952–1954* 5:730–732; and PREM 11/372. OR C.C. (53) 14th Conclusions, Minute 4, BNA.

49. Pierre Guillen, "Les chefs militaires français," *Revue d'histoire de la deuxième guerre mondiale et des conflits contemporains* 33 (January 1983): 22.

50. "Telegram," March 2, 1953, PREM 11/373, BNA; and "Memorandum by the Secretary of State for Foreign Affairs," 23 March 1953, PREM 11/373, BNA.

51. See Philippe Vial, "La Quatrième et son maréchal: essai sur le comportement politique d'Alphonse Juin (1945–1956)," in Oliver Forcade, Eric Duhamel, and Philippe Vial, eds., *Militaires en République (1870–1962): Les officiers, le pouvoir et la vie publique en France* (Paris: Publications de la Sorbonne, 1999), 164.

52. Quoted in "23 Days to Paris," *Time* 61 (January 12, 1953): 24. For the text of the entire speech, see "Bordereau d'Envoi," January 6, 1953, René Mayer Papers 363 AP 23 "CED et affaires militaires," AN.

53. Quoted in Guillen, "Les chefs militaires français," 22–23.
54. French Ambassador to Rome Jacques Fouques du Parc warned of domestic opposition to the EDC Treaty. See "Télégramme à l'Arrivée," February 19, 1953, AMAE, Secrétariat Général, CED III, 68.
55. Trouble was brewing in Morocco and Tunisia.
56. "Compte rendu de la réunion restreinte du Comté de Direction tenue le 11 Février 1953, au Palais de Chaillot," AMAE, Secrétariat Général, CED III, 68.
57. For an English translation of the note submitted by France, see "The Ambassador in France to the Department of State," February 13, 1953, *FRUS 1952–1954* 5:721–722; 722–724, 725–726.
58. "The Ambassador in France to the Department of State," February 12, 1953, *FRUS 1952–1954* 5:719–721.
59. "Procés-Verbal, Séance du 24 février 1953," AMI 23/2/2, FJME.
60. "The United States Observer to the Interim Committee of the European Defense Community to the Department of State," February 27, 1953, *FRUS 1952–1954* 5:741–743; and "Télégramme à l'Arivée," February 26, 1953, AMAE, Secrétariat Général, CED III, 68. See also *L'Année Politique 1953,* 327; *DOSB* 30, no. (March 16, 1953); and Dockrill, *Britain's Policy for West German Rearmament, 1950–1955,* 115–116. See also "The Secretary of State to the Embassy in France," March 6, 1953, *FRUS 1952–1954* 5:755–756.
61. Yoram Gorziski and Oleg Khlevniuk, *Cold Peace: Stalin and the Soviet Ruling Circle, 1949–1953* (New York: Oxford University Press, 2004), 100.
62. Matthew Evangelista, "'Why Keep Such an Army?' Khrushchev's Troop Reductions," Cold War International History Project (CWIHP) working paper 19 (December 1997), 4, 33.
63. Sétif was located in the Department of Constantine, in North Africa.
64. Quoted in Fursdon, *The European Defense Community,* 211. See also Poidevin, "La France devant le problème de la C.E.D.," 54.
65. Jean Doisse and Maurice Vaïsse, *Diplomatie et outil militaire (1871–1969)* (Paris: Imprimerie nationale, 1987), 424.
66. The Interim Committee, which was created at the Paris Conference, was charged with implementing the EDC Treaty.
67. "Compte rendu de la réunion restreinte du Comté de Direction tenue le 9 mars 1953 à Rome," AMAE, Secrétariat Général, CED III, 68.
68. France had suggested initially that the NAC instruct SACEUR to act favorably on any request to withdraw troops, a proposal rejected by the others.
69. "Editorial Note," *FRUS 1952–1954* 5:775.
70. *L'Année Politique 1953,* 336–337, 603; Poidevin, "La France devant le problème de la C.E.D.," 55; Fursdon, *The European Defense Community,* 217; and Editorial Note, *FRUS 1952–1954,* 5:775.
71. Quoted in Guillen, "Les chefs militaires français," 23.
72. "Juin Urges Delay On European Army," *New York Times,* March 1953, 1; and "French Concessions," *Times* [London], March 28, 1953, 5.
73. Quoted in "Gaps in N.A.T.O. Defenses," *Times* [London], April 6, 1953, 5.

74. Poidevin, "La France devant le problème de la C.E.D.," 56; and Guillen, "Les chefs militaires français," 23–25. See also Europe 1944–1960, Généralités, AMAE, CED, 71.

75. Vincent Auriol Papers, 552 AP 46, 4AU6/Dr 4, CDN, mars-avril 1953, AN. Juin would pay a price for speaking out so openly. On August 18, 1953, Prime Minister Pleven reorganized France's armed forces in a way that took power and responsibility from Juin. He retained his position as vice president of the conseil supérieur des forces armies and as the permanent councilor of the government. See Vial, "La Quatrième et son maréchal," 166–167.

76. Letter, Juin to Mayer, April 21, 1953, SHAT, Fonds Juin, Dossier 4: CED 1952–1954.

77. Letter, Mayer to Juin, April 22, 1953, SHAT, Fonds Juin, Dossier 4: CED 1952–1954.

78. See *FRUS 1952–1954* 6:534ff.; "Memorandum of Discussion at the 131st Meeting of the National Security Council, Wednesday, February 11, 1953," *FRUS 1952–1954* 2:236, 264; and "Memorandum of Discussion at the 137th Meeting of the National Security Council on Wednesday, March 18, 1953," *FRUS 1952–1954* 1:592–595.

79. Quoted in Brian Duchin, " 'The Agonizing Reappraisal': Eisenhower, Dulles, and the European Defense Community," *Diplomatic History* 16, no. 2 (Spring 1992): 203–204.

80. "The President's News Conference of March 19, 1953," *PPPUS: DDE 1953*, no. 31; and "The President's News Conference of March 26, 1953," ibid., no. 37.

81. Duchin, " 'The Agonizing Reappraisal,' " 204–205. Humphrey firmly believed in balanced budgets, even if they required cutting defense spending.

82. Quoted in Duchin, " 'The Agonizing Reappraisal,' " 204.

83. "The Defense Budget, Fiscal Year 1954: Statement by the Secretary of Defense before the Armed Services Subcommittee of the Committee on Appropriations, House of Representatives," May 11, 1953, cited in *Documents on American Foreign Relations 1953*, ed. Peter V. Curl (New York: Harper & Brothers, 1954), 52–62.

84. AMAE, Europe 1944–1960, Allemagne, 370.

85. "Memorandum of Discussion at the 138th Meeting of the National Security Council," March 25, 1953, *FRUS 1952–1954* 6:1323–1325.

86. "The United States Observer to the Interim Committee of the European Defense Committee to the Department of State," March 24, 1953, *FRUS 1952–1954* 6:1319–1325.

87. Wall, *The United States and the Making of Postwar France*, 268.

88. René Mayer Papers, AN 363 AP 22; *FRUS 1952–1954* 13:429–464; Dockrill, *Britain's Policy for West German Rearmament, 1950–1955*, 119; and Wall, *The United States and the Making of Postwar France*, 267–268.

89. "Memorandum by John J. McCloy," March 15, 1953, *FRUS 1952–1954* 7:405–408.

90. "Memorandum by the Director of the Bureau of German Affairs to the Secretary of State," March 30, 1953, *FRUS 1952–1954* 8:416–419.
91. Thomas W. Maulucci, Jr., "Konrad Adenauer's April 1953 Visit to the United States," paper delivered at the Society for Historians of American Foreign Relations Conference, June 21–24, 1996, Boulder, CO; and Ronald Granieri, *The Ambivalent Alliance: Konrad Adenauer, the CDU/CSU, and the West, 1949–1966* (Providence, RI: Berghahn Books, 2003), 60–61.
92. Charles Wighton, *Adenauer: A Critical Biography* (New York: Coward-McCann, 1964), 181.

6. The Death of Stalin

1. Robert Service, *Stalin: A Political Biography* (Cambridge, MA: Harvard University Press, 2005), 571–580; John J. Yurechko, "The Day Stalin Died: American Plans for Exploiting the Soviet Succession Crisis of 1953," *The Journal of Strategic Studies* 3 (1980): 44–73; M. Steven Fish, "After Stalin's Death: The Anglo-American Debate Over a New Cold War," *Diplomatic History* 10, no 4 (fall 1986): 333–355; David Mayers, "After Stalin: The Ambassadors and America's Soviet Policy, 1953–1962," *Diplomacy and Statecraft* 5 (1994): 213–247; Simon Sebag Montifiore, *Stalin: The Court of the Red Tsar* (New York: Knopf, 2004), 614; Amy Knight, *Beria: Stalin's First Lieutenant* (Princeton, NJ: Princeton University Press, 1995), 176; and Yoram Gorlizki and Oleg Khlevniuk, *Cold Peace: Stalin and the Soviet Ruling Circle, 1945–1953* (New York: Oxford University Press, 2004), 3, 10–11, 17.
2. For an excerpt of Malenkov's March speech, see Denise Folliot, ed., *Documents on International Affairs 1953* [hereafter cited as *DIA*] (London: Oxford University Press, 1956), 11–13. Some observers argue that Malenkov sincerely wanted to relieve international tensions because he feared that a continued Cold War might end in disaster for everyone. They also believe that Beria, Malenkov's closest ally, supported him in this view. See Service, *Stalin*, 591; James Richter, "Reexamining Soviet Policy Towards Germany During the Beria Interregnum," Cold War International History Project (CWIHP) Working Paper No. 3 (June 1992), 5–6; and Knight, *Beria*, 182. Beria also moved to dismantle the gulag, a prison system that incarcerated over 2.5 million people for political "crimes." He insisted that many of them "do not represent a serious danger to society." Quoted in Gorlizki and Khlevniuk, *Cold Peace*, 131. Amy Knight argues that Khrushchev also wanted to institute a policy of political liberalization. See Knight, *Beria*, 184.
3. For the text of Eisenhower's "Chance for Peace" speech, see *PPPUS: DDE 1953* (Washington, D.C.: U.S. G.P.O., 1960), 179–188. For more on the Austrian question, see Günter Bischof, "Eisenhower, the Summit, and the Austrian Treaty, 1953–1955," in *Eisenhower: A Centenary Assessment*, ed. Günter Bischof and Stephen E. Ambrose (Baton Rouge: Louisiana State University Press, 1995), 136–161.

4. Gorlizki and Khlevniuk, *Cold Peace,* 167. Beria was arrested on June 26, 1953, nine days after the uprising in East Germany. Had this uprising not occurred, it would have made it more difficult for his rival, Nikita Khrushchev, to oust him. Ironically, Khrushchev himself later began a policy of liberation and de-Stalinization once he gained power. See Knight, *Beria,* 193–194. James Richter argues that the Soviet leadership did not recommend that East Germany abandon socialism; rather, the July 2 document indicated that Soviet policy aimed at the "recovery of the political situation in the GDR." He also writes that "The Soviet leadership agreed to adopt a more conciliatory tone toward the West in an effort to divide the Western alliance, to encourage the activity of Western 'progressive forces,' particularly the West German Social Democrats, and, consequently, to prevent German rearmament." See Richter, "Reexamining," 9–10.

5. Bischof, "Eisenhower, the Summit, and the Austrian Treaty, 1953–1955," 141, 145; and "The Ambassador in the United Kingdom to the Department of State," May 12, 1953, *FRUS 1952–1954* 6:985–986. CIA Director Allen Dulles told the NSC that the Soviet Union had been waging a "peace offensive" since Stalin's death in an effort to "divide the Western allies." See David G. Coleman, "Eisenhower and the Berlin Problem, 1953–1953," *Journal of Cold War Studies* 2 (2000): 3–34; quote at 14.

6. See Peter Boyle, ed., *The Churchill-Eisenhower Correspondence, 1953–1955* (Chapel Hill: University of North Carolina Press, 1990); and Saki Dockrill, *Britain's Policy for West German Rearmament, 1950–1955* (New York: Cambridge University Press, 1991), 124.

7. For the text of Churchill's remarks, see Parliamentary Debates (Hansard) (New York: Cambridge, 1991), Cols. 895–898.

8. French Foreign Minister Georges Bidault warned weeks before that the Soviet Union would launch a disingenuous "peace offensive." See "Record of a meeting held at the Quai d'Orsay on April 25, 1953," Selwyn Lloyd Papers, SELO 5/27, Churchill College, Cambridge University.

9. Thomas J. Maulucci, Jr., "Konrad Adenauer's April 1953 Visit to the United States," paper delivered at the Society for Historians of American Foreign Relations Conference, June 21–24, 1996; and "Chancellor Adenauer to President Eisenhower," May 29, 1953, *FRUS 1952–1954* 7:460–463. Any mention of Potsdam terrified Adenauer. He remarked that "Bismarck has spoken of his ever-present nightmare of a coalition against Germany. I too have a nightmare. My nightmare is called Potsdam. The danger [to Germany] of a collective policy by the Four Great Powers has existed since 1945 . . . and has continued to exist since the founding of the Federal Republic." Quoted in Charles Wighton, *Adenauer: A Critical Biography* (New York: Coward-McCann, 1964), 186.

10. Franz-Josef Strauss, the vice president of the CDU parliamentary group and a federal minister without portfolio, regretted the decision, contending that it would be exploited by Moscow. AMAE, Europe 1944–1960, 71.

11. Manfred Overesch, "The Alternative Prospect: The Plan of a Neutralized United Germany," in *Power in Europe?* II: *Great Britain, France, Germany, and Italy and the Origins of the EEC, 1952–1957,* ed. Ennio Di Nolfo (Berlin and New York: Walter de Gruyter, 1992), 93; and Dockrill, *Britain's Policy for West German Rearmament, 1950–1955,* 124.

12. *L'Année Politique 1953,* 480; and Raymond Poidevin, "La France devant le problème de la C.E.D.: Incidences nationales et internationales (été 1951 à été 1953)," *Revue d'histoire de la duexième guerre mondiale et des conflits contemporains* 33 (January 1983): 55–56.

13. France provided the United States with a full briefing on the session. See "The Ambassador in France to the Department of State," May 14, 1953, *FRUS 1952–1954* 5:844–845.

14. Office Universitaire de recherche socialiste [hereafter OURS] Archives Guy Mollet [hereafter AGM] 57: Dossier Allemagne; "Conventions Franco-Sarroises," *Notes et Études Documentaires,* 25 no. 1.756 (Juin 1953), 51 pp.; and Poidevin, "La France devant le problème de la C.E.D.," 55–56. For the text of the conventions, see *L'Année Politique 1953,* 611–622.

15. Folliot, *DIA 1953,* 222.

16. Quoted in Jean Lacouture, *Pierre Mendès France,* trans. George Holoch (New York: Holmes & Meier, 1984), 194.

17. Irwin M. Wall, *The United States and the Making of Postwar France, 1945–1954* (New York: Cambridge University Press, 1991), 271; and Lacouture, *Pierre Mendès France,* 199.

18. Joseph Laniel became prime minister on June 27.

19. Wall, *The United States and the Making of Postwar France,* 271.

20. Quoted in Pierre Mendès France, *Oeuvres complètes,* vol. 2: *Une Politique de l'Economie, 1943–1954* (Paris: Éditions Gallimard, 1985), 468–479.

21. "Record of the Sixth CINCUSAREUR-HICOG Commanders Conference, Heidelberg, June 29, 1953, 1:30 P.M.," *FRUS 1952–1954* 7:1602–1608.

22. Dockrill, *Britain's Policy for West German Rearmament, 1950–1955,* 127; and OURS/AGM 58.

23. Fish, "After Stalin's Death," 339; and Gordon D. Drummond, *The Social Democrats in Opposition, 1949–1960: The Case Against Rearmament* (Norman: University of Oklahoma Press, 1982), 105.

24. Coleman, "Eisenhower and the Berlin Problem," 12–13, 15.

25. "Memorandum of Discussion at the 150th Meeting of the National Security Council, Thursday, June 18, 1953," *FRUS 1952–1954* 7:1586–1590.

26. Edward M. Fursdon, *The European Defense Community: A History* (New York: St. Martin's Press, 1980), 220; and Frank Giles, *The Locust Years: The Story of the Fourth Republic, 1946–1983* (New York: Carroll & Graf, 1994), 183.

27. Due to the RPF's devastating defeat in May municipal elections, de Gaulle announced on May 6 that he was returning "liberty" to those deputies elected under his name in 1951. A group of RPF deputies formed subse-

quently a successor party, the Union des Républicains d'Action sociale (URAS).

28. Denise Artaud, "Indochina and the European Defense Community," in *Dien Bien Phu and the Crisis of Franco-American Relations, 1954–1955,* ed. Lawrence A. Kaplan, Denise Artaud, and Mark Rubin (Wilmington, DE: Scholarly Resources, 1990), 257.

29. These talks replaced the proposed Bermuda Heads of State conference that had been postponed due to Churchill's stroke. For U.S. documentation, see *FRUS 1952–1954* 5:1608–1696. See also "Communiqué of the Meetings of the Foreign Ministers of the United States, the United Kingdom, and France," July 14, 1953, *FRUS 1952–1954* 5:1703–1708.

30. Quoted in Dockrill, *Britain's Policy for West German Rearmament, 1950–1955,* 127–128.

31. Ibid., 128.

32. AMAE, Europe 1944–1960, Généralités, 72.

33. Brian R. Duchin, " 'The Agonizing Reappraisal': Eisenhower, Dulles, and the EDC," *Diplomatic History* 16 (1992): 208–209.

34. "Memorandum," July 21, 1953, *FRUS 1952–1954* 5:798–801.

35. NSC-160/1, August 17, 1953, *FRUS 1952–1954* 7:510–520; Hans-Jürgen Grabbe, "Konrad Adenauer, John Foster Dulles, and West German Relations," in Richard H. Immerman, ed., *John Foster Dulles and the Diplomacy of the Cold War* (Princeton, NJ: Princeton University Press, 1989) 115–116; and Rolf Steininger, "John Foster Dulles, the European Defense Community, and the German Question," in ibid., 84–85.

36. Quoted in Dockrill, *Britain's Policy for West German Rearmament, 1950–1955,* 129.

37. Duchin, " 'The Agonizing Reappraisal,' " 205.

38. See the remarks of James B. Connant, the U.S. HICOG, to Dulles, November 13, 1953, RG 59, RPPS, C & A Files, Germany, 1950–1953, Box 16, NARA. See also Dulles' reply to Connant, November 20, 1953, Alfred M. Gruenther Papers, NATO, Box 1, Top Secret Correspondence, DDEL.

39. "The Secretary of State to the Chancellor of the Federal Republic of Germany," November 20, 1953, *FRUS 1952–1954* 5:854–855; and James G. Hershberg, " 'Explosion in the Offing': German Rearmament and American Diplomacy, 1953–1955," *Diplomatic History* 16 (1992): 511–549.

40. Quoted in "Future of the Saar," *Times* [London] October 29, 1953, 7. See also Drummond, *The Social Democrats in Opposition,* 112.

41. "Paper Prepared in the Department of State," November 18, 1953, *FRUS 1952–1954* 5:841–851.

42. "Probable Short-Term Developments in French Policy," November 24, 1953, *FRUS 1952–1954* 6:1393–1396. NIEs are authoritative interdepartmental intelligence assessments of foreign policy problems. They reflect the collective views of the CIA, the Departments of State, the army, the air force, and the Joint Staff. Another response to France's disquiet was the U.S. campaign to allay French fears with regard to American-Soviet relations. The United

States continued what many U.S. officials believed a fruitless exchange of high-level diplomatic notes with the Soviet Union largely to assure France that every effort was being made to negotiate peacefully with Moscow. See also "The Secretary of State to the Embassy in the United Kingdom," October 13, 1953, *FRUS 1952–1954* 7:654–656.

43. "Etat-Major Particulier du Maréchal de France," November 17, 1953, SHAT, Fonds Juin, Dossier 4, CED, (1953).

44. Both men are quoted in "Tortured Mind," *Time* 42 (November 30, 1953): 28.

45. The NATO solution would entail overriding French objections and integrating the Federal Republic directly into NATO. The United States would reject this option. See "Meeting in the Secretary's Office 11:30–12:30, August 25, 1954," John Foster Dulles State Papers, box 64, Seeley Mudd Library, Princeton University. I thank Marc Trachtenberg for providing me a copy of this document.

46. *FRUS 1952–1954* 5:1774–1786; ibid., 1801–1803; ibid., 874; and *L'Année Politique 1953,* 445–448. None of the EDC countries had yet ratified the treaty.

47. Quoted in Fish, "After Stalin's Death," 352.

48. "Memorandum of Discussion at the 174th Meeting of the National Security Council," December 10, 1953, RG 59, RPPS 1947–1953, C&A Files, Box 29, Europe 1952–1953, NARA.

49. Quoted in Donald Cameron Watt, "Britain and German Security, 1944–1955," in Foreign and Commonwealth Office Historical Branch, Occasional Paper No. 3 (November 1989), 50.

50. Both Eisenhower and Dulles refused to consider alternatives to the EDC—at least publicly. According to Eisenhower, "any projected alternative to the EDC will present problems no less acute and difficult to solve." Quoted in Boyle, *The Churchill-Eisenhower Correspondence,* 115–118.

51. Gregory Mitrovich, *Undermining the Kremlin: America's Strategy to Subvert the Soviet Bloc, 1947–1956* (Ithaca, NY: Cornell University Press, 2000), 148; Robert R. Bowie and Richard H. Immerman, *Waging Peace: How Eisenhower Shaped an Enduring Cold War Stragtegy* (New York: Oxford University Press, 1998), 165, 249; Valur Ingimundarson, "The Eisenhower Administration, the Adenauer Government, and the Political Uses of the East German Uprising in 1953," *Diplomatic History* 20, no. 3 (summer 1996): 381–409; and László Borhi, "Rollback, Liberation, Containment, or Inaction? U.S. Policy and Eastern Europe in the 1950s," *Journal of Cold War Studies* 1, no. 3 (fall 1999): 67–110. See also NSC 174, "United States Policy Toward the Soviet Satellites in Eastern Europe," December 11, 1953, Declassified Documents Reference System. By the mid-1950s, the Soviet Union began producing intercontinental ballistic missiles despite doubts about their robustness in the face of modern air defenses. See Steven J. Zaloga, "Soviet/Russian Strategic Nuclear Forces, 1945–2000," in *The Military History of the Soviet Union,* ed. Robin Hingham and Frederick W. Kagen (New York: Palgrave, 2002), 202.

52. For documentation on the "New Look" as it related to U.S. military policy, see *FRUS 1952–1954,* vol. 2. For the role it would play in the context of NATO, see *FRUS 1952–1954* 5:482–570. In point of fact, the New Look was not altogether "new." Its roots can be found in the policies and decisions of the Truman administration. See Robert A. Wampler, "Conventional Goals and Nuclear Promises: The Truman Administration and the Roots of the NATO New Look," in Francis H. Heller and John Gillingham, eds., *NATO: The Founding of the Atlantic Alliance and the Integration of Europe* (New York: St. Martin's Press, 1997), chap. 16; Marc Trachtenberg, "The Nuclearization of NATO and U.S.-West European Relations," in Heller and Gillingham, *NATO,* chap. 19; and Bowie and Immerman, *Waging Peace,* chaps. 5–9.

53. See "Memorandum of Discussion at the 166th Meeting of the National Security Council, Tuesday 13 October 1953," *FRUS 1952–1954* 2:534–550; "Memorandum of Discussion at the 168th Meeting of the National Security Council, Tuesday October 29, 1953," *FRUS 1952–1954* 2:567–576; and NSC 162/2, October 30, 1953 *FRUS 1952–1954,* 2:577–597.

54. "Statement of the Secretary of State to the North Atlantic Council," December 14, 1953, *FRUS 1952–1954* 5:461–468.

55. At his December 16, 1953 press conference, Eisenhower was questioned as to whether he would ask Congress for a change in the law that would allow the United States to share nuclear weapons with its allies. Eisenhower replied that it "depends on the circumstances and what will meet the needs of the military situation . . . Now if that becomes necessary, why, I see no reason why you shouldn't do it to advance the interests of the United States." Quoted in *PPPUS: DDE 1953* (Washington, D.C.: U.S. G.P.O., 1960), 831–846.

56. NATO later adopted this thinking as MC 48. For a discussion of the great significance of MC 48, see Wampler, "Conventional Goals and Nuclear Promises"; Marc Trachtenberg, *A Constructed Peace: The Making of the European Settlement, 1945–1963* (Princeton, NJ: Princeton University Press, 1999); and Marc Trachtenberg, "The Nuclearization of NATO," in Marc Trachtenberg, *History and Strategy* (Princeton, NJ: Princeton University Press, 1991), 153–168. See also Dulles's letter to Eisenhower discussing a grand settlement of the cold war in Mitrovich, *Undermining the Kremlin,* 151. For the full text of MC 48, see Gregory W. Pedlow, ed., *NATO Strategy Documents, 1949–1969* (Belgium: SHAPE Historical Office, 1997), 321–331.

57. Dwan, "Jean Monnet and the European Defense Community," 153. See also Philippe Vial, "Limites et contradiction d'une méthode: Monnet et les débuts de la construction communautaire (1950–1954)," in *Cinquante ans après la declaration Schuman, histoire de la construction européenne,* ed. Michel Catala (Nantes: Ouest Editions, 2002), 45–101.

58. See Robert M. Wampler, "Conventional Goals and Nuclear Promises," 356; and Lawrence S. Kaplan, *The United States and NATO: The Enduring Alliance* (Boston: Twayne Publishers, 1988), 142–144.

59. This was not the only time U.S. officials took into account Soviet security needs. See "Proposed Talks With the Soviets" October 12, 1953, RG 59, RPPS, 1947–1953, C&A Files, Box 29, NARA; and Borhi, "Rollback, Liberation, Containment, or Inaction?," 68, 92–95.

60. Terminating the Occupation Statute, signed on November 29, 1949, between the Allied High Commission and Adenauer, would have restored sovereignty to the Federal Republic, in theory allowing it withdraw from NATO if it chose to do so.

61. Department of State, *Bulletin* 30 (4 January 1954): 3–7.

62. Quoted in *Le Monde*, December 15, 1953, 3; "Dulles Cautions Europe to Ratify Army Treaty Soon," *New York Times*, December 15, 1953, 1, 15; and "Report on the Ministerial Meeting of the North Atlantic Council, December 14–16, held at the Palais de Chaillot, Paris," December 23, 1953, *Documents on Canadian External Relations*.

63. See, for example, Duchin, "The 'Agonizing Reappraisal,' " 201–221. Evidence exists, however, that French officials encouraged Dulles to take this hard line. See Dwan, "Jean Monnet and the European Defence Community."

64. Cited in Pierre Guillen, "Les chefs militaires français, le réarmement d'Allemange et la CED, 1950–1954." *Revue d'histoire de la deuxième guerre mondiale et des conflits contemporains* 33 (January 1983): 6.

7. The End of the Affair

1. Letter, January 27, 1954, Alphonse Juin Papers, SHAT; and Bernard Pujo, *Juin, maréchal de France* (Paris: A. Michel, 1988), 302–304.

2. For an extract of Juin's speech in Auxerre, see Alphonse Juin Papers, Dossier 4, EDC (1954), SHAT. For the complete text, see *Le Figaro*, March 29, 1954. For a subsequent speech in Saumur, see *L'Année Politique 1954*, 19–20; and Georgette Elgey, *La République des contradictions, 1951–1954* (Paris: Fayard, 1968), 590.

3. Alphonse Juin Papers, March 30, 1954, Dossier 4, CED, (1954), SHAT; and Pujo, *Juin*, 304.

4. Pujo, *Juin*, 305–307. The French government was not the only body irritated by Juin's speech; at its April meeting, the NAC unanimously adopted a resolution condemning his statements, though it would vote to retain him in the position of Commander in Chief of Allied Forces in Central Europe. Letter of March 31, 1954, Alphonse Juin Papers, Dossier 4, EDC (1954), SHAT.

5. Pujo, *Juin*, 307–309; and *L'Année Politique 1954*, 19–23; 338–339.

6. *Réunions des ministres des Affaires étrangères des États-Unis, de France, de Grande-Bretagne et d'U.R.S.S., Berlin, 25 janvier-18 février 1954 (séances plénieres)*, (Paris: Imprimerie nationale, 1955); *L'Année Politique 1954*, 304–310, 314–330; *FRUS 1952–1954* 7:601ff.; *Documents Relating to the Meeting of Foreign Ministers of France, the United Kingdom, the Soviet Union and the United States of America*, Cmd 9080 (London: HMSO, 1954); Earl of Avon, *The Memoirs of the Rt Hon Sir Anthony Eden: Full Circle* (London:

Cassell, 1960); and Edward M. Fursdon, *The European Defense Community: A History* (New York: St. Martin's, 1980), 234–246.

7. Rolf Steininger, "John Foster Dulles, the European Defense Community, and the German Question," in *John Foster Dulles and the Diplomacy of the Cold War*, ed. Richard N. Immerman (Princeton, NJ: Princeton University Press, 1990), 838–836. The Western powers proposed that the meeting open January 4, but the Soviet Union suggested January 25 instead, an offer the West accepted on January 1. For the text of the January 1, 1954, U.S. note and the December 26, 1953, Soviet note, see Department of State, *Bulletin* 30 (January 11, 1954): 43–44.

8. For the text of the Eden memorandum, see Department of State, *Bulletin* 30 (February 8, 1954): 186–187. See also "The United States Delegation at the Berlin Conference to the Department of State," February 16, 1954, *FRUS 1952–1954* 7:1117–1112; and *Documents Diplomatiques Français, 1954,* Vol. 1 (21 juillet–31 décembre 1954) (Paris: Imprimerie nationale, 1987), 4.

9. Fursdon, *The European Defense Community*, 236–36. France was the one exception because it opposed Germany's entry into NATO.

10. Department of State, *Bulletin* 30 (February 8, 1954): 184–186.

11. Department of State, *Bulletin* 30 (February 15, 1954): 228–229; and Department of State, *Bulletin* 30 (February 22, 1954): 269–270. See also *DDF 1954,* 1, fn. 3; and Gordon Drummond, *The Social Democrats in Opposition, 1949–1960: The Case Against Rearmament* (Norman: University of Oklahoma Press, 1982), 115.

12. Quoted in Irwin M. Wall, *The United States and the Making of Postwar France* (New York: Cambridge University Press, 1990), 272–273. Dulles also made his feelings known to Bidault, telling him that France had to act or face the consequences of a shift in U.S. policy toward Europe. See Brian Duchin, "The 'Agonizing Reappraisal': Eisenhower, Dulles, and the European Defense Community," *Diplomatic History* 16 (1992): 213.

13. Quoted in Frank Costigliola, *France and the United States: The Cold Alliance Since World War II* (New York: Twayne Publishers, 1992), 91.

14. AMAE, Europe 1944–1960, Généralités, CED, 73, 119–120; and Drummond, *The Social Democrats in Opposition,* 116.

15. Fursdon, *The European Defense Community,* 243–244. See also *New York Times,* February 23, 1954.

16. Steininger, "John Foster Dulles, the European Defense Community, and the German Question," 87.

17. Telegram, March 16, 1954, AMAE Europe 1944–1960/Généralités, CED, vol. 73.

18. For a discussion of the great significance of MC 48, see Robert A. Wampler, "Conventional Goals and Nuclear Promises: The Truman Administration and the Roots of the NATO New Look," in *NATO: The Founding of the Atlantic Alliance and the Integration of Europe*, ed. Francis H. Heller and John R. Gillingham (New York: St. Martin's, 1992); Marc Trachtenberg, *A Constructed Peace: The Making of the European Settlement, 1945–1963* (Princeton, NJ: Princeton University Press, 1999); Marc Trachtenberg, "The

Nuclearization of NATO," in Marc Trachtenberg, *History and Strategy* (Princeton, NJ: Princeton University Press, 1991). For the full text of MC 48, see Gregory W. Pedlow, ed., *NATO Strategy Documents, 1949–1969* (Belgium: SHAPE Historical Office, 1997), 321–331.

19. "Annual Message to the Congress on the State of the Union," January 7, 1954, *PPUS DDE 1954* (Washington, D.C.: U.S. G.P.O., 1960), 10–11.

20. Department of State, *Bulletin* 30 (25 January 1954): 107–110.

21. Signed in April 1949, the North Atlantic Treaty allowed members to withdraw from the organization after twenty years.

22. "U.S. and U.K. Assurances on NATO and EDC [January, 1954?]," *FRUS 1952–1954* 5:873–877.

23. Wall, *The United States and the Making of Postwar France*, 270.

24. "Memorandum of Discussion at the 187th Meeting of the National Security Council," March 4, 1954, *FRUS 1952–1954* 5:886–890. Eisenhower premised these assurances on a conceit: he wanted to begin reducing U.S. forces on the Continent in two years, when the Europeans were able to take up the slack.

25. Saki Dockrill, *Britain's Policy for West German Rearmament, 1950–1955* (New York: Cambridge University Press, 1991), 136.

26. Parl. Debs., H. of C., Sess. 1953–54, Cols. 1141–1147.

27. Department of State, *Bulletin* 30 (April 26, 1954), 619–621.

28. *L'Année Politique 1954*, 344–345.

29. Department of State, *Bulletin* 30 (April 26, 1954), 619–621.

30. AMAE, Europe 1944–1960, Généralités, CED, 73.

31. Ibid., 256–257.

32. Wall, *The United States and the Making of Postwar France*, 275.

33. Stanley Karnow, *Vietnam: A History*, rev. ed. (New York: Viking Penguin, 1991), 212–214; George Herring and Richard Immerman, "Eisenhower, Dulles, and Dien Bien Phu: 'The Day We Didn't Go to War Revisited,'" *Journal of American History* 71 (September 1984): 87–90; Jean Lacouture, *Pierre Mendès France* (New York: Holmes & Meier Publishers, 1984), 239–240; and Bernard B. Fall, *Hell in a Very Small Place: The Siege of Dien Bien Phu* (New York: Da Capo Press, 1966), 301–313. For the most recent treatment of U.S. plans to save France, see John Prados, *Operation Vulture* (New York: ibooks inc., 2002).

34. Fall, *Hell in a Very Small Place*, 309.

35. "The Ambassador in France to the Department of State," June 14, 1954, *FRUS 1952–1954* 13:1687–1689.

36. Karnow, *Vietnam*, 216.

37. Fall, *Hell in a Very Small Place*, 415–416.

38. Pierre Mendès France, *Oeuvres complètes*, Tome II: *Une Politique de l'Economie, 1943–1954* (Paris: Editions Gallimard, 1985), 541–557.

39. Jean-Jacques Becker, *Histoire politique de la France depuis 1945* (Paris: Armand Colin, 1992), 61; and Jean-Pierre Rioux, *The Fourth Republic, 1944–1958*, trans. Godfrey Rogers (New York: Cambridge University Press, 1989), 227. René Coty succeeded Vincent Auriol as President on January 16, 1954.

40. Mendès France, *Oeuvres Completes,* Tome III: *Gouverner, c'est choisir, 1954–1955* (Paris: Gallimard, 1986), 54–56.

41. *Journal Officiel de la République Française, 1954 Débats Parlementaire Assemblée nationale* (Paris: Imprimerie des Journaux officiels, 1954), 2992–3007. Mendès France also assumed the foreign minister portfolio.

42. See the note from Leon Fuller, the deputy director of the Office of German Political Affairs, to Robert Bowie, the director of the Policy Planning Staff, "Reappraisal in London, Bonn and Paris," June 21, 1954, RG 59, RPPS, 1954, Box 87, NARA.

43. Charles Wighton, *Adenauer: A Critical Biography* (New York: Coward-McCann, 1964), 203; Institut Pierre Mendes France [hereafter IPMF], CED, 2.

44. George-Henri Soutou, "La France, L'Allemagne, et les accords de Paris," *Relations internationales,* no. 52 (Winter 1987): 460.

45. "Memorandum by the Joint Chiefs of Staff to the Secretary of Defense," June 25, 1954, *FRUS 1952–1954* 5:994–995.

46. "Joint Statement Issued by Prime Minister Churchill and President Eisenhower," June 29, 1954, *FRUS 1952–1954* 5:989–990; "Agreed United States-United Kingdom Secret Minute on Germany and the EDC" [June 28, 1954?], *FRUS 1952–1954* 5:988–989; and FO 371/109579, BNA.

47. See "Report of Anglo-American Study Group on Germany, Held in London, July 5–12 1954," *FRUS 1952–1954* 5:997–1018; FO 371/109579, BNA; and "Telegram," 5 July 1954, AMAE, Secrétariat Général, CED III, vol. 72.

48. See the minute that Frank Roberts sent to Minister of State Selwyn Lloyd, July 13, 1954, FO 371/109579, BNA. Another British official, Pat Hancock, head of the Foreign Office's Central Department, passed along the same information to the Canadians. See July 12, 1954, FO 371/109579, BNA.

49. CED, Carton II, IPMF.

50. *DDF 1954,* 17.

51. Note from P. Baudet to Alexandre Parodi, Georges Boris, and André Pelabon, July 3, 1954, IPMF/CED/Carton II. In fact, Guerin de Beaumont cancelled his trip to Bonn. See "Télégram à l'Arivée," July 3, 1954, AMAE Secrétariat Général, CED III, 72.

52. Letter, Kluthe to Mendès France, July 15, 1954, IPMF, CED, Carton II.

53. Letter, Mendès France to Kluthe, July 25, 1954, IPMF, CED, Carton II.

54. Letter, Kluthe to Mendès France, August 5, 1954, IPMF, CED, Carton II.

55. Letter, Mendès France to Kluthe, August 9, 1954, IPMF, CED, Carton II.

56. Karnow, *Vietnam,* 218; and Prados, *Operation Vulture,* 273.

57. "Telegram," Mendès France to Paris, July 10, 1954, quoted in Georgetta Elgey, *La République des Tourmentes, 1954–1959* (Paris: Fayard, 1992), 125. See also Letter, Mendès France to Moch, July 11, 1954, IPMF, Défense, Carton I. See "Entretien avec M. Pierre Mendès France" (Conducted by Roger Massip), January 29, 1981, FJME.

58. Accords de Paris, Dulles Oral History Project, IPMF; and Duchin, "The 'Agonizing Reappraisal,'" 215. See also "Memorandum of Conversation," January 13, 1954, *FRUS 1952–1954* 5:1018.

59. Karnow, *Vietnam,* 220; and Prados, *Operation Vulture,* 274–275.

60. See "Entretien avec M. Pierre Mendès France" (Conducted by Roger Massip), January 29, 1981, FJME.

61. On August 13, Mendès France persuaded his cabinet to accept five protocols that he intended to attach to the EDC Treaty in order to make it more acceptable to the French parliament. Three anti-EDC ministers—Jacques Chaban Delmas, General Pierre Koenig, and Maurice Lemaire—offered to resign. See "Entretien avec M. Pierre Mendès France" (Conducted by Roger Massip), January 29, 1981, FJME.

62. Article 13 of the NAT allows members to withdraw after twenty years while the EDC was to last fifty years. This discrepancy increased French deputies' fears that Britain and the United States would drop all support for the EDC, and perhaps Western defense in general, once the NATO Treaty expired. See "US and UK Commitments to the EDC," March 25, 1953, RG 59, ROERA, 1946–1953, Files of J. Graham Parsons, Box 2, NARA.

63. Once again Bruce and Monnet urged the United States to pressure France in order to preserve the supranational features of the EDC. The two men also enlisted the Belgium foreign minister Paul-Henri Spaak in the effort. See Renata Dwan, "Jean Monnet and the European Defense Community, 1950–1954," *Cold War History* 1, no. 3 (April 2001): 154. See also F. Roy Willis, *France, Germany, and the New Europe, 1945–1967* (Stanford: Stanford University Press, 1968), 181. Mendés France later declared that Bruce's actions worked against him. See "Entretien avec M. Pierre Mendès France" (Conducted by Roger Massip), January 29, 1981, FJME.

64. *Documents Diplomatiques Français 1954, Annexes (21 juillet–31 décembre)* (Paris: Imprimèrie nationale, 1987), 133–141; and "Prime Minister Churchill to the Secretary of State," August 24, 1954, *FRUS 1952–1954* 5:1077–1079.

65. Despite his suggestion, Dillon passed over this alternative to the EDC, and instead warned of the consequences should France vote down the treaty. See "The Ambassador in France to the Department of State," August 24, 1954, *FRUS 1952–1954* 5:1071–1077.

66. DDF 1954, 230–231, 254–255; and Soutou, "La France, l'Allemagne et les accords de Paris," 460.

67. Jean Lacouture, *Pierre Mendès France,* trans. George Holoch (New York: Holmes and Meier, 1984), 273–278.

68. "The Ambassador in France to the Department of State," August 31, 1954, *FRUS 1952–1954* 6:1443–1445.

69. Dwight D. Eisenhower, *The White House Years: Mandate for Change, 1953–1956* (Garden City, NY: Doubleday, 1963), 404.

70. Ibid., 403–404. The fact that Dulles believed France still required proof of U.S. resolve after four years of effort is suggestive of America's desire or capacity to coerce France.

71. Donald Cameron Watt, "Britain and German Security, 1944–1955" in FCO Occasional Papers, No. 3 (November 1989), 50.

72. *Times* [London], "Germany After the French Vote," September 4, 1954), 6; and Ronald J. Granieri, *The Ambivalent Alliance: Konrad Adenauer, the CDU/CSU, and the West, 1949–1966* (Providence, RI: Berghahn Books, 2003), 60–61.

73. Pierre Guillen, "Les chefs militaires français, le réarmement d'Allemangne et la CED (1950–1954)," *Revue d'histoire de la deuxième guerre mondiale et des conflits contemporains* 33 (January 1983): 6.

74. For the standard account of the "New Look," see John Lewis Gaddis, *Strategies of Containment: A Critical Appraisal of Postwar American National Security Policy* (Oxford: Oxford University Press, 1982), chap. 5.

75. Guillen, "Les chefs militaires," 6–7.

76. Ibid., 6–7. Catroux quoted in Jean Delmas, "Military Power in France," in *Power in Europe? II: Great Britain, France, Germany and Italy and the Origins of the EEC 1952–1957,* ed. Ennio di Nolfo (New York: Walter de Gruyter, 1992), 240.

77. According to his memoirs, Eden came up with this idea on September 5 while taking a bath. See Anthony Eden, *Full Circle: The Memoirs of Anthony Eden* (London: Cassell & Company Ltd., 1960), 168–170. See also "The Secretary of State to Foreign Secretary Eden," September 8, 1954, *FRUS 1952–1954* 5:1155–1156; *DDF 1954,* 328–330; and Dockrill, *Britain's Policy for West German Rearmament 1950–1955,* 142.

78. George-Henri Soutou, "La France, l'Allemagne et les accords de Paris," *Relations internationales* no. 52 (winter 1987): 460; and René Massigli, *Une comedie des erreurs, 1943–1956* (Paris: Plon, 1978), 461–462.

79. Dwight D. Eisenhower, *Mandate for Change: The White House Years, 1953–1956* (Garden City, NY: Doubleday, 1963), 404; "Foreign Secretary Eden to the Secretary of State," September 13, 1954, *FRUS 1952–1954* 5:1184–1185; "The Secretary of State to Foreign Secretary Eden," September 14, 1954, *FRUS 1952–1954* 5:1192–1194; Steininger, "John Foster Dulles," 105; Fursdon, *The European Defense Community,* 315; and Massigli, *Une comedie des erreurs,* 463.

80. Fursdon, *The European Defense Community,* 316–317.

81. "Report on the Secretary of State's Conversations With Chancellor Adenauer and Foreign Secretary Eden," September 16–17, 1954, September 20, 1954, *FRUS 1952–1954* 5:1209–1223.

82. *DDF 1954,* 398–399, 400–401.

83. Soutou, "Les accords de Paris," 462; Massigli, *Une comédie des erreurs,* 467; and Granieri, *The Ambivalent Alliance,* 81.

84. *FRUS 1952–1954* 5:1294–1366. For the text of the Final Act, see Department of State, *Bulletin* 31 (October 11, 1954): 515–528; and Soutou, "Les accords de Paris," 463.

85. *FRUS 1952–1954* 5:1351–1366; and *DDF 1954, Annexes,* 175ff.

86. On the final day of the Paris Conference, accords were signed clearing the way for the entry of Germany and Italy into the WEU, and the restoration of Germany's sovereignty and her entry into NATO. Adenauer also agrees to allow a referendum on the "Europeanization" of the Saar. All that remained

was parliamentary ratification. Consult Department of State, *Bulletin* 31 (November 15, 1954): 719–733 for related documents.

87. "Diary Entry by the President's Press Secretary," December 24, 1954, *FRUS 1952–1954* 5:1520–1523.
88. The second vote was tied to a question of confidence. "The Ambassador in France to the Department of State," December 24, 1954, *FRUS 1952–1954* 5:1519–1520.
89. Department of State, *Bulletin* 32 (January 3, 1955): 9–14; Wampler, "Conventional Goals and Nuclear Promises," 368–369; and Dockrill, "Cooperation and Suspicion," 167–169.
90. Quoted in Delmas, "Military Power in France," 241.
91. "The Secretary of State to Prime Minister Mendès France," December 30, 1954, *FRUS 1952–1954* 5:1538; and *DDF 1954*, 985–986. The French Senate, which also had to ratify the treaty, did so in March.
92. Quoted in Steininger, "John Foster Dulles," 107.

Conclusion

1. This point contradicts an argument made in one of the most influential books ever written on international relations theory. See Kenneth Waltz, *Theory of International Politics* (New York: McGraw-Hill, 1979).
2. Arthur A. Stein and Richard N. Rosecrance, eds., *The Domestic Bases of Grand Strategy* (Ithaca, NY: Cornell University Press, 1993).
3. For a recent example of the praise heaped on Eisenhower's handling of foreign policy, see Robert R. Bowie and Richard H. Immerman, *Waging Peace: How Eisenhower Shaped an Enduring Cold War Strategy* (Oxford: Oxford University Press, 2000).

Sources

Archival Collections

Belgium

NATO ARCHIVES, BRUSSELS
Direction des archives, Service public fédéral des Affaires étrangères, Commerce
   extérieure et Coopération au développement, Brussels

France

Archives nationales, Paris
   F60 (Archives of the President du Conseil)
   Vincent Auriol Papers (courtesy of the Centre d'histoire de Science Po)
   Georges Bidault Papers (courtesy of Mme. Bidault)
   René Mayer Papers
   Jules Moch Papers (courtesy of Mr. Moch)
   René Pleven Papers
Centre d'histoire de Science Po, Paris
   Wilfrid Baumgartner Papers (courtesy of Jean-Noël Jeanneney)
   Alexander Parodi Papers
Institut Pierre Mendès France, Paris
   Pierre Mendès France Papers
Ministère des Affaires Étrangères, Paris
   Y—Internationale, 1944–49
   Z—Europe, 1944–49
   Allemagne
   Généralités

Grande-Bretagne
URSS
EU [Europe], 1949–55
Allemagne
Sarre
B—Amérique, sous séries Etats-Unis, 1944–52
Direction des Affaires Economiques/Service de Coopération Economique, 1945–60
Henri Bonnet Papers
Rene Massigli Papers
Robert Schuman Papers
Ministère de l'économie, des finances et de l'industrie, Paris
Office Universitaire de la recherche socialiste, Paris
Guy Mollet Papers
Service historique de l'armée de l'air
Service historique de la marine
Henri Térel Papers
Service historique de l'armée de terre
Clement Blanc Papers
Paul Ely Papers
Alphonse Juin Papers

Switzerland

Fondation Jean Monnet pour l'Europe
Jean Monnet Papers

United Kingdom

Bodleian Library, Oxford University
Clement Attlee Papers
Churchill Archives Centre, Cambridge University
Sir Winston Churchill Papers
Sir John Colville Papers
Duff Cooper Papers
Herbert Miles Gladwyn Jebb Papers
Philip John Noel-Baker Papers
Selwin-Lloyd Papers
Imperial War Museum, London
Field Marshal Viscount Montgomery of Alamein Papers
Liddell Hart Center for Military Archives, London
Sir William Elliot Papers
Liddell Hart Papers
Lord Ismay Papers
London School of Economics
Ernest Davies Papers

National Archives, Kew, Richmond, Surrey
  CAB 129
  Cabinet Memoranda
  FO 371
  Foreign Office Political Files
  PREM 11
  Prime Minister's Office, Correspondence and Papers, 1951-64
  Anthony Eden Papers
Wren Library, Trinity College, Cambridge University
  Robert A. Butler Papers

United States

Air Force Historical Research Agency, Maxwell AFB
Library of Congress, Washington, DC
  W. Averell Harriman Papers
Nathan Marsh Pusey Library, Harvard University
  James B. Conant Papers
National Archives and Records Administration, Washington, DC
  Record Group 59, General Records of the Department of State
  Decimal Files
  Lot Files
  Memoranda to the President
  Records of the Office of European Affairs
  Records of the Policy Planning Staff
Harry S. Truman Library, Independence, Missouri
  Dean Acheson Papers
  William L. Clayton Papers
  Clayton-Thorp Office Files
  Harry S. Truman Papers
  President's Confidential File
  President's Official File
  President's Secretary's File
Dwight D. Eisenhower Presidential Library, Abilene, Kansas
  John Foster Dulles Papers
  Papers of Dwight D. Eisenhower (Ann Whitman File)
  Administration File
  DDE Diaries
  Dulles-Herter Series
  International Series
  NSC Series
  Alfred Gruenther Papers
  C. D. Jackson Papers
  Lauris Norstad Papers
  White House Office, National Security Council Staff Papers

RAND Corp, Santa Monica
Seeley Mudd Library, Princeton University
  George F. Kennan Papers
Sterling Memorial Library, Yale University
  Hanson Baldwin Papers
Virginia Historical Society, Richmond, Virginia
  David K. E. Bruce Papers

Published Primary Sources

L'Année Politique. Paris: Editions du Grand Siècle, 1944–1955.
Beyer, Henry, ed. *Robert Schuman: L'Europe par la reconciliation franco-allemande*. Lausanne: Fondation Jean Monnet pour l'Europe, 1986.
Churchill-Eisenhower Correspondence, 1953–1955. Edited by Peter G. Boyle. Chapel Hill: University of North Carolina Press, 1990.
Documents on British Policy Overseas. Series II, vols. 1–3. London: HMSO, 1986–1989.
Executive Sessions of the Senate Foreign Relations Committee, vol. 2, *Eighty-First Congress, First and Second Sessions, 1949–1950*. Washington, D.C.: U.S. G.P.O., 1951.
Fondation Jean Monnet pour l'Europe. *Jean Monnet–Robert Schuman correspon-dance, 1947–1953*. Lausanne, 1986.
Lipgens, Walter, and Wilfried Loth, eds. *Documents on the History of European Integration*. Vol. 3. *1945–1950*. Berlin/New York: Walter de Gruyter, 1988.
Ministère des Affaires Etrangères, Commission de publication des documents diplomatiques français. *Documents Diplomatiques Français*. Paris, 1987–.
Papers of Dwight David Eisenhower. The Presidency: The Middle Way. Vols. 14–16. Edited by Louis Galambos and Daun Van Lee. Baltimore, MD: Johns Hopkins University Press, 1996.
Royal Institute of International Affairs. *Documents on Germany under Occupa-tion, 1945–1954*. Edited by Beate Ruhm von Oppen. Oxford: Oxford University Press, 1955.
U.S. Department of State. *Foreign Relations of the United States, 1945–1954*. Washington, D.C.: USGPO, 1972–1987.
U.S. Joint Chiefs of Staff. *Records of the Joint Chiefs of Staff*. Part 2. *1946–1953: Europe and NATO*. Frederick, MD: University Publications of America, 1979–1981. Microfilm.

Memoirs and Diaries

Acheson, Dean. *Present at the Creation: My Years in the State Department*. New York: W. W. Norton, 1969.
Adenauer, Konrad. *Memoirs, 1945–1953*. Translated by Beate Ruhm von Oppen. Chicago: Henry Regnery Company, 1965.
Alphand, Herve. *L'etonnement de etre*. Paris: Fayard, 1977.

Aron, Raymond. *Memoirs: Fifty Years of Political Reflection*. Translated by George Holoch. New York: Holmes and Meier, 1990.

Auriol, Vincent. *Journal du Septennat, 1947–1954*. 7 vols. Paris: Armand Colin, 1970–1975.

Berard, Armand. *Un ambassadeur se souvient: Washington et Bonn, 1945–1955*. Paris: Pion, 1978.

Bidault, Georges. *Resistance: The Political Autobiography of Georges Bidault*. Translated by Marianne Sinclair. New York: Praeger, 1967.

Bloch-Laine, François. *Profession: Fonctionnaire*. Paris: Seuil, 1976.

Chauvel, Jean. *Commentaire: D'Alger a Berne, 1944–1952*. Vol. 2. Paris: Fayard, 1972.

Clay, Lucius D. *Decision in Germany*. New York: Doubleday, 1950.

Cooper, Duff. *Old Men Forget: The Autobiography of Duff Cooper*. New York: Dutton, 1954.

Debre, Michel. *Trois Républiques pour une France: Mémoires*. Vol. 2, *Agir, 1946–1958*. Paris: Albin Michel, 1988.

de Gaulle, Charles. *Discours et messages*. Vol. 1, *1940–1946*. Paris: Pion, 1970.

———. *Discours et messages*. Vol. 2, *1946–1958*. Paris: Pion, 1970.

Dumaine, Jacques. *Quai d'Orsay (1945–1951)*. Translated by Alan Davidson. London: Chapman and Hall, 1958.

Eden, Anthony. *Full Circle: The Memoirs of Sir Anthony Eden*. London: Cassell, 1960.

Eisenhower, Dwight D. *The White House Years: Mandate for Change, 1953–1956*. New York: Doubleday, 1963.

Kennan, George F. *Memoirs (1925–1950)*. New York: Bantam, 1969.

Massigli, Rene. *Une comédie des erreurs, 1943–1956*. Paris: Pion, 1978.

Mendes France, Pierre. *Œuvres complètes*. Vol. 2, *Une politique de l'économie, 1943–1954*. Vol. 3, *Gouverner c'est choisir, 1954–1955*. Paris: Gallimard, 1985–1986.

Moch, Jules. *Une si longue vie*. Paris: Robert Laffont, 1976.

Monnet, Jean. *Memoires*. Paris: Fayard, 1976.

Seydoux, François. *Mémoires d'owtre Rhin*. Paris: Grasset, 1975.

Teitgen, Paul-Henri. *Faites entrer Ie temoin suivant*. Rennes: Oaest-France, 1988.

Williams, Philip M., ed. *The Diary of Hugh Gaitskell, 1945–1956*. London: Jonathan Cape, 1983.

Index

ABC weapons, 161–162

Acheson, Dean: Acheson as a hardliner, 72, 79, 172n6; discussions with Schuman, 77–78, 79; EDC, 15, 26–28, 32, 63–65, 67, 79, 91, 200n63; Franco-American relations, 58–59, 63–65, 67, 72, 79, 84, 86, 96, 172n6; German rearmament, 17, 19–20, 26–28, 32, 34–35, 41, 46–47, 50, 67, 72, 73–74, 77, 88; HICOG, 50, 64; Indochina, 19–20, 86, 96; Lisbon, 84, 86, 96; NAC, 26–28, 67, 84; NATO, 65, 84; nuclear balance, 53; Occupation of Germany, 88, 91; Petersburg Conference, 77–78; Pleven Plan, 53, 91; Senate Foreign Relations Committee, 86; Shuman Plan, 19–20, 26–28, 65; Soviet Union, 53, 88, 186n60; Treaty of Bonn, 91; tripartite meetings, 19–20, 65, 91; West German-American relations, 15, 17, 84, 88; Western rearmament, 53, 73–74. *See also* German rearmament: Acheson

Adenauer, Konrad, 148, 162; Berlin Conference, 139, 141; contractual agreements, 73, 119; domestic politics, 15, 36–37, 46–48, 77, 91, 105–106, 118, 125, 127–128, 139, 141, 150, 154, 159, 163, 178n39, 188n69, 188–189n71, 190n1, 196n3, 205n30; EDC, 15, 46–47, 75, 79, 91, 105–106, 112–113, 118–120, 123, 125, 127–128, 150, 154, 157, 159, 196n3, 200n63; Franco–West German relations, 19, 36–38, 44, 46, 72, 73–75, 79, 91, 103, 105, 108, 112, 119–120, 123, 125, 128–129, 150–151, 154, 157, 159, 161,

163, 173n11, 178n40; German sovereignty, 47, 73–74, 79, 91, 119–120, 123, 161, 215n60, 220–221n86; NATO, 48, 75, 77, 157, 159, 161, 164, 196n3, 215n60, 220–221n86; Occupation Statute, 214n60; Paris Conference, 62, 79, 220–221n86; Petersburg Conference, 51, 62; Pleven Plan, 62; relationship with Mendès France, 125, 150–151, 154, 157, 159, 163; relationship with Schuman, 103; rivalry with Schumacher, 46–47; Saar, 75, 105–106, 108–109, 119–120, 123, 128–129, 154, 173n11, 196n3, 220–221n86; Shuman Plan, 19; Soviet–West German relations, 36, 38, 42, 47, 72, 112–113, 119, 123, 139, 159, 163; Treaty of Bonn, 91; West German–American relations, 15, 36–38, 42, 47, 62, 72, 74, 77–79, 91, 108–109, 119–120, 125 128, 151, 158, 161; WEU, 161, 220–221n86. *See also* ABC weapons; German rearmament: Adenauer; Kluthe, H. A.; Westbindung

Alexander, Czar, 130

Algeria, 165. *See also* North Africa

Allied High Commission (AHC), 39, 48, 65, 91, 186n60, 188–189n71, 196n5, 215n60

Alphand, Hervé, 60, 63–64, 89, 103, 112

American imperialism, 4

Arc de Triomph, 138

Atlantic Alliance, 18, 41–42, 45, 55, 73, 78–79, 81, 90, 125, 134, 159, 163–164, 172n3; Acheson's hardline, 72, 73; EDC, 75, 78–79, 90, 100, 134, 137;

71, 104, 147, 151; 1953 four-power
summit proposal, 122–123, 126–127,
130, 132, 139; Bermuda Summit,
130–132; French Parlimentary vote on
the EDC, 157–159
Claussonne, François Seydoux de, 205n35
Clay, Lucius D., 14, 18, 178n51
Cleveland Plain Dealer, 15, 178n40
Cologne, 15, 174n9
Cominform, 70
Communism: fear of, 16, 176n26; France
and containment, 4, 35, 56, 86, 107,
141, 174n9, 176n26; United States and
containment, 4, 26, 33, 41, 99, 121,
133, 166, 187n64. *See also* Parti
Communiste Français (PCF); Rollback
Conant, James B., 161
Congress of the National Union of Reserve
Officers, 114
Contractual Agreements on German
Sovereignty, 73, 91, 104–105, 119,
200n62
Costigliola, Frank, 4
Coty, René, 150, 217n39
Council of Europe, 20, 57
Council of Foreign Ministers (CFM), 10,
46, 130, 173n2, 174n12
Czechoslovakia, 11, 181n5

Daladier, Edouard, 95, 130
DC 6/1, 13, 176n28
DC 28, 13
De Gaulle, Charles, 9, 18, 35, 187n65,
211–212n27. *See also* Gaullists
De Larminat, Edgar, 92
De Lattre de Tassigny, Jean, 56
Defense Committee (DC), 12–13, 24, 30,
39, 190n23
Dehler, Thomas, 128
Denmark, 172n3
Dien Bien Phu, 148–149
Dietz, Maria, 190n1
Dillon, Douglas, 109, 141, 149, 157–158,
163, 219n65
Direction Politique, 160
Draper, William, 107
Dulles, Allen, 210n5
Dulles, John Foster, 117, 127, 141, 150,
167, 219n70; American pressure on
European allies, 104, 106–109,
117–119, 131, 133–135, 145, 158, 161,
215n63, 216n12, 219n70; Berlin
Conference, 139–140; Bermuda Summit,

131; connecting EDC and NATO, 145,
151; criticism of Eden Plan, 160–161;
France and the EDC, 107–109,
118–119, 133–135, 155, 158, 160–162,
187n63, 205–206n40, 206n42, 215n63,
216n12, 219n70; Franco-German
rapprochement, 18, 20, 128, 133;
friendship with Monnet, 202n4;
Indochina War, 148–149, 155; London
Conference, 161–162; Mendès France,
150, 155, 163–164; United States
support for EDC, 106, 151, 202n4,
213n50; United States–Soviet Union
relations, 121–122, 126, 139–140, 167
Dunn, James C., 96, 105, 205n29
Duroselle, Jean-Baptiste, 4–5

East Berlin, 125
East Germany, 36, 88, 95, 122, 125,
172n3, 181n5, 209–210n4
Eden, Anthony: Anglo-American relations,
131, 161; Anglo-French relations, 71,
89, 104, 161, 201–202n85; Berlin
Conference, 139–140; British
continental policy, 71, 89, 160, 162;
Brussels Conference, 156; EDC, 71,
89–90, 109, 128, 146, 156–157, 160,
200n63; chair of the London
Conference, 161; German unification,
139; post-EDC plans, 160–162, 220n77;
Treaty of Bonn, 91. *See also* Eden Plan
Eden Plan, 140, 160–161
Eisenhower, Dwight, 99, 194n54, 203n14;
Bermuda Summit, 130–132; criticism of
Truman Administration, 99–100;
Indochina War, 142, 148–149; nuclear
weapons, 101–102, 132–133, 144, 167,
214n55; SACEUR, 39, 48, 50, 60–62,
68, 77, 187–188n65; United States
economy, 99–102, 116–117, 119, 144,
202n1, 203n14; United States–Soviet
relations, 121–123, 125–126. *See also*
Eisenhower Administration
Eisenhower Administration: efforts to
establish the EDC, 98, 100, 106–107,
118–120, 127–128, 131–132, 145–147,
151, 162, 166, 213n50; Eisenhower's
Cold War strategies, 99–101; Franco-
American relations, 99, 100, 119–120,
133, 140, 142, 146–149, 158, 162–164,
167, 202n4, 206n42; response to East
Berlin uprising, 125–126; United States
military presence in Europe, 6, 128, 133,